100 Christmas Carols

ISBN 0-634-08190-X

HAL•LEONARD®
CORPORATION

7777 W. BLUEMOUND RD. P.O. BOX 13819 MILWAUKEE, WI 53213

In Australia Contact:
Hal Leonard Australia Pty. Ltd.
22 Taunton Drive P.O. Box 5130
Cheltenham East, 3192 Victoria, Australia
Email: ausadmin@halleonard.com

Visit Hal Leonard Online at
www.halleonard.com

contents

4 Angels from Heaven

5 Angels from the Realms of Glory

6 Angels We Have Heard on High

10 As Each Happy Christmas

14 As Lately We Watched

16 As with Gladness Men of Old

18 Away in a Manger (Kirkpartick)

20 Away in a Manger (Murray)

22 A Baby in the Cradle

11 Bells Over Bethlehem

24 Beside Thy Cradle Here I Stand

26 The Boar's Head Carol

28 A Boy Is Born in Bethlehem

30 Break Forth, O Beauteous, Heavenly Light

32 Bring a Torch, Jeannette Isabella

34 Carol of the Birds

27 A Child Is Born in Bethlehem

36 Child Jesus Came to Earth This Day

38 Christ Is Born This Evening

40 Christ Was Born on Christmas Day

42 Christians, Awake! Salute the Happy Morn

41 The Christmas Tree with Its Candles Gleaming

44 Come, All Ye Shepherds

45 Come, Thou Long-Expected Jesus

48 Coventry Carol

52 Dance of the Sugar Plum Fairy

54 A Day, Bright Day of Glory

56 Deck the Hall

58 Ding Dong! Merrily on High!

49 The First Noël

60 The Friendly Beasts

62 From Heaven Above to Earth I Come

66 Fum, Fum, Fum

68 Go, Tell It on the Mountain

70 God Rest Ye Merry, Gentlemen

63 Good Christian Men, Rejoice

72 Good King Wenceslas

74 The Happy Christmas Comes Once More

76 Hark! The Herald Angels Sing

78 He Is Born, The Holy Child (Il Est Ne, Le Divin Enfan

80 Here We Come A-Wassailing

82 The Holly and the Ivy

73 I Am So Glad on Christmas Eve

84 I Heard the Bells on Christmas Day

86 I Saw Three Ships

88 In the Field with Their Flocks Abiding

91 In the Silence of the Night

92 It Came Upon the Midnight Clear

94 Jesu, Joy of Man's Desiring

100 Jesus Holy, Born So Lowly

102 Joy to the World	154 Shout the Glad Tidings
104 Lo, How a Rose E'er Blooming	156 Silent Night
106 Masters in This Hall	158 The Simple Birth
108 Neighbor, What Has You So Excited?	160 Sing, O Sing, This Blessed Morn
110 Noël! Noël!	162 Sing We Now of Christmas
112 O Bethlehem	164 Sleep, Holy Babe
114 O Christmas Tree	166 Sleep, O Sleep, My Precious Child
116 O Come, All Ye Faithful (Adeste Fideles)	168 The Snow Lay on the Ground
97 O Come Away, Ye Shepherds	170 The Star of Christmas Morning
118 O Come, Little Children	151 Star of the East
120 O Come, O Come Immanuel	172 Still, Still, Still
122 O Come Rejoicing	174 There's a Song in the Air
124 O Holy Night	176 Toyland
128 O Let Us All Be Glad Today	202 'Twas the Night Before Christmas
130 O Little Town of Bethlehem	178 The Twelve Days of Christmas
119 O Sanctissima	182 A Virgin Unspotted
132 Of the Father's Love Begotten	184 Watchman, Tell Us of the Night
134 On Christmas Night	186 We Three Kings of Orient Are
136 Once in Royal David's City	188 We Wish You a Merry Christmas
138 Pat-A-Pan (Willie, Take Your Little Drum)	190 Wexford Carol
140 Rejoice and Be Merry	192 What Child Is This?
141 Ring Out, Ye Wild and Merry Bells	194 When Christ Was Born of Mary Free
144 Rise Up, Shepherd, and Follow	196 When Christmas Morn Is Dawning
146 Shepherd! Shake Off Your Drowsy Sleep	198 While Shepherds Watched Their Flocks
148 Shepherd's Cradle Song	200 Winds Through the Olive Trees

ANGELS FROM HEAVEN

Traditional Hungarian

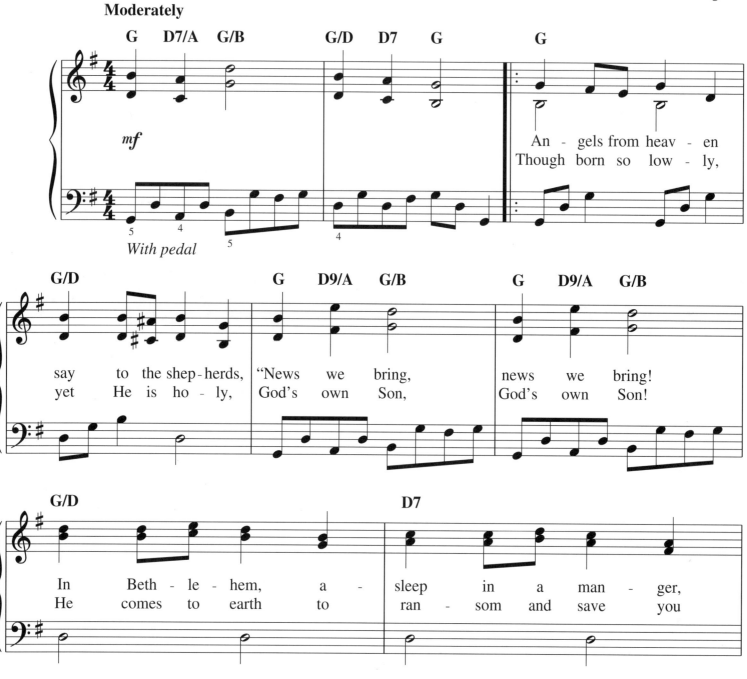

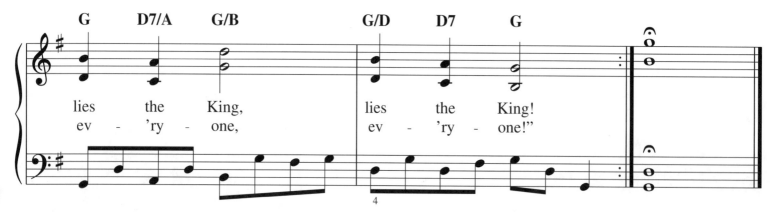

Lyrics:
An - gels from heav - en
Though born so low - ly,
say to the shep - herds,
yet He is ho - ly,
"News we bring,
God's own Son,
news we bring!
God's own Son!
In Beth - le - hem, a -
He comes to earth to
sleep in a man - ger,
ran - som and save you
lies the King,
ev - 'ry - one,
lies the King!
ev - 'ry - one!"

ANGELS FROM THE REALMS OF GLORY

Words by JAMES MONTGOMERY
Music by HENRY T. SMART

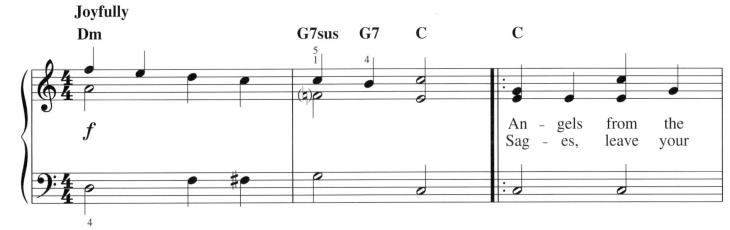

Angels from the
Sag - es, leave your

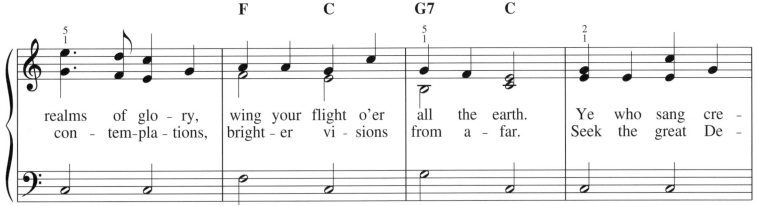

realms of glo - ry,
con - tem-pla - tions,

wing your flight o'er
bright - er vi - sions

all the earth.
from a - far.

Ye who sang cre -
Seek the great De -

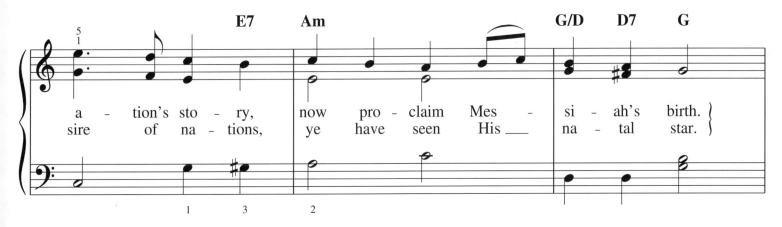

a - tion's sto - ry,
sire of na - tions,

now pro - claim Mes -
ye have seen His

si - ah's birth.
na - tal star.

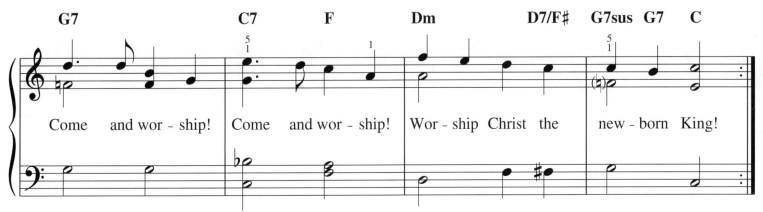

Come and wor - ship!

Come and wor - ship!

Wor - ship Christ the

new - born King!

ANGELS WE HAVE HEARD ON HIGH

Traditional French Carol
Translated by JAMES CHADWICK

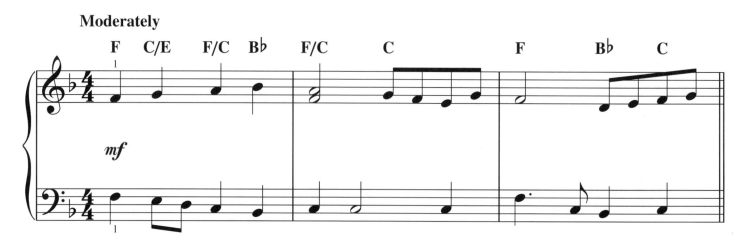

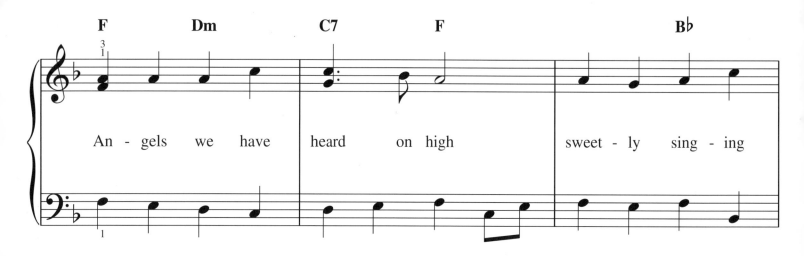

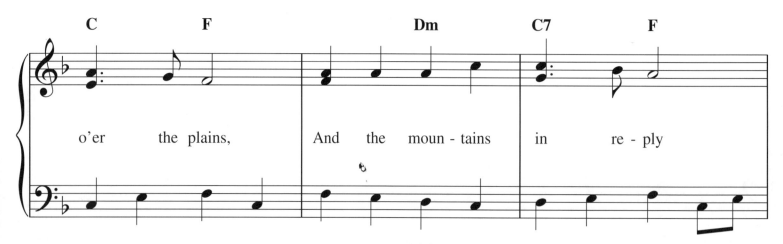

ech - o - ing their joy - ous strains. Glo -

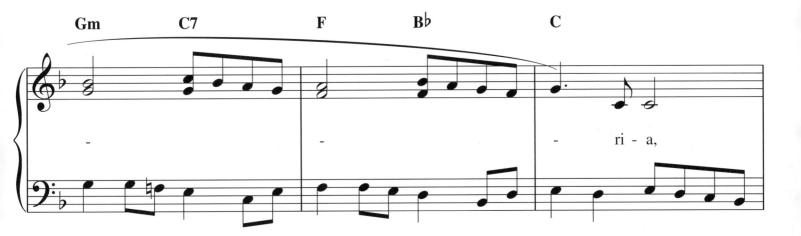

- ri - a,

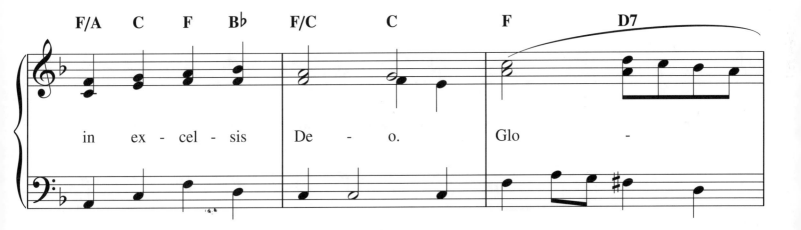

in ex - cel - sis De - o. Glo -

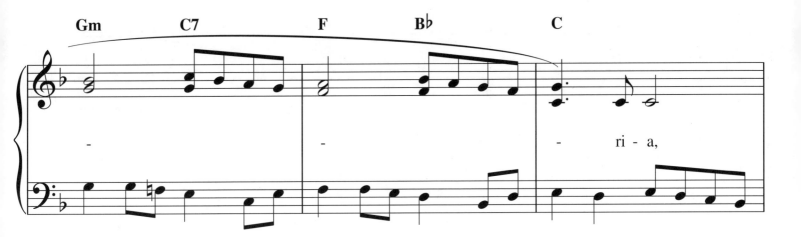

- ri - a,

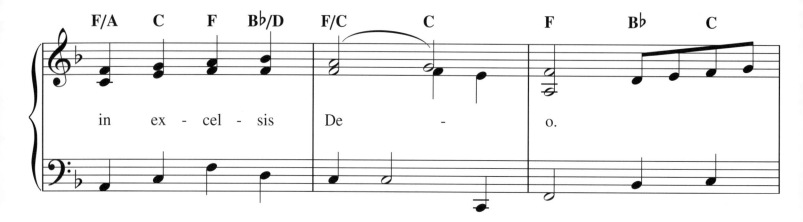

in ex - cel - sis De - o.

Shep - herds why this ju - bi - lee, why your joy - ous

mf

strains pro - long? What the glad - some tid - ings be

which in - spire your heav'n - ly song? Glo -

f

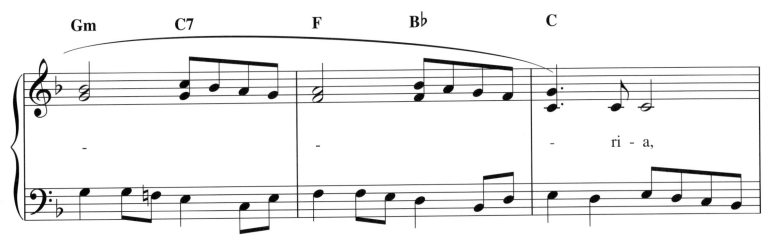

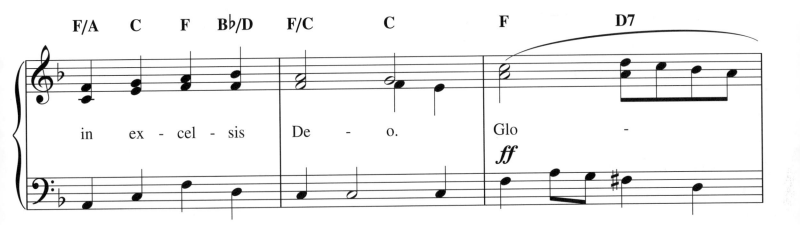

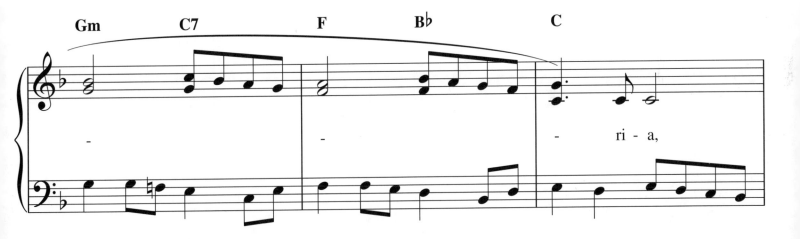

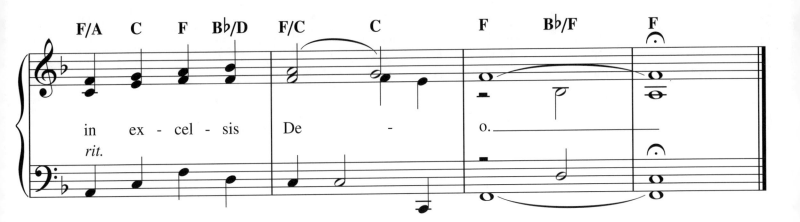

AS EACH HAPPY CHRISTMAS

Traditional

Happily

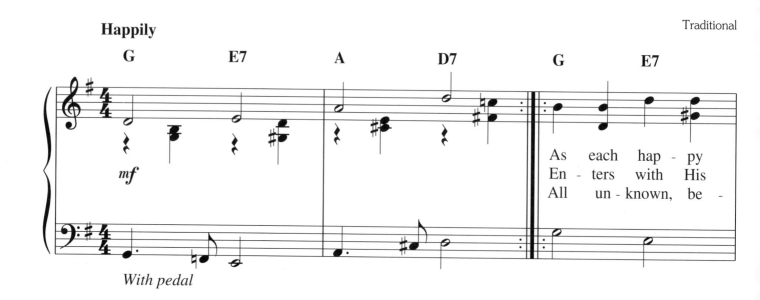

As each hap-py
En-ters with His
All un-known, be -

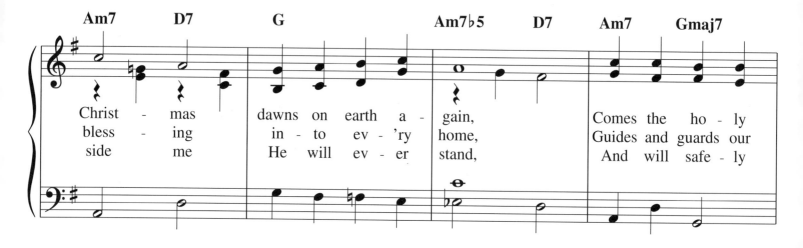

Christ - mas   dawns on earth a - gain,   Comes the ho - ly
bless - ing   in - to ev-'ry   home,   Guides and guards our
side   me   He will ev - er   stand,   And will safe - ly

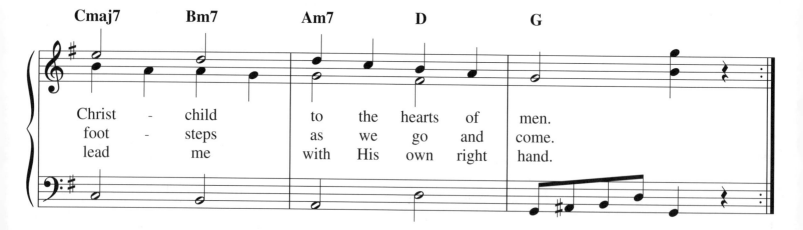

Christ - child   to the hearts of   men.
foot - steps   as we go and   come.
lead   me   with His own right   hand.

BELLS OVER BETHLEHEM

Traditional Andalucian Carol

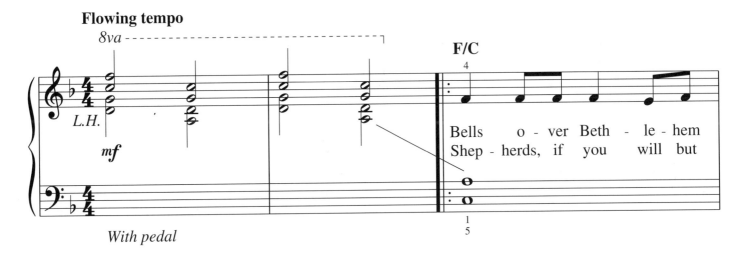

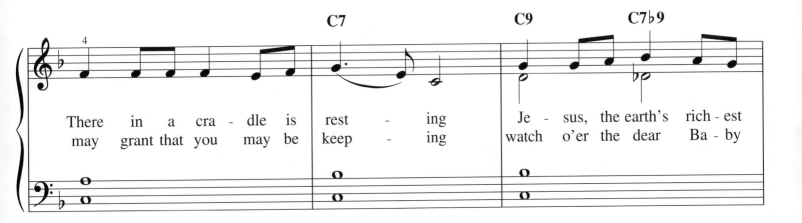

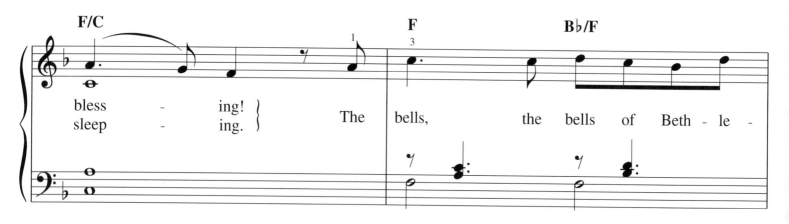

bless - ing! } The bells, the bells of Beth - le -
sleep - ing. }

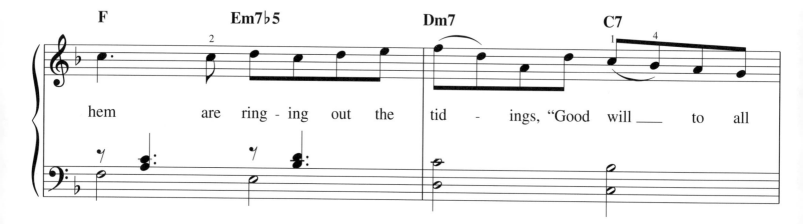

hem are ring - ing out the tid - ings, "Good will ___ to all

men!" Leave your sheep ___ and come, O shep - herds,

pres - ents bring the Babe so low - ly. ___ Bring some cheese ___ and

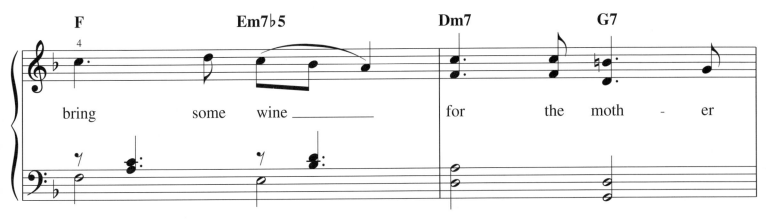

bring   some   wine _____   for   the   moth - er

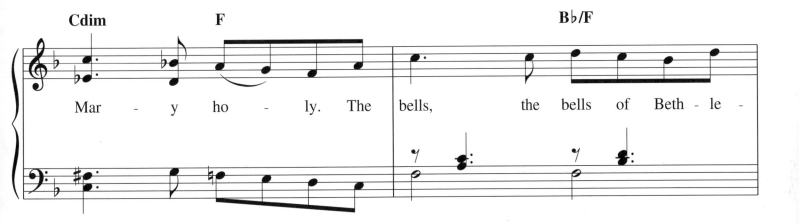

Mar - y   ho - ly.   The   bells,   the   bells   of   Beth - le -

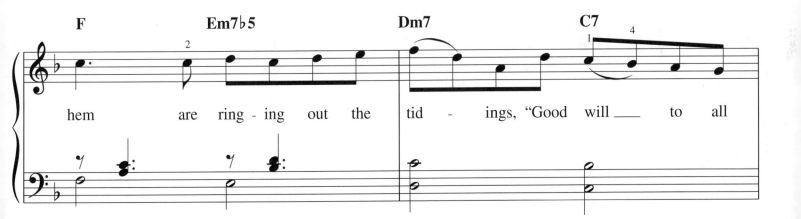

hem   are   ring - ing   out   the   tid - ings,   "Good   will ____   to   all

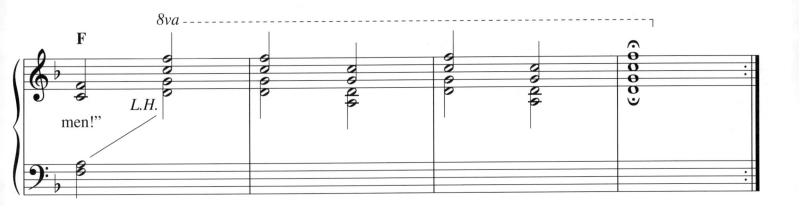

men!"

AS LATELY WE WATCHED

19th Century Austrian Carol

Moving gently

1. As late - ly we watched o'er ___ our ___ fields through the night, a star there was seen; and
2. King of such beauty was ___ ne' - er be - fore seen of ___ such ___ glo - ri - ous light!
3. *(See additional verse)*

star Mar - y was His Mother so ___ like ___ to a ___ queen.

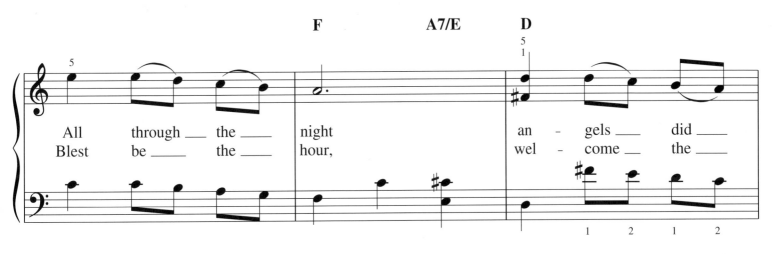

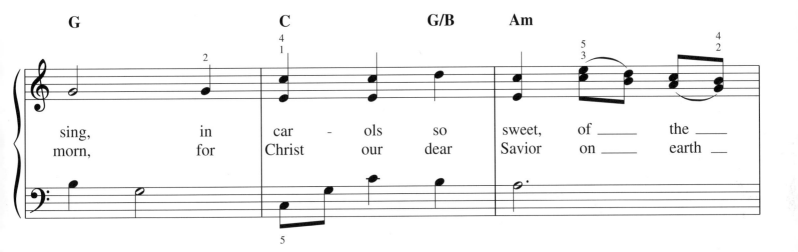

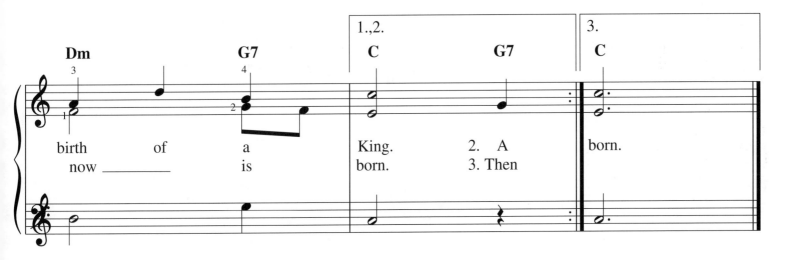

Additional Verse

3. Then shepherds, be joyful
   Salute your liege King;
   Let hills and dales ring
   To the song that ye sing:
   Blest be the hour,
   Welcome the morn,
   For Christ our dear Savior,
   On earth now is born.

AS WITH GLADNESS MEN OF OLD

Words by WILLIAM CHATTERTON DIX
Music by CONRAD KOCHER

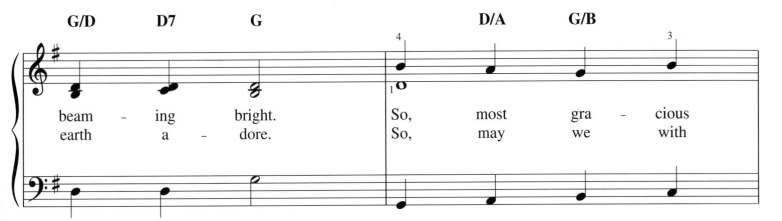

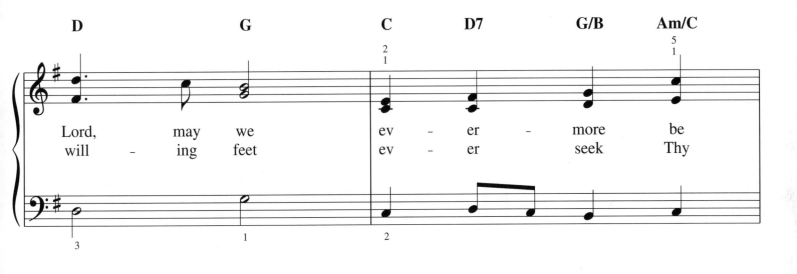

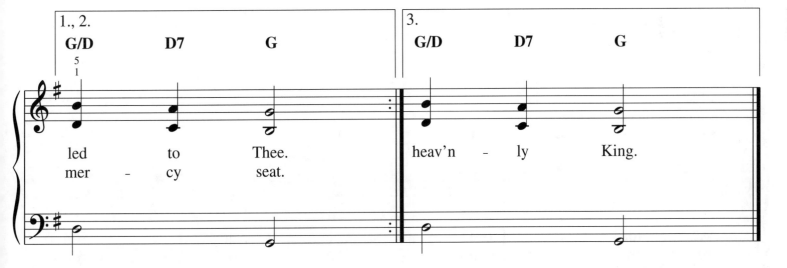

Additional Verse

3. As they offered gifts most rare,
   At that manger rude and bare,
   So may we with holy joy,
   Pure and free from sin's alloy,
   All our costliest treasures bring,
   Christ, to Thee our heav'nly King.

AWAY IN A MANGER

Traditional
Words by JOHN T. McFARLAND (v.3)
Music by WILLIAM J. KIRKPATRICK

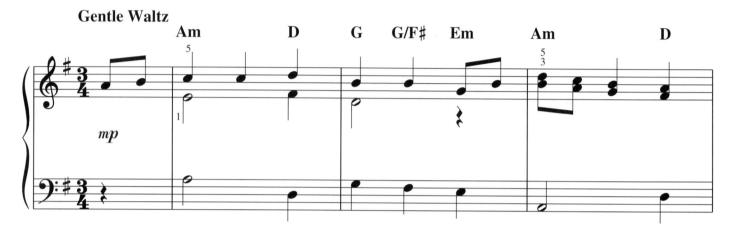

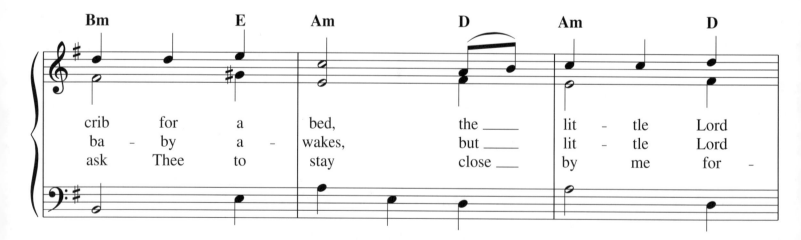

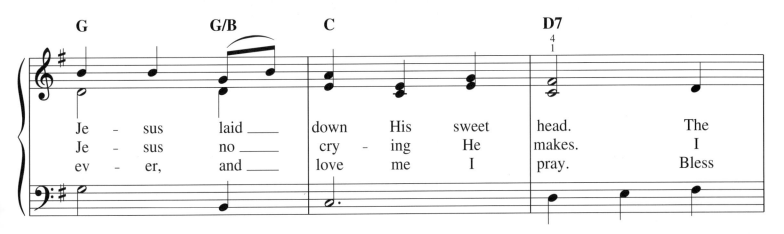

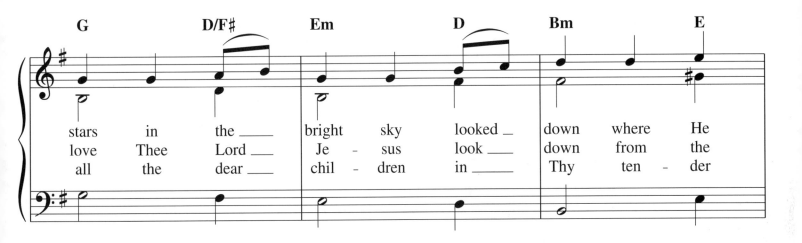

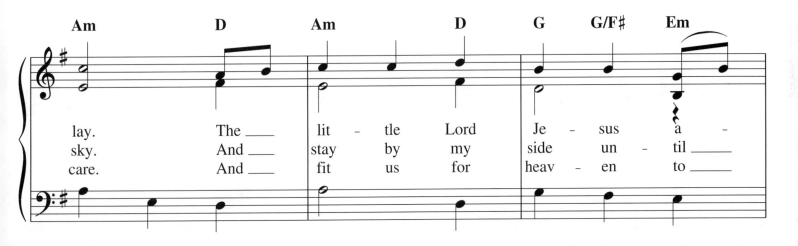

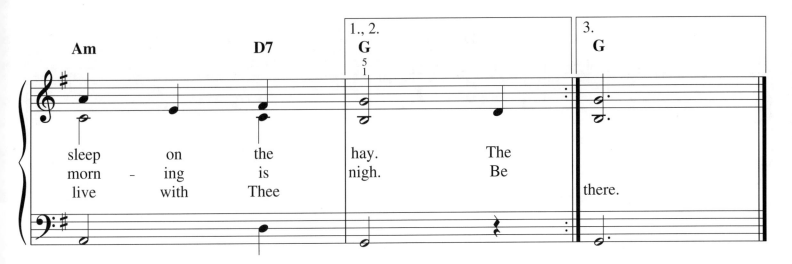

AWAY IN A MANGER

Traditional
Words by JOHN T. McFARLAND (v.3)
Music by JAMES R. MURRAY

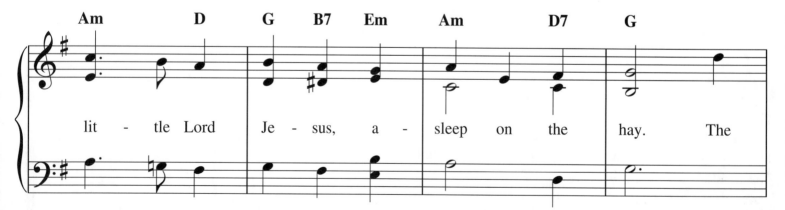

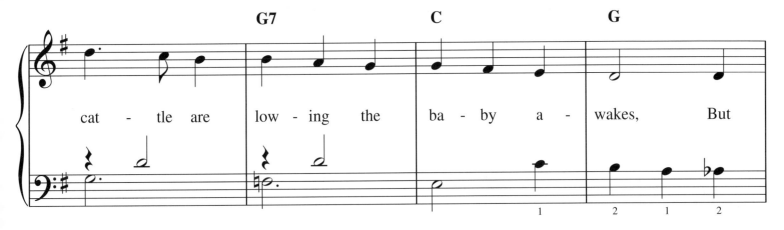

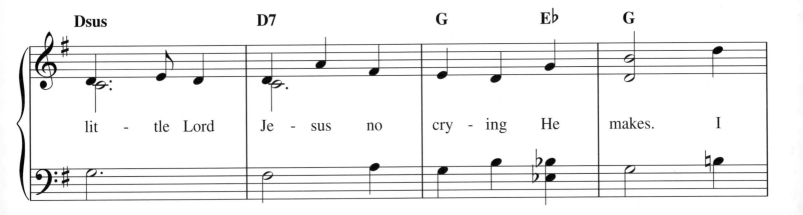

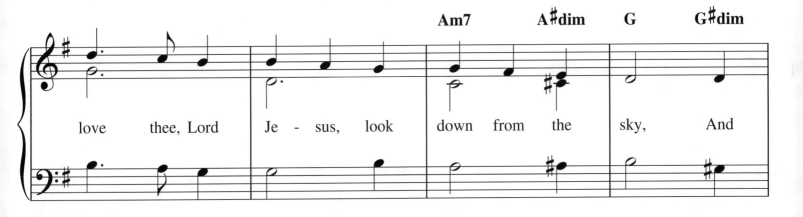

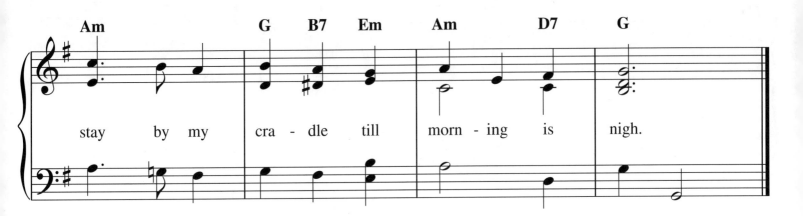

A BABY IN THE CRADLE

By D.G. CORNER

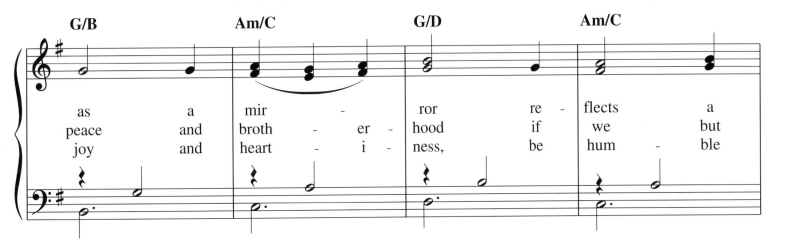

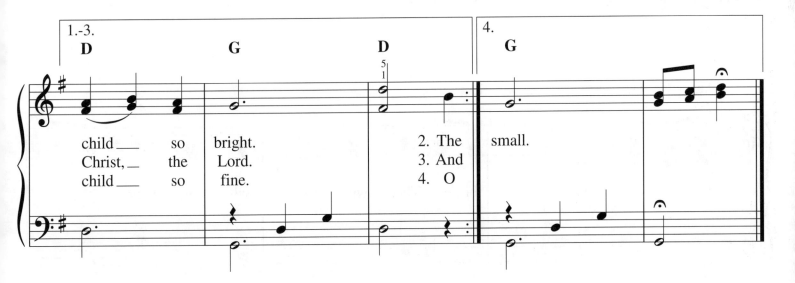

Additional Verse

4. O Jesus, dearest Savior,
   Although Thou art so small,
   With Thy great love o'erflowing
   Come flooding through my soul,
   Thou lovely Babe so small.

BESIDE THY CRADLE HERE I STAND

Words by PAUL GERHARDT
Translated by REV. J. TROUTBECK
Music from the *Geistliche Gesangbuch*
Harmonized by J.S. BACH

Slowly with feeling

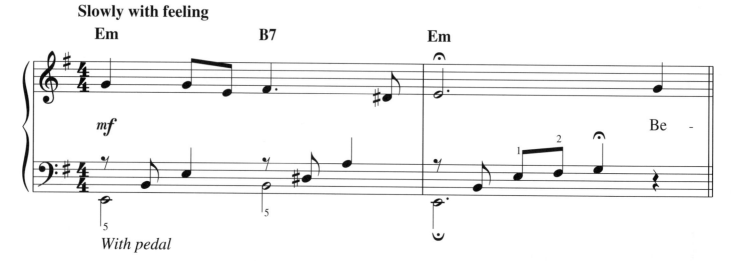

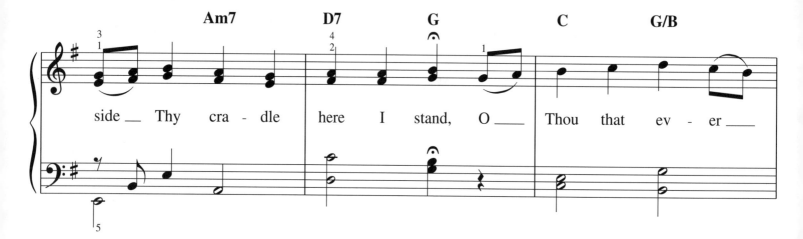

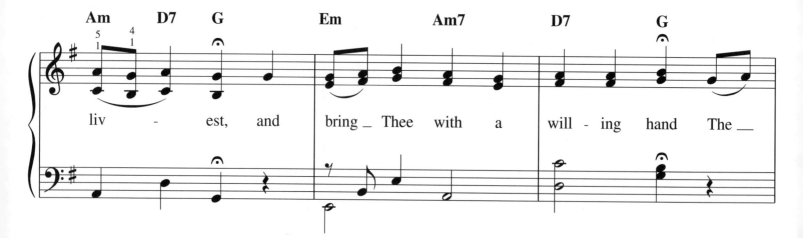

ver - y gifts Thou ___ giv - est. Ac -

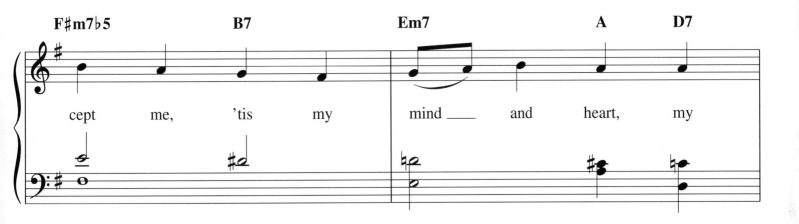

cept me, 'tis my mind ___ and heart, my

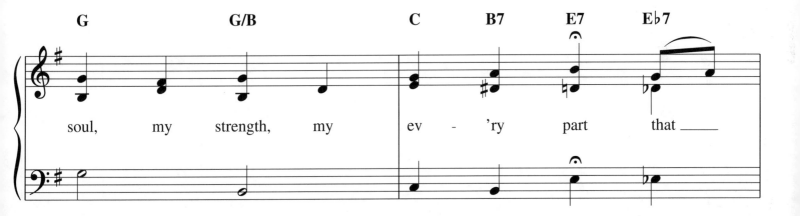

soul, my strength, my ev - 'ry part that ___

Thou from me re - quir - est.

THE BOAR'S HEAD CAROL

Traditional English

With spirit

The boar's head in hand bear I, Be -
boar's head I un - der - stand, The

decked with bays and rose - mar - y. And I pray you, my mas - ters
fin - est dish in all the land. Which is thus all be - decked with

mer - ry be, *Quot es - tis in con - vi - vi - o.* *Ca - put a - pri*
gay gar - land, Let us ser - vi - re can - ti - co.

de - fe - ro, *Red - dens lau - des Do - mi - no.* The *Do - mi - no.*

A CHILD IS BORN IN BETHLEHEM

14th-Century Latin Text adapted by NICOLAI F.S. GRUNDTVIG
Traditional Danish Melody

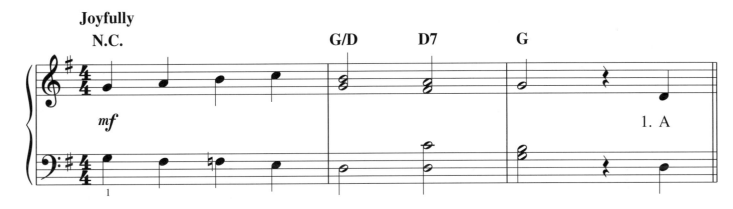

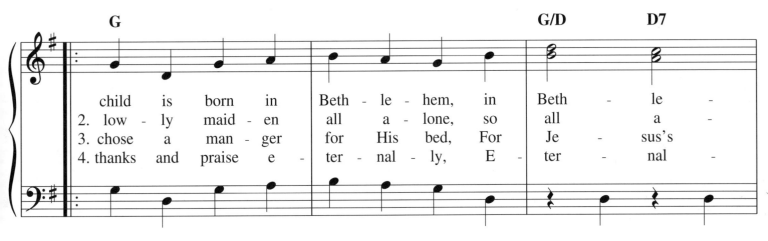

child is born in Beth - le - hem, in Beth - le -
2. low - ly maid - en all a - lone, so all a -
3. chose a man - ger for His bed, For Je - sus's
4. thanks and praise e - ter - nal - ly, E - ter - nal -

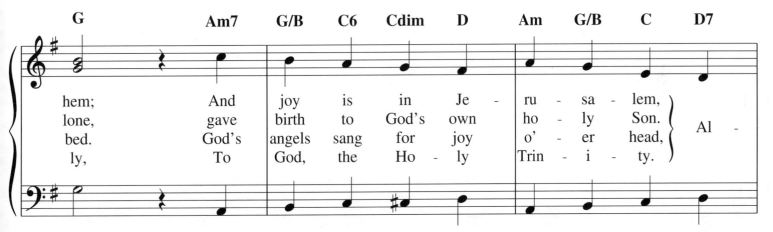

hem; And joy is in Je - ru - sa - lem,
lone, gave birth to God's own ho - ly Son.
bed. God's angels sang for joy o' - er head,
ly, To God, the Ho - ly Trin - i - ty.
Al -

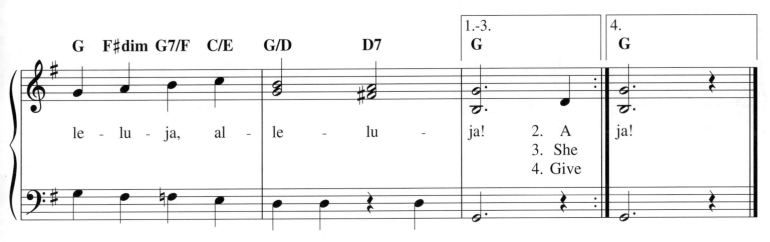

le - lu - ja, al - le - lu - ja! 2. A ja!
3. She
4. Give

A BOY IS BORN IN BETHLEHEM

Traditional

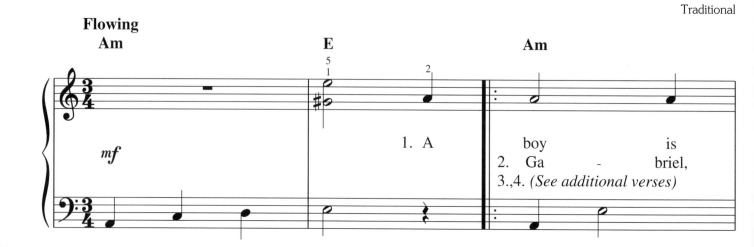

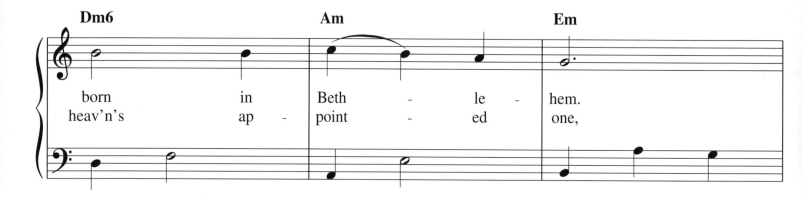

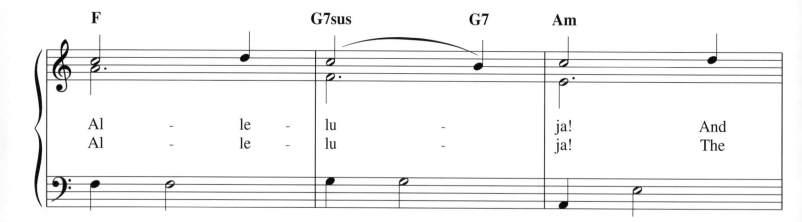

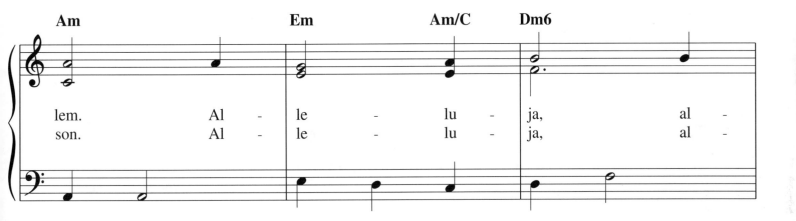

Additional Verses

3. The wisest kings of Orient.
   Alleluja!
   Gold, frankincense, and myrrh present.
   Alleluja, alleluja!

4. Laud to the Holy Trinity.
   Alleluja!
   All thanks and praise to God most high.
   Alleluja, alleluja!

BREAK FORTH, O BEAUTEOUS, HEAVENLY LIGHT

Words by JOHANN RIST
Translated by JOHN TROUTBECK
Melody by JOHANN SCHOP
Arranged by J.S. BACH

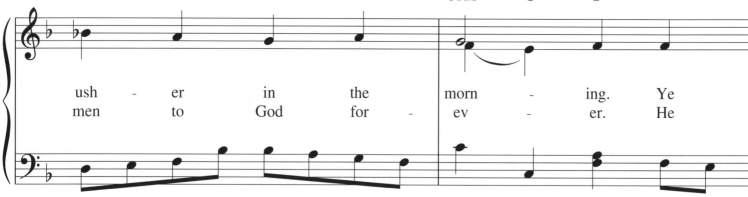

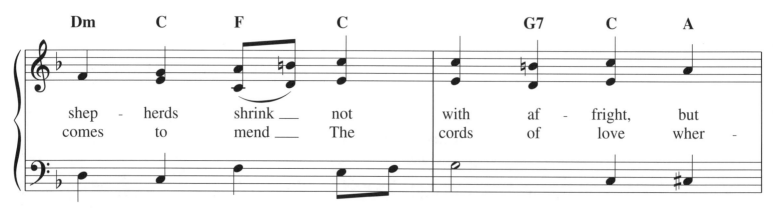

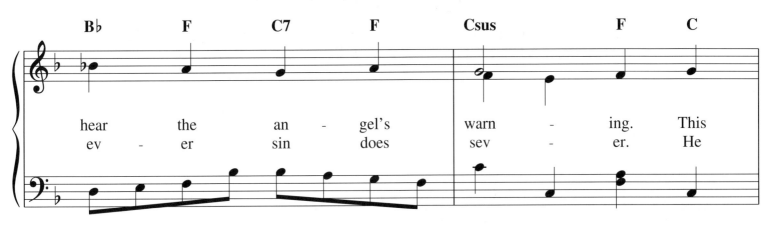

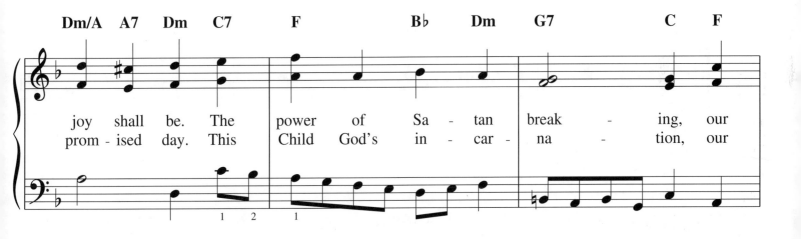

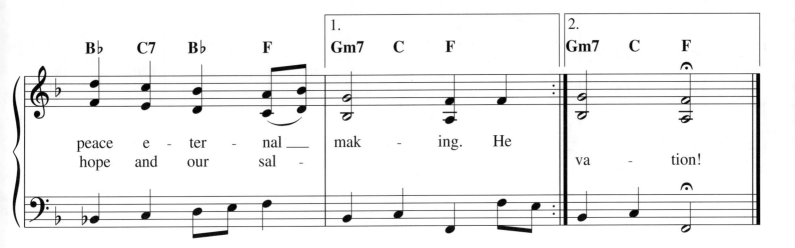

BRING A TORCH, JEANNETTE ISABELLA

17th Century French Provençal Carol

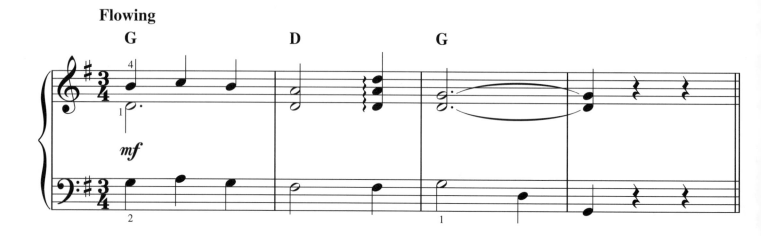

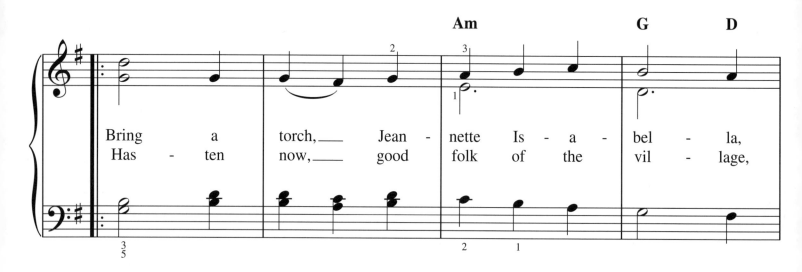

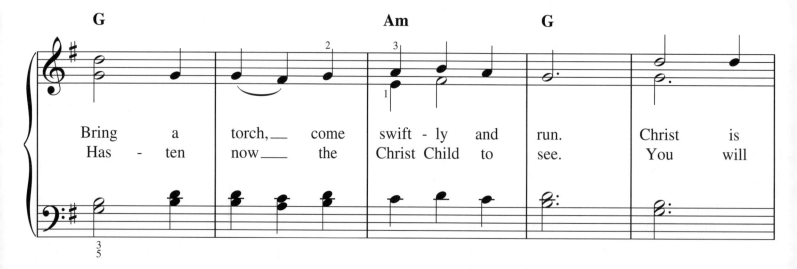

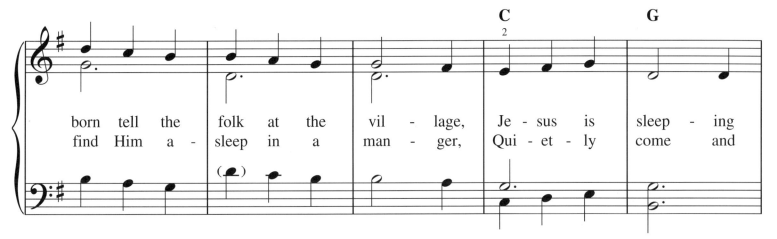

born tell the | folk at the | vil - lage, | Je - sus is | sleep - ing
find Him a - | sleep in a | man - ger, | Qui - et - ly | come and

in His | cra - dle. | Ah, _____ | Ah, _____
whis - per | soft - ly. | Hush, _____ | Hush, _____

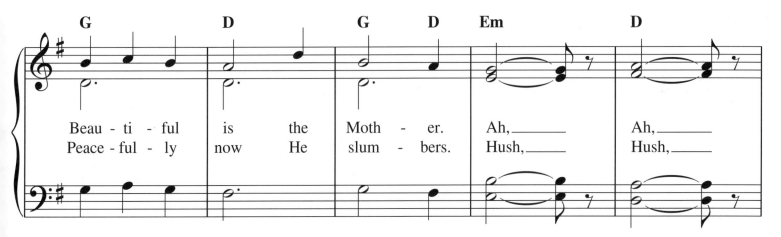

Beau - ti - ful | is the | Moth - er. | Ah, _____ | Ah, _____
Peace - ful - ly | now He | slum - bers. | Hush, _____ | Hush, _____

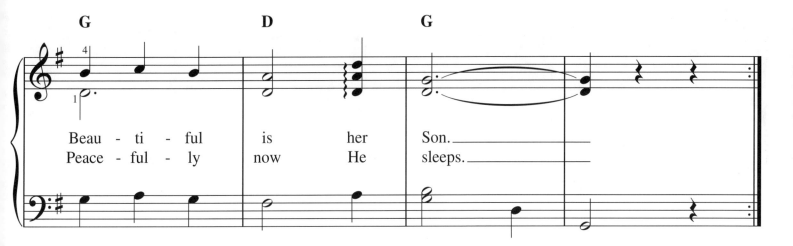

Beau - ti - ful | is her | Son. _____
Peace - ful - ly | now He | sleeps. _____

CAROL OF THE BIRDS

Traditional Catalonian Carol

Like Calypso Ballad

1. Up - on this ho - ly night, when God's great star ap -
2. night - in - gale is first to bring his song of
3.,4. *(See additional verses)*

pears, and floods the earth with bright - ness: birds'
cheer, and tell us of his glad - ness: Je -

voic - es rise in song, and war - bling all night long, ex -
sus, our Lord, is born to free us from all sin, and __

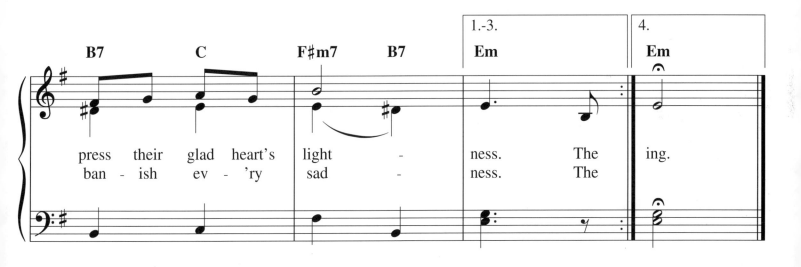

Additional Verses

3. The answ'ring Sparrow cries:
   "God comes to earth this day
   Amid the angels flying."
   Trilling in sweetest tones,
   The Finch his Lord now owns:
   "To Him be all thanksgiving."
   Trilling in sweetest tones,
   The Finch his Lord now owns:
   "To Him be all thanksgiving."

4. The Partridge adds his note:
   "To Bethlehem I'll fly,
   Where in the stall He's lying."
   There, near the manger blest,
   I'll build myself a nest,
   And sing my love undying.
   There, near the manger blest,
   I'll build myself a nest,
   And sing my love undying.

CHILD JESUS CAME TO EARTH THIS DAY

Traditional Carol

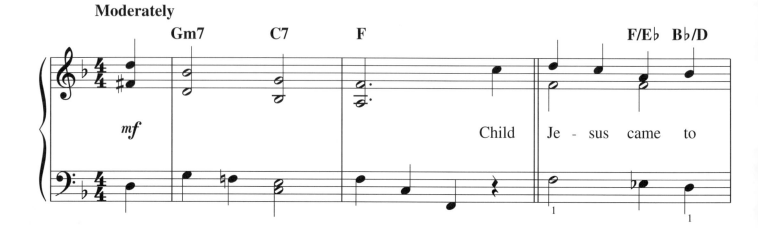

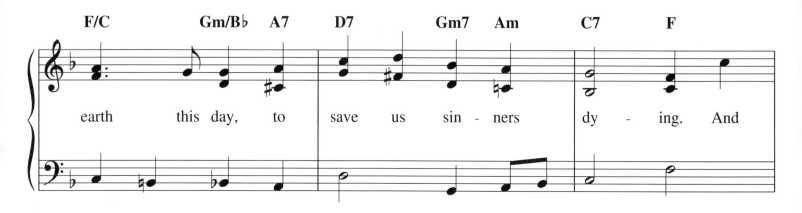

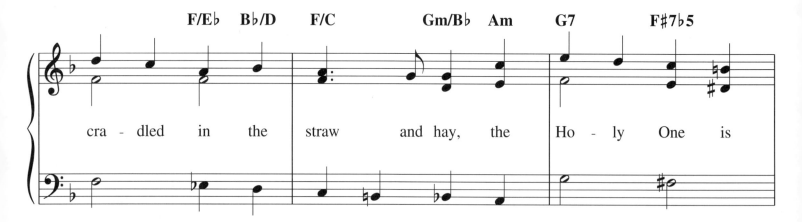

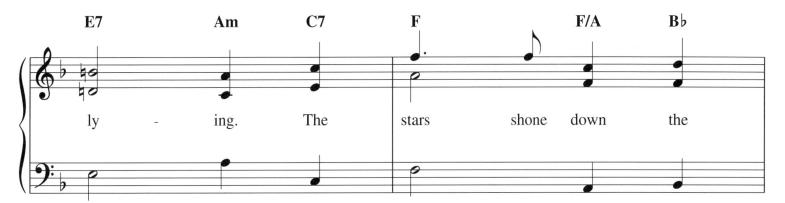

ly - ing. The stars shone down the

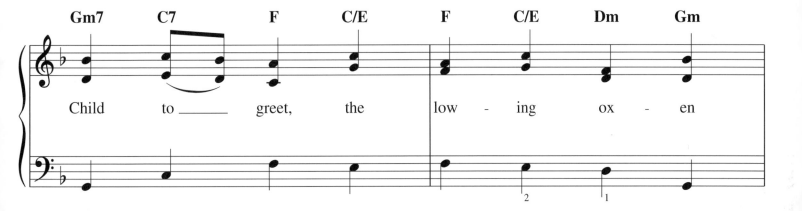

Child to _____ greet, the low - ing ox - en

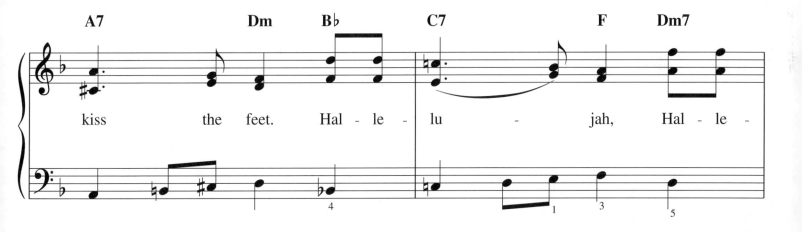

kiss the feet. Hal - le - lu - jah, Hal - le -

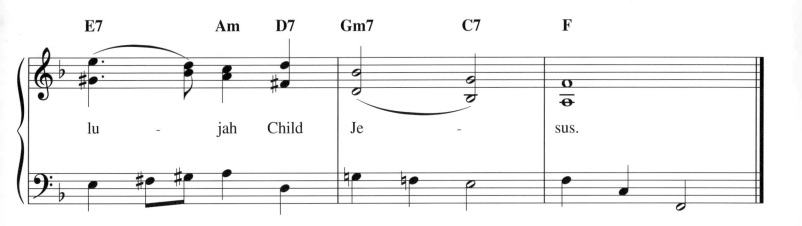

lu - jah Child Je - sus.

CHRIST IS BORN THIS EVENING

Traditional

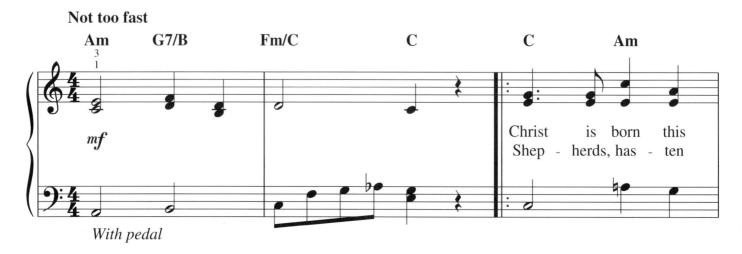

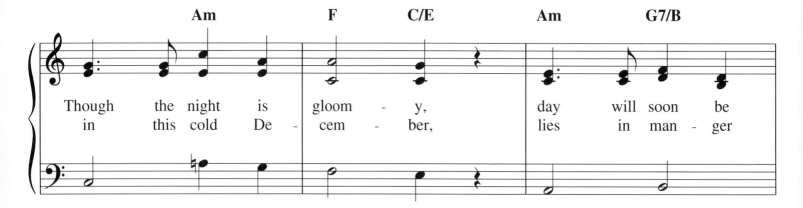

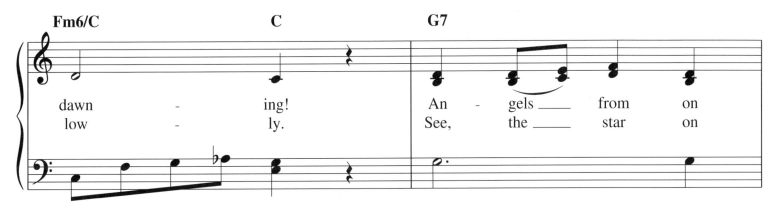

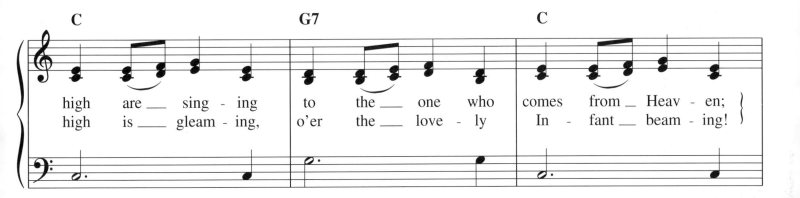

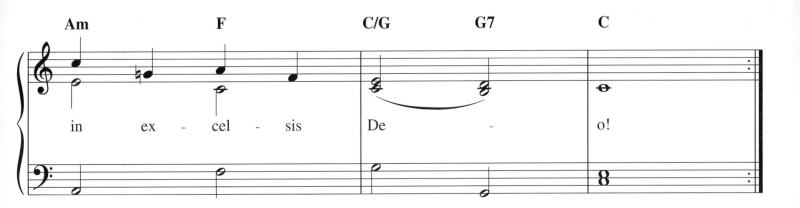

CHRIST WAS BORN ON CHRISTMAS DAY

Moderately bright

Traditional

Christ was born on Christ - mas day, Wreath the hol - ly,
He is born to set us free, He is born our
Let the bright red ber - ries glow, Ev - 'ry - where in
Chris - tian men re - joice and sing, 'Tis the birth - day

twine the bay, Christ - us na - tus ho - di - e; The
Lord to be, Ex Ma - ri - a Vir - gin - e; The
good - ly show; Christ - us na - tus ho - di - e; The
of a King, Ex Ma - ri - a Vir - gin - e; The

Babe, the Son, the Ho - ly One of Mar - y.
God, the Lord, by all a - dored for - ev - er.
Babe, the Son, the Ho - ly One of Mar - y.
God, the Lord, by all a - dored for - ev - er.

THE CHRISTMAS TREE WITH ITS CANDLES GLEAMING

Traditional Czech Text
Traditional Bohemian-Czech Tune

Like a lullabye

With pedal

The Christ-mas

tree, with its can-dles gleam-ing, a glow is kin-dling in all our hearts.
stand round the glit-'ring treas-ure, their eyes are spar-kling, their spir-its bright.
heart, you of-fer bless-ing, for ev-'ry par-ent as well as child.

It speaks of God's pure love-light stream-ing; it brings us hope, and joy im-parts.
O sweet re-mind-er of love's full meas-ure, our shin-ing sym-bol of heav'n-ly light!
For young and old, your bea-cons beck-'ning lead us to Je-sus, sweet and mild.

1.,2. The chil-dren
For ev-'ry

3. mild.

CHRISTIANS, AWAKE!
SALUTE THE HAPPY MORN

Traditional

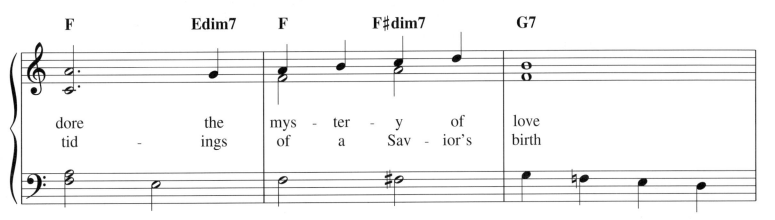

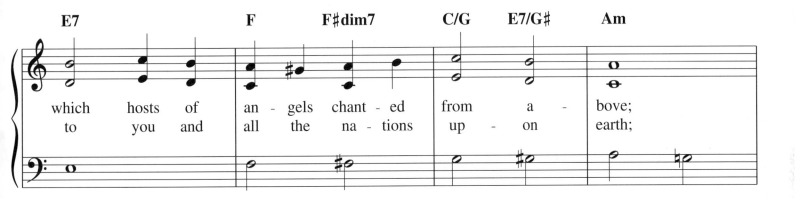

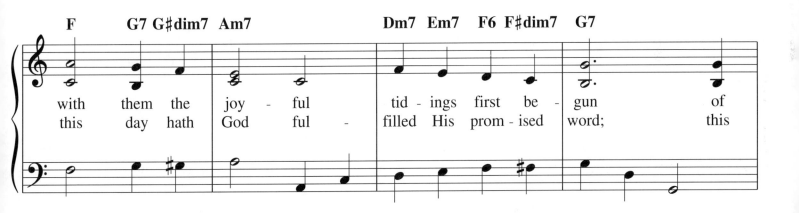

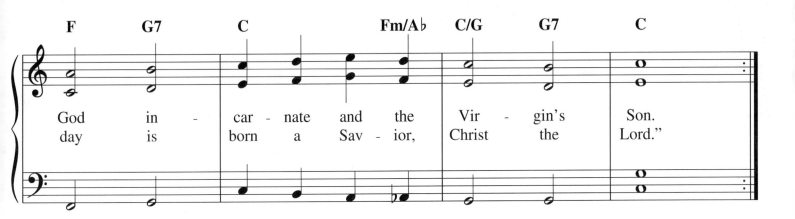

COME, ALL YE SHEPHERDS

Traditional Czech Text
Traditional Moravian Melody

Happily

Come, all ___ ye ___ shep - herds, ___ such ___ won - ders ___ en -

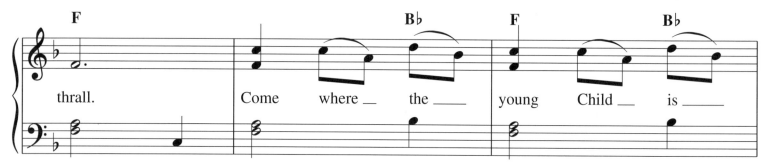

thrall. Come where ___ the ___ young Child ___ is ___

laid in ___ a ___ stall. This day to us a Sav - ior is giv - en,

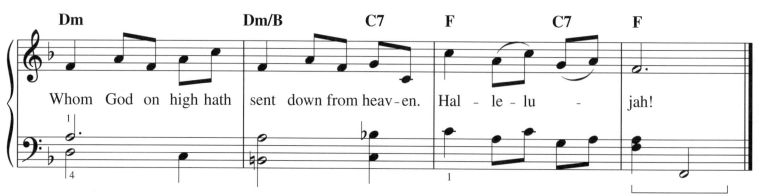

Whom God on high hath sent down from heav - en. Hal - le - lu - jah!

COME, THOU LONG-EXPECTED JESUS

Words by CHARLES WESLEY
Music by ROWLAND HUGH PRICHARD

With reverence

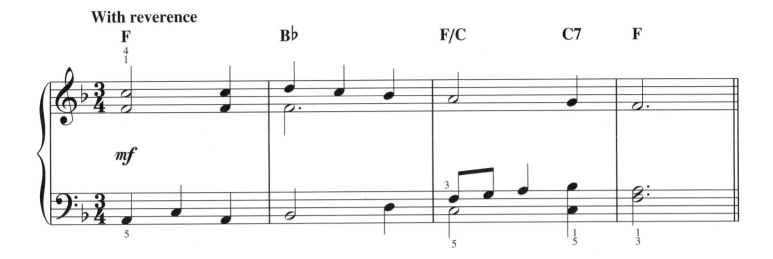

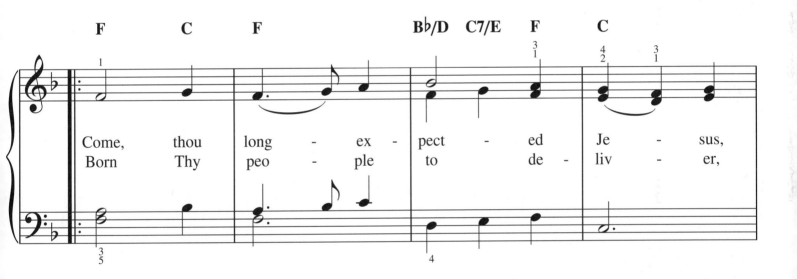

Come, thou long - ex - pect - ed Je - sus,
Born Thy peo - ple to de - liv - er,

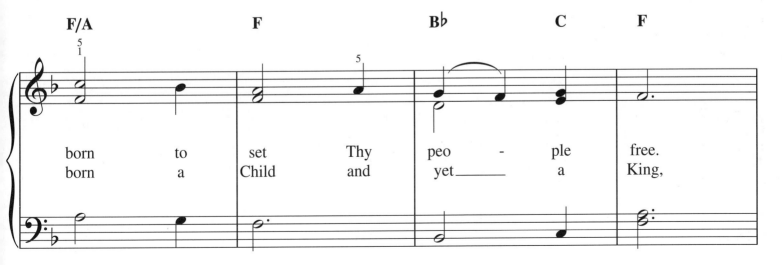

born to set Thy peo - ple free.
born a Child and yet_____ a King,

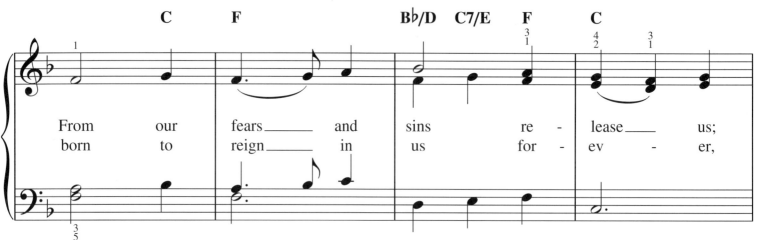

From our   fears____ and   sins   re - lease____ us;
born   to   reign____ in   us   for - ev - er,

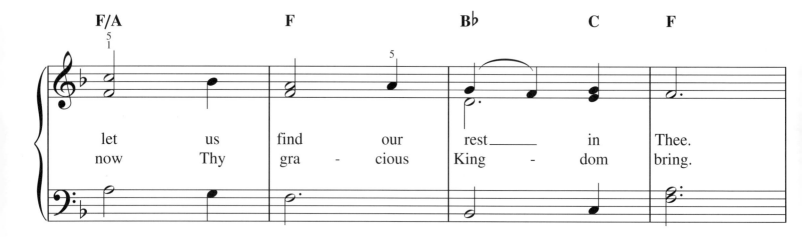

let   us   find   our   rest____ in   Thee.
now   us Thy   gra - cious   King - dom   bring.

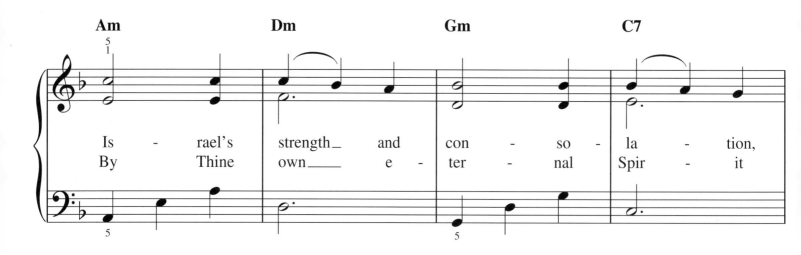

Is - rael's   strength_ and   con - so - la - tion,
By   Thine   own____ e - ter - nal   Spir - it

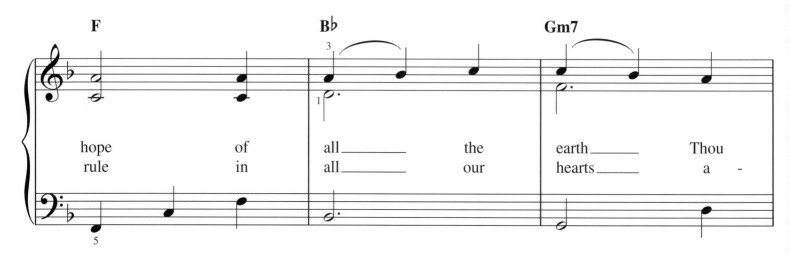

hope   of   all_____ the   earth____ Thou
rule   in   all_____ our   hearts____ a -

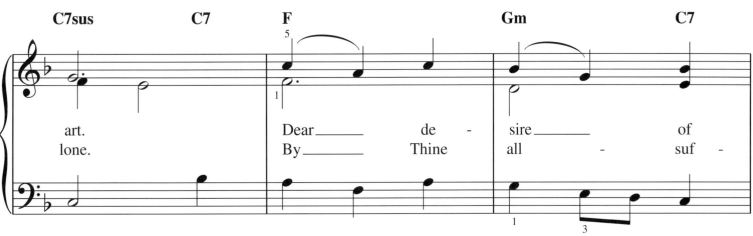

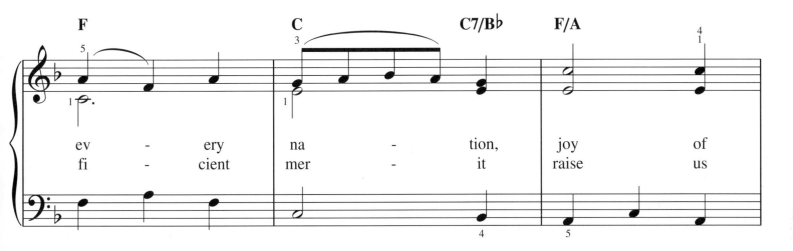

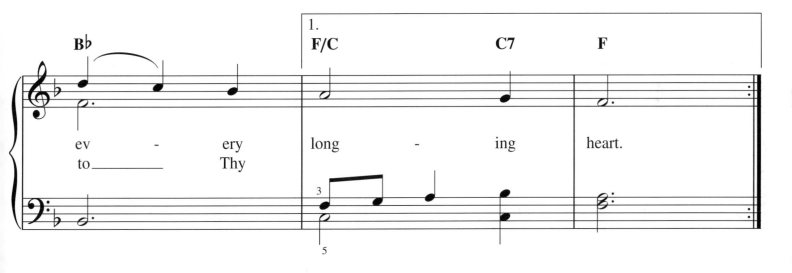

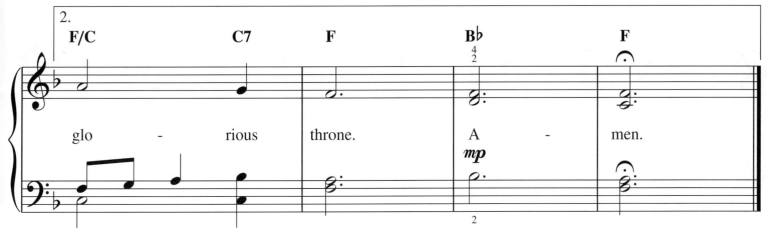

COVENTRY CAROL

Words by ROBERT CROO
Traditional English Melody

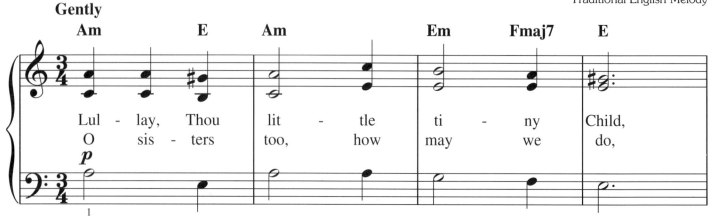

Lul - lay, Thou lit - tle ti - ny Child,
O sis - ters too, how may we do,

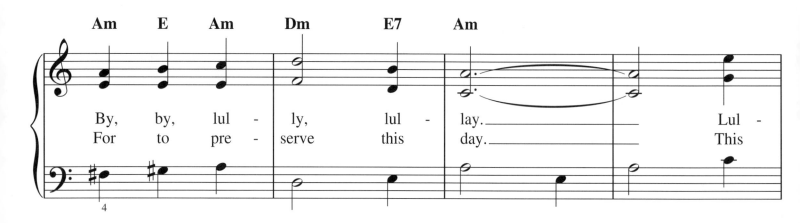

By, by, lul - ly, lul - lay.
For to pre - serve this day.
Lul -
This

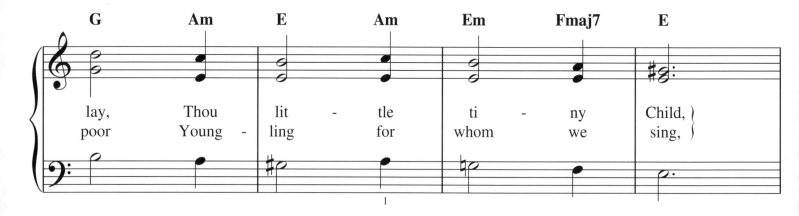

lay, Thou lit - tle ti - ny Child,
poor Young - ling for whom we sing,

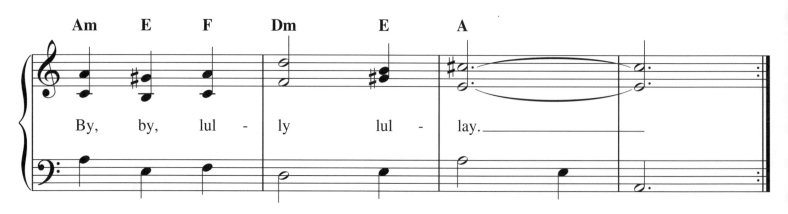

By, by, lul - ly lul - lay.

THE FIRST NOËL

17th Century English Carol
Music from W. Sandy's *Christmas Carols*

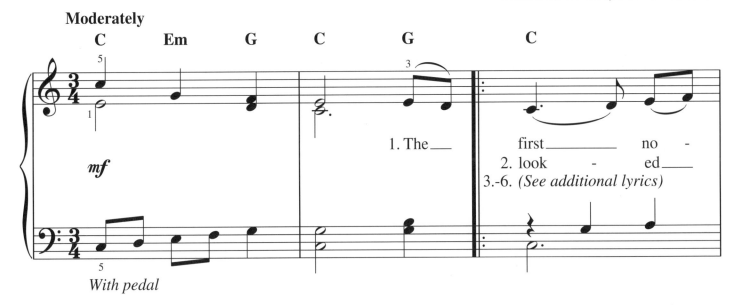

Moderately

1. The first no -
2. look - ed
3.-6. *(See additional lyrics)*

mf

With pedal

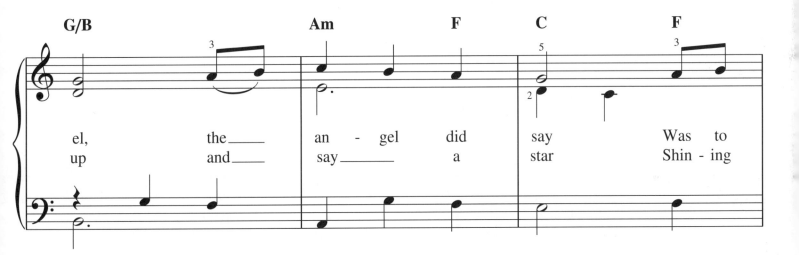

el, the an - gel did say Was to
up and say a star Shin - ing

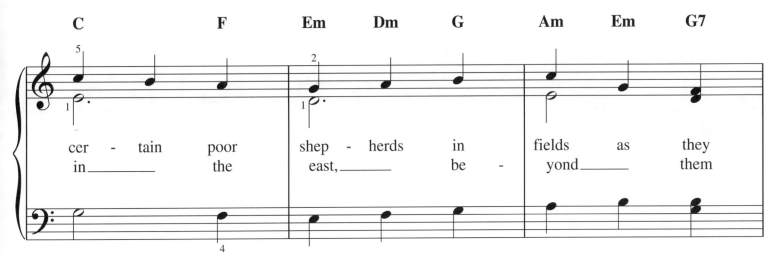

cer - tain poor shep - herds in fields as they
in the east, be - yond them

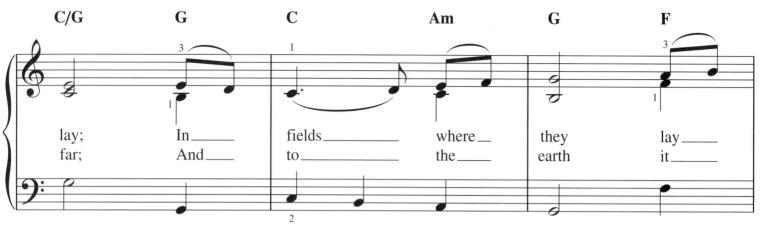

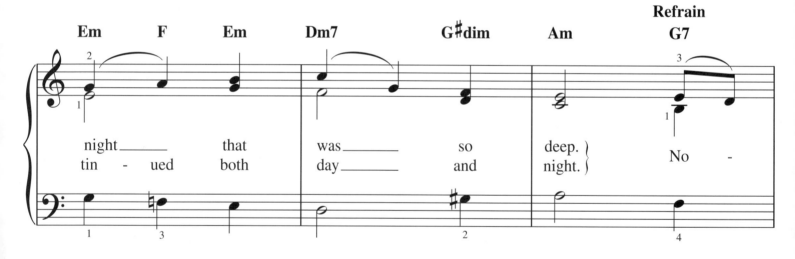

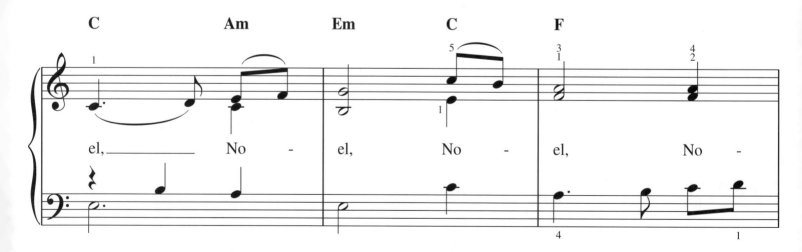

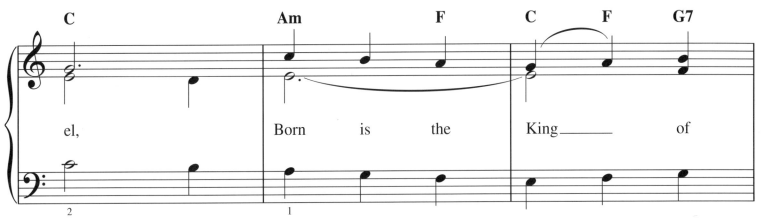

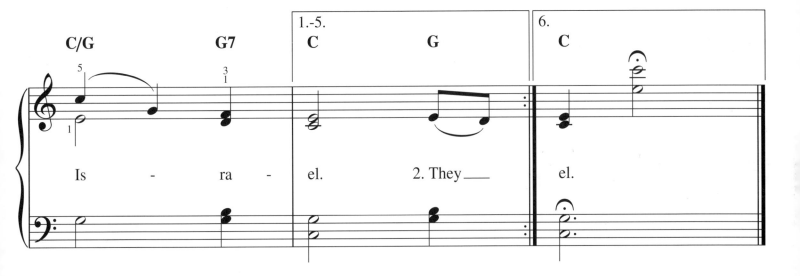

Additional Lyrics

3. And by the light of that same star,
   Three wise men came from country far.
   To seek for a King was their intent,
   And to follow the star wherever it went.
   Refrain

4. This star drew nigh to the northwest;
   O'er Bethlehem it took its rest.
   And there it did both stop and stay,
   Right over the place where Jesus lay.
   Refrain

5. Then entered in those wise men three,
   Full rev'rently upon their knee;
   And offered there in His presence,
   Their gold and myrrh and frankincense.
   Refrain

6. Then let us all with one accord
   Sing praises to our heav'nly Lord,
   That had made heav'n and earth of naught,
   And with His blood mankind hath bought.
   Refrain

DANCE OF THE SUGAR PLUM FAIRY

By PYOTR IL'YICH TCHAIKOVSKY

Not too slow, daintily

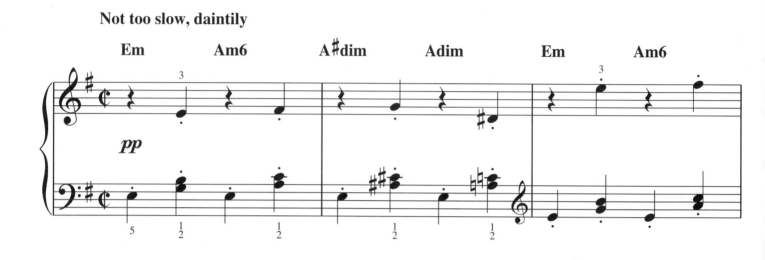

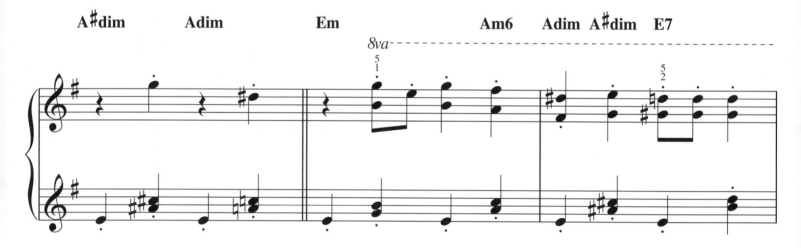

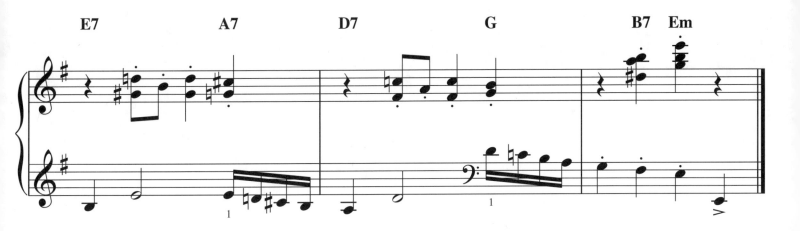

A DAY, BRIGHT DAY OF GLORY

Traditional

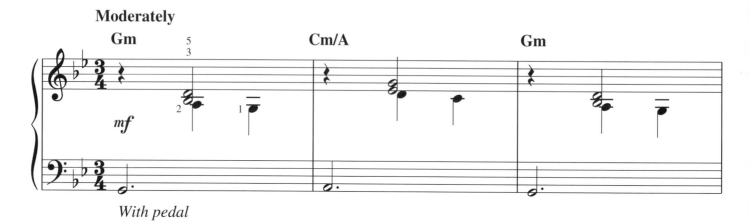

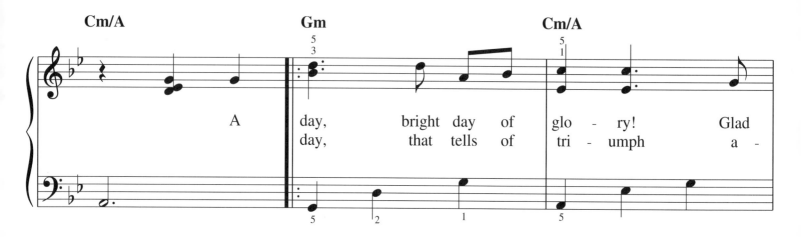

A day, bright day of glory! Glad
day, that tells of tri - umph a -

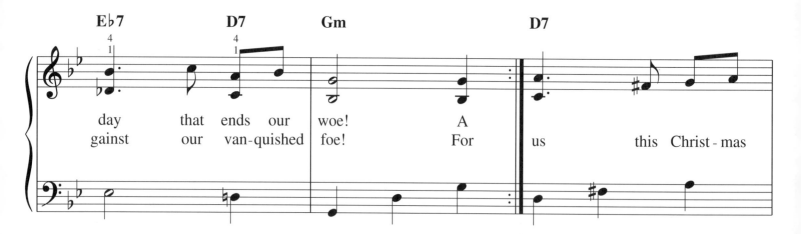

day that ends our woe! A For
gainst our van-quished foe! us this Christ - mas

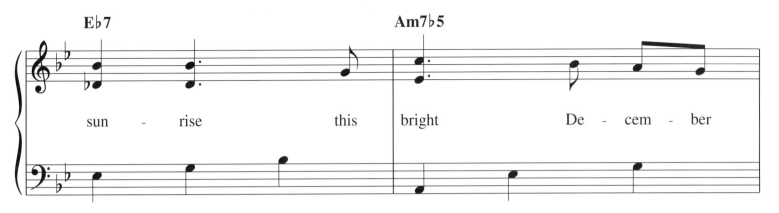

sun - rise   this | bright   De - cem - ber

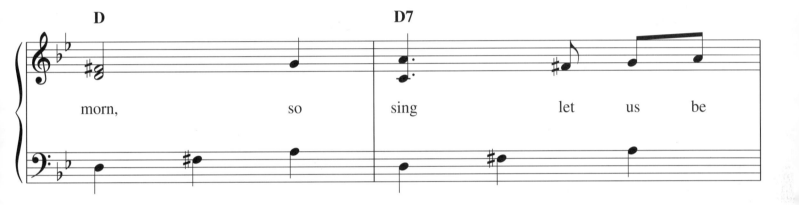

morn,   so | sing   let   us   be

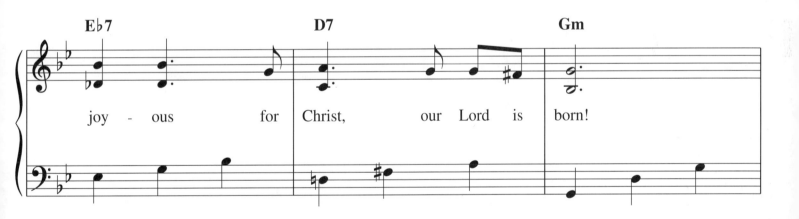

joy - ous   for | Christ,   our Lord is | born!

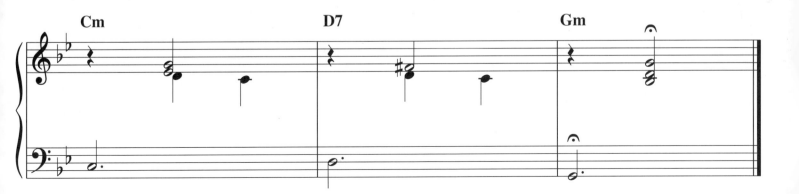

DECK THE HALL

Traditional Welsh Carol

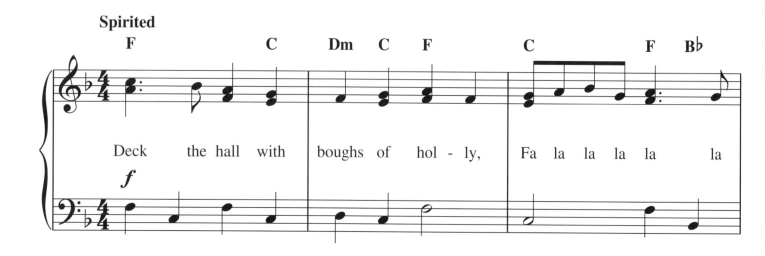

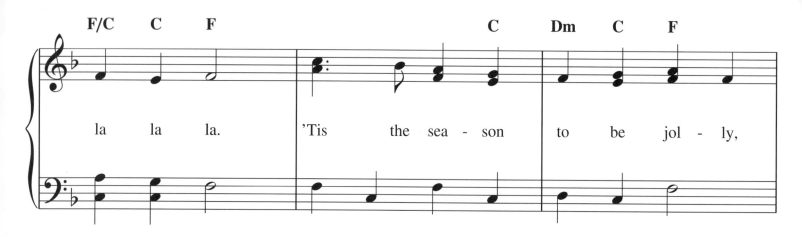

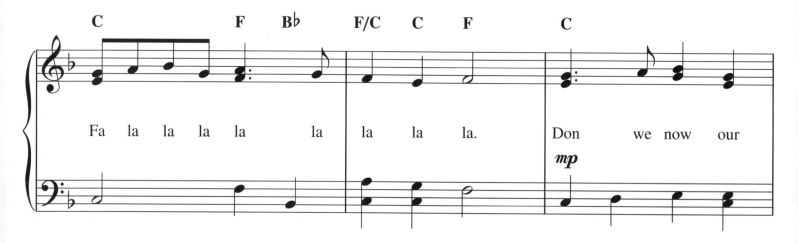

gay ap-par-el, Fa___ la fa___ la la la la.

cresc.

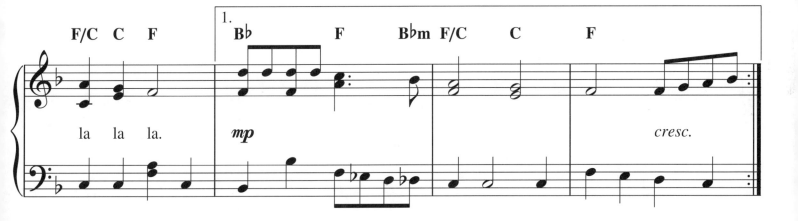

Troll the an - cient Yule - tide car - ol, Fa la la la la la

f

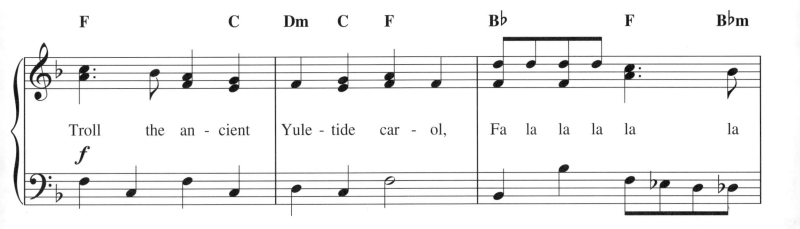

1.

la la la. Fa la la la la la la la la

mp *cresc.*

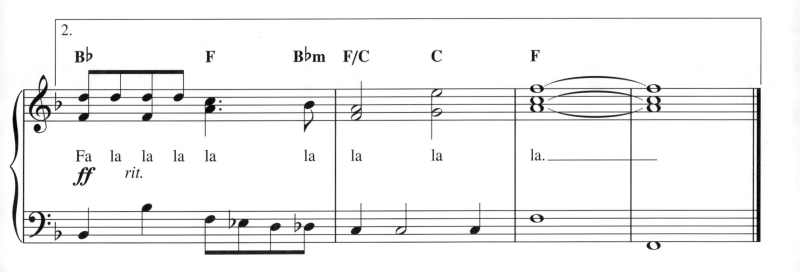

2.

Fa la la la la la la la la.___

ff *rit.*

DING DONG! MERRILY ON HIGH!

French Carol

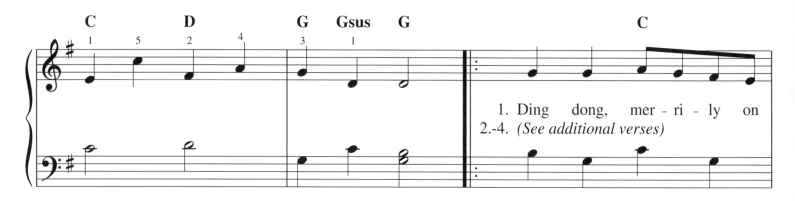

1. Ding dong, mer - ri - ly on
2.-4. *(See additional verses)*

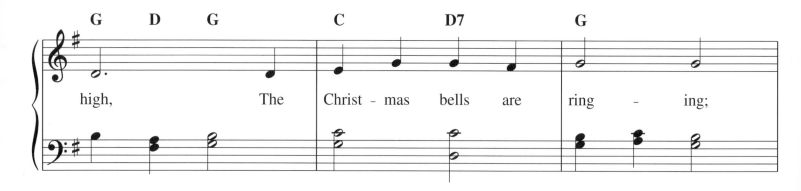

high, The Christ - mas bells are ring - ing;

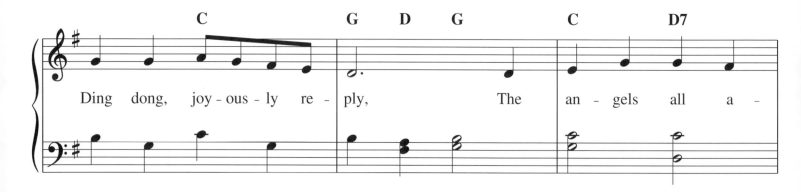

Ding dong, joy - ous - ly re - ply, The an - gels all a -

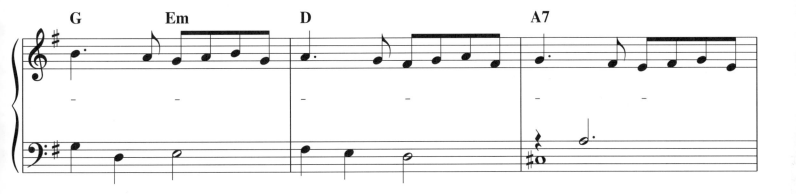

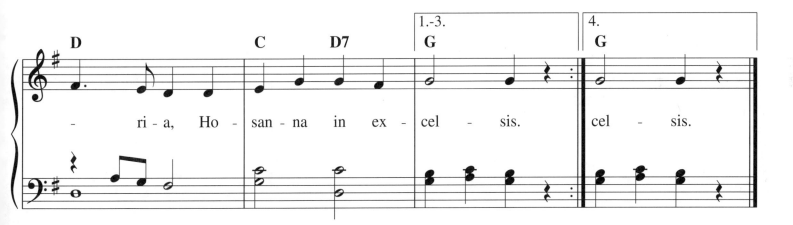

Additional Verses

2. Ding dong, carol all the bells,
   Ring out the Christmas story;
   Ding dong, sound the good noels,
   God's Son has come in glory.
   Refrain

3. Praise Him! People far and near,
   And join the angels' singing.
   Ding dong, everywhere we hear
   The Christmas bells a-ringing.
   Refrain

4. Hear them ring this happy morn!
   Our God a gift has given;
   Ding dong, Jesus Christ is born!
   A precious Child from heaven.
   Refrain

THE FRIENDLY BEASTS

Traditional English Carol

Moderately

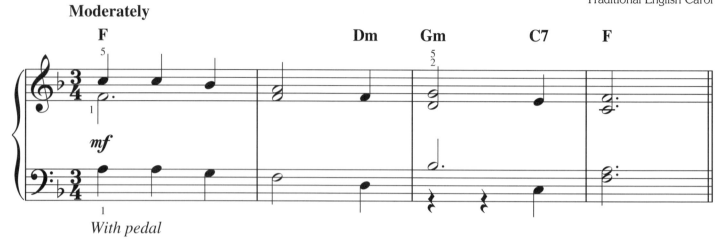

With pedal

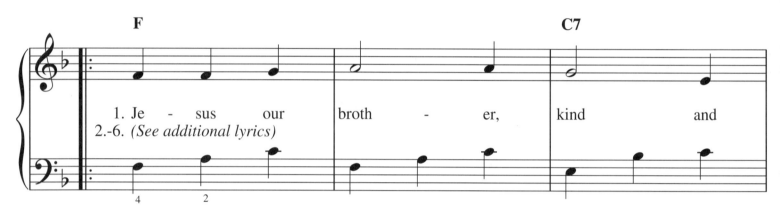

1. Je - sus our broth - er, kind and
2.-6. *(See additional lyrics)*

good Was hum - bly born in a

sta - ble rude, And the friend - ly beasts a -

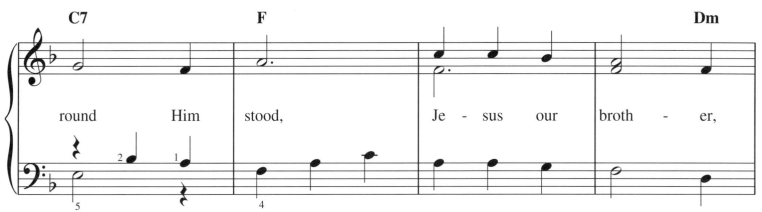

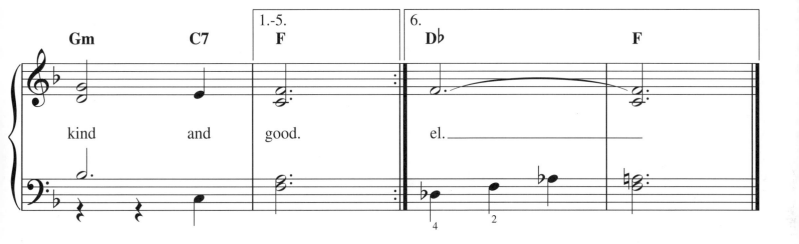

Additional Lyrics

2. "I," said the donkey, shaggy and brown,
"I carried His mother up hill and down;
I carried her safely to Bethlehem town."
"I," said the donkey, shaggy and brown.

3. "I," said the cow all white and red,
"I gave Him my manger for His bed;
I gave Him my hay to pillow His head."
"I," said the cow all white and red.

4. "I," said the sheep with curly horn,
"I gave Him my wool for His blanket warm;
He wore my coat on Christmas morn."
"I," said the sheep with curly horn.

5. "I," said the dove from the rafters high,
"I cooed Him to sleep so He would not cry;
We cooed Him to sleep, my mate and I."
"I," said the dove from the rafters high.

6. Thus every beast by some good spell,
In the stable dark was glad to tell
Of the gift he gave Emanuel,
The gift he gave Emanuel.

FROM HEAVEN ABOVE TO EARTH I COME

Words and Music by
MARTIN LUTHER

GOOD CHRISTIAN MEN, REJOICE

14th Century Latin Text
Translated by JOHN MASON NEALE
14th Century German Melody

With spirit

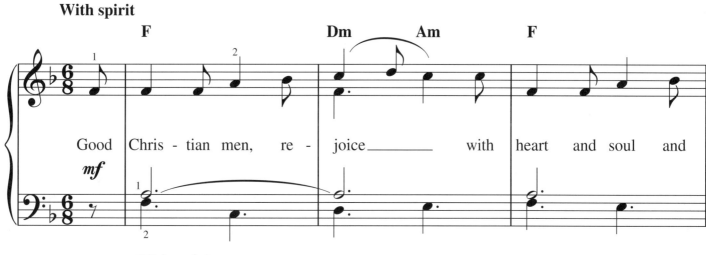

Good Chris - tian men, re - joice_____ with heart and soul and

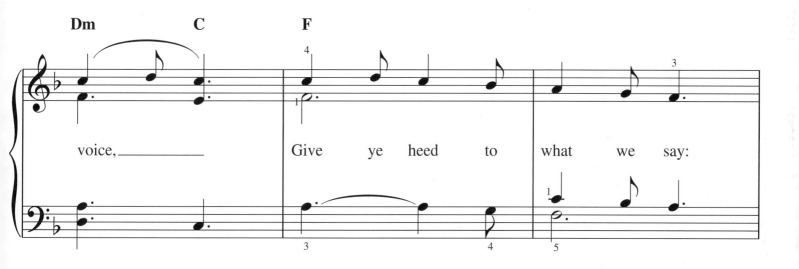

voice,_____ Give ye heed to what we say:

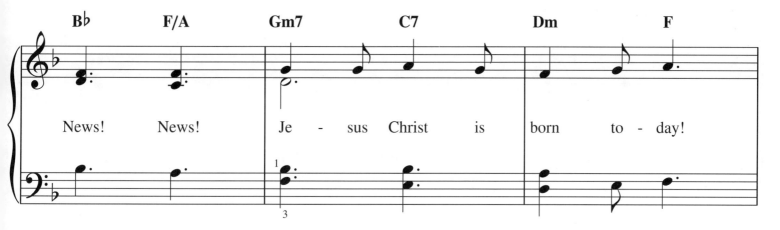

News! News! Je - sus Christ is born to - day!

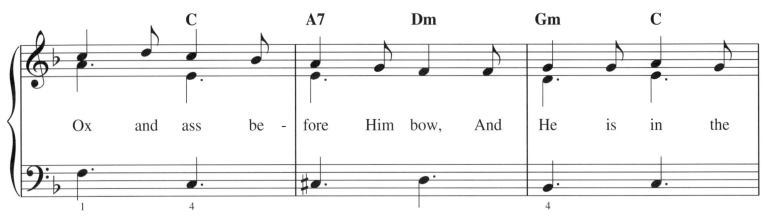

Ox and ass be - fore Him bow, And He is in the

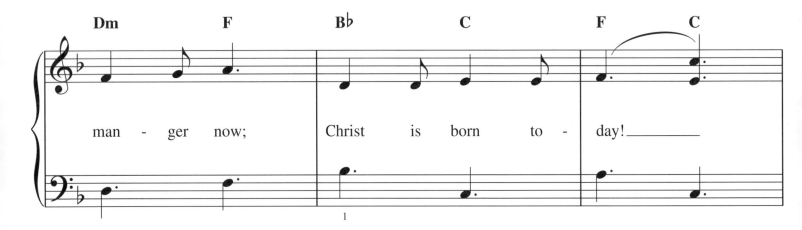

man - ger now; Christ is born to - day! Christ is born to -

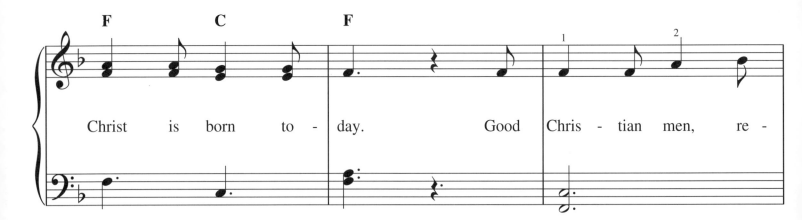

day. Good Chris - tian men, re -

joice_____ with heart and soul and voice_____

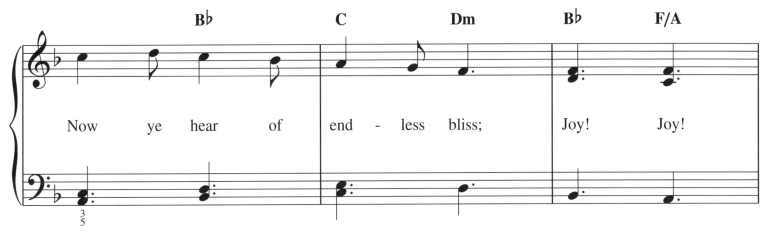

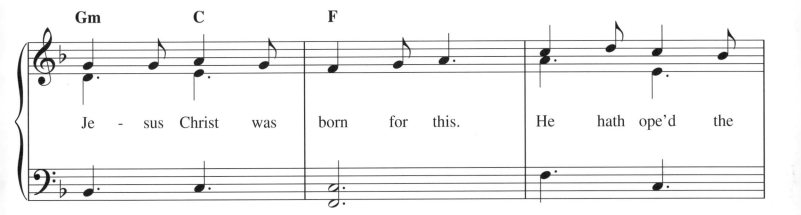

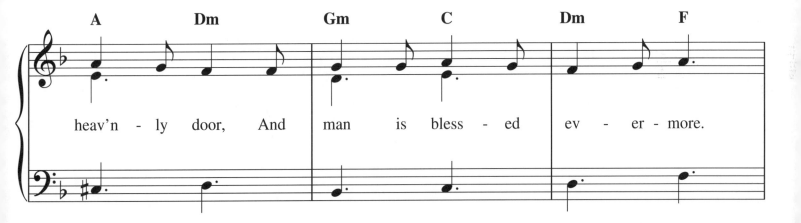

FUM, FUM, FUM

Traditional Catalonian Carol

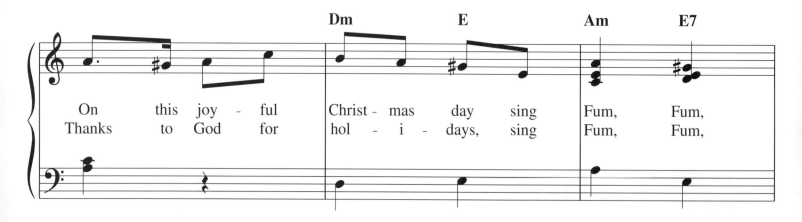

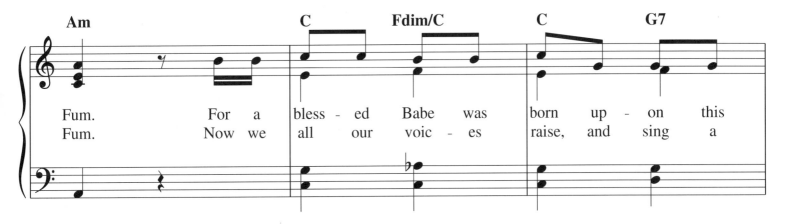

Am | C | Fdim/C | C | G7

Fum.   For a bless - ed Babe was born up - on this
Fum.   Now we all our voic - es raise, and sing a

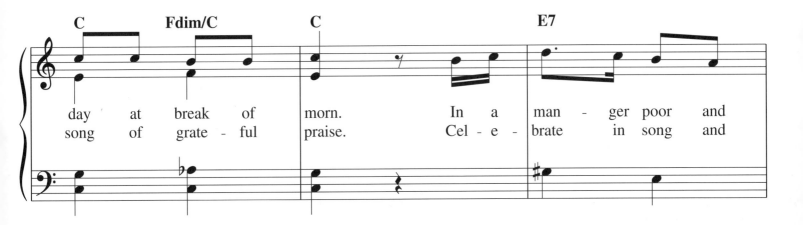

C | Fdim/C | C | E7

day at break of morn.   In a man - ger poor and
song of grate - ful praise.   Cel - e - brate in song and

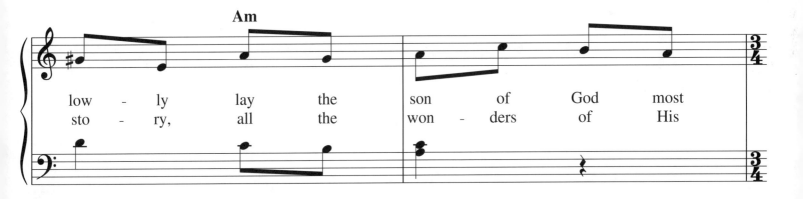

Am

low - ly lay the son of God most
sto - ry, all the won - ders of most His

E | Am | E7 | 1. Am | 2. Am

ho - ly, Fum, Fum, Fum.
glo - ry, Fum, Fum,   Fum.

GO, TELL IT ON THE MOUNTAIN

African-American Spiritual
Verses by JOHN W. WORK, JR.

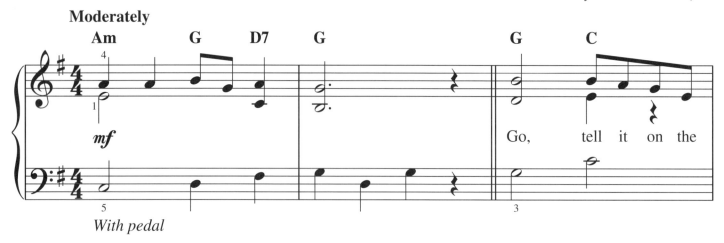

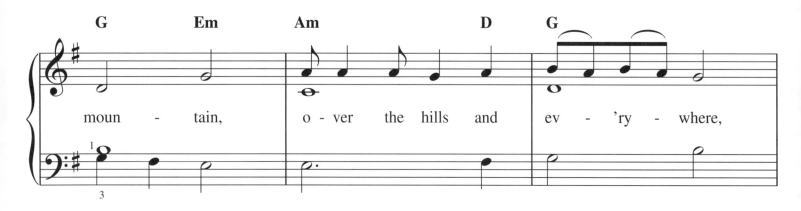

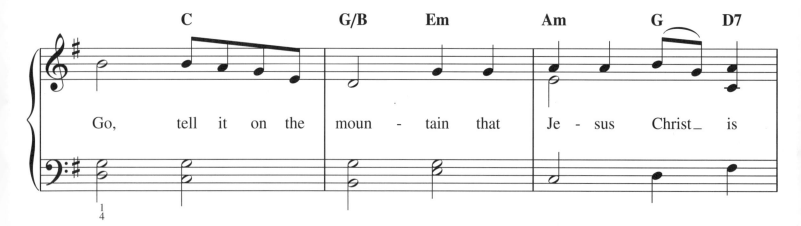

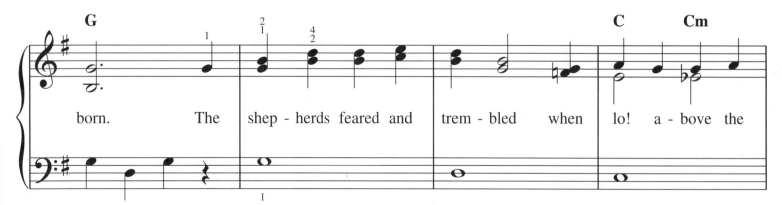

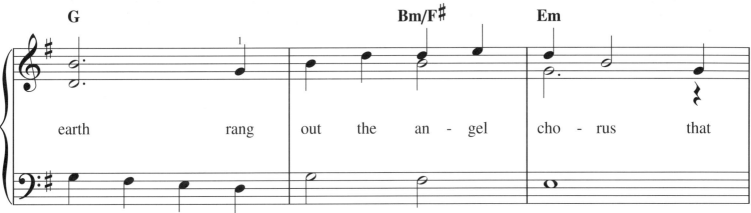

earth   rang   out the an - gel   cho - rus   that

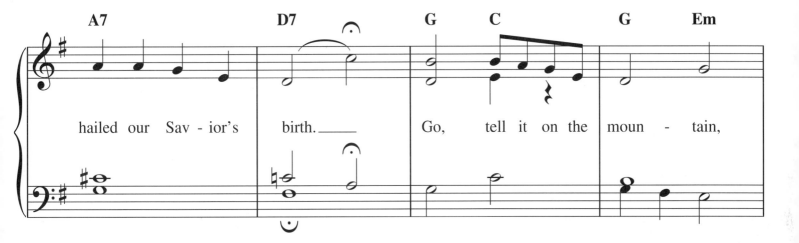

hailed our Sav - ior's   birth._____   Go,   tell it on the moun - tain,

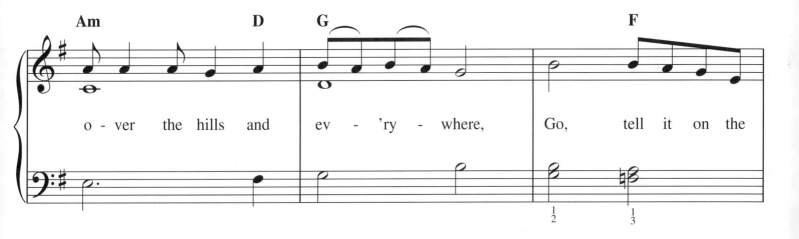

o - ver the hills and   ev - 'ry - where,   Go,   tell it on the

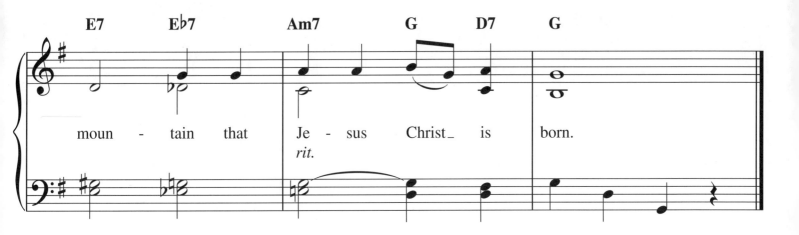

moun - tain that   Je - sus Christ_ is   born.

GOD REST YE MERRY, GENTLEMEN

19th Century English Carol

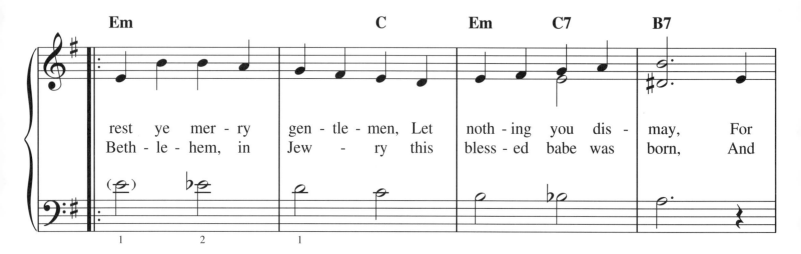

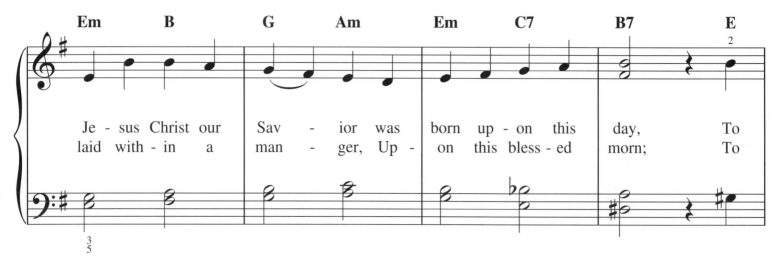

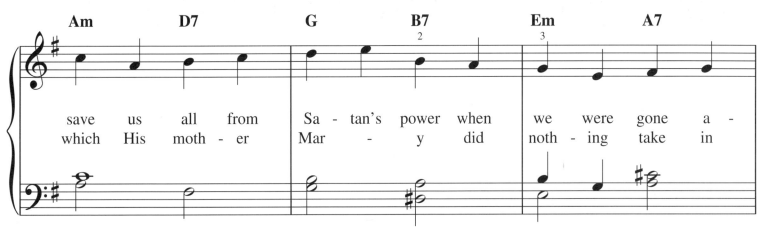

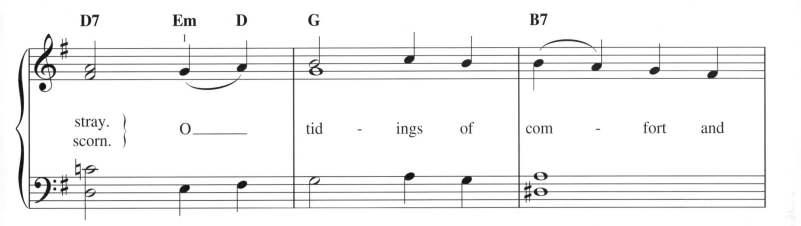

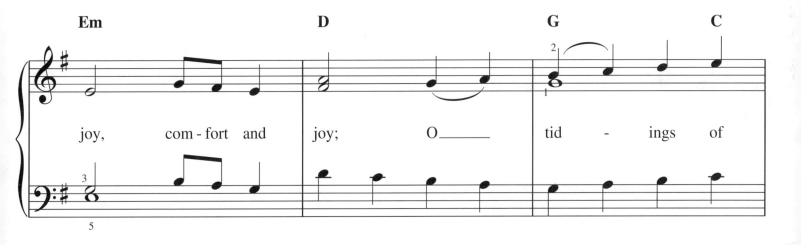

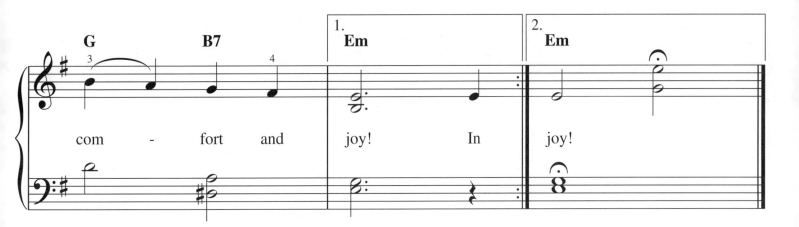

GOOD KING WENCESLAS

Words by JOHN M. NEALE
Music from *Piae Cantiones*

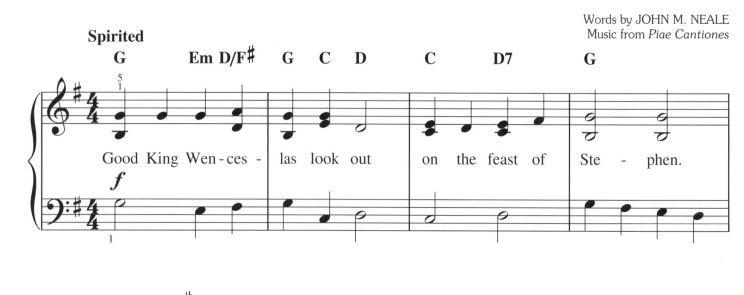

Good King Wen-ces- las look out on the feast of Ste - phen.

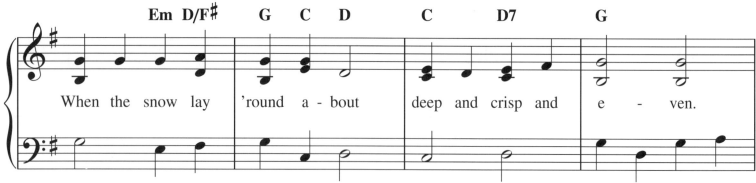

When the snow lay 'round a - bout deep and crisp and e - ven.

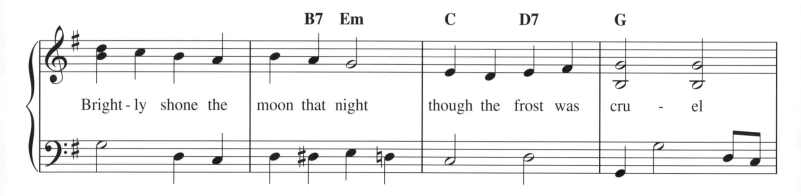

Bright-ly shone the moon that night though the frost was cru - el

when a poor man came in sight gath-'ring win - ter fu - el.

I AM SO GLAD ON CHRISTMAS EVE

Words by MARIE WEXELSEN
Music by PEDER KNUDSEN

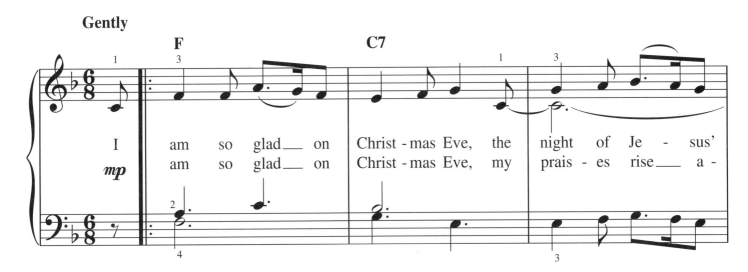

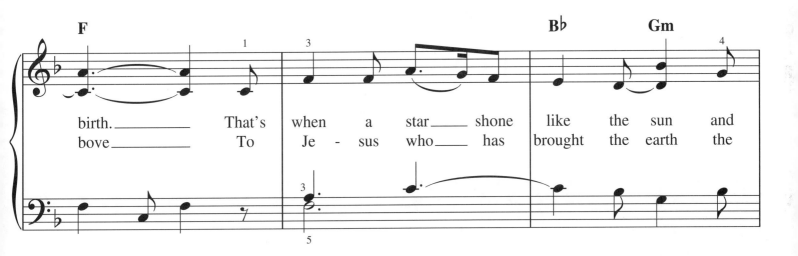

THE HAPPY CHRISTMAS COMES ONCE MORE

Words by NICOLAI F.S. GRUNDTVIG
Music by C. BALLE

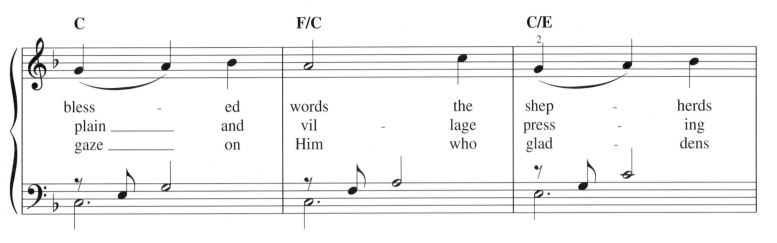

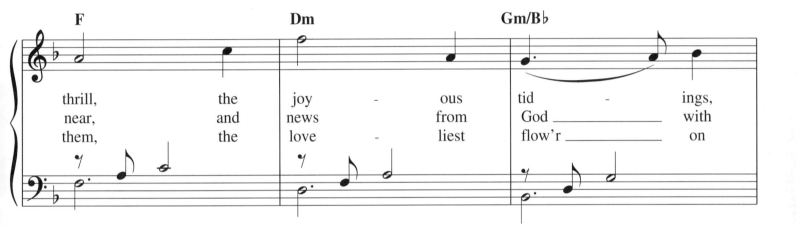

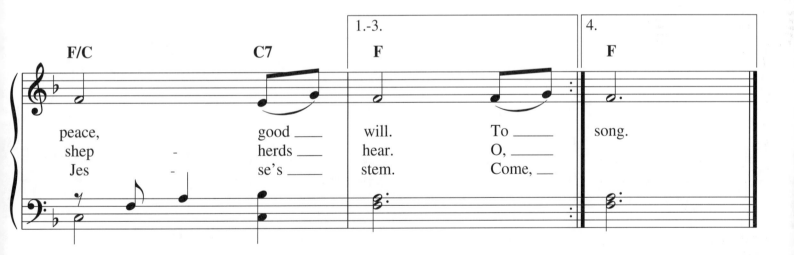

Additional Verse

4. Come, Jesus, glorious heav'nly Guest,
   Keep Thine own Christmas in our breast;
   Then David's harp-string, hushed so long
   Shall swell our jubilee of song.

HARK! THE HERALD ANGELS SING

Words by CHARLES WESLEY
Altered by GEORGE WHITEFIELD
Music by FELIX MENDELSSOHN-BARTHODLY
Arranged by WILLIAM H. CUMMINGS

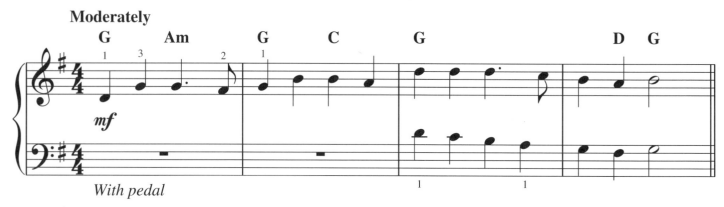

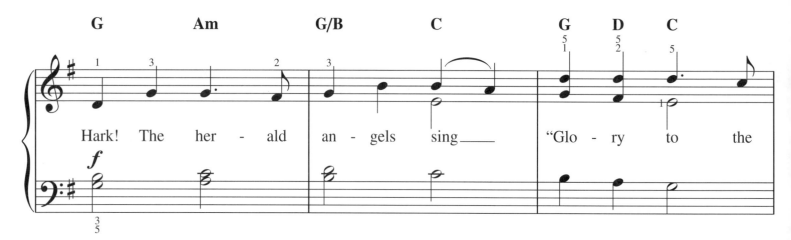

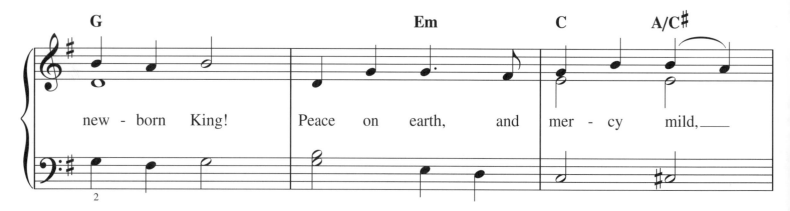

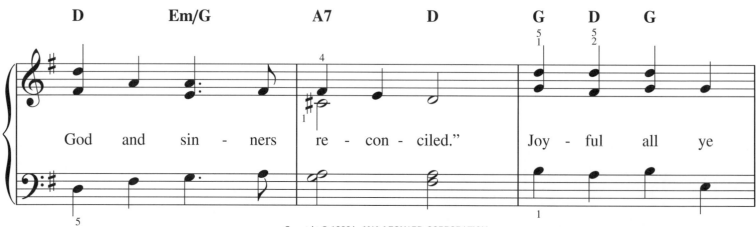

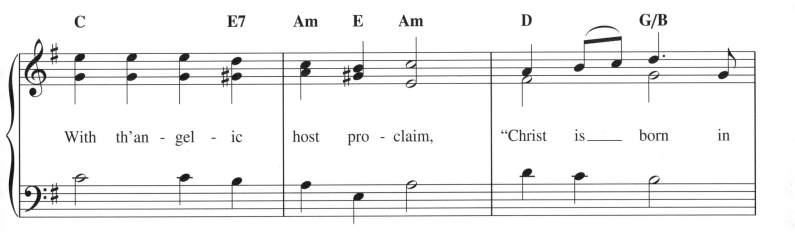

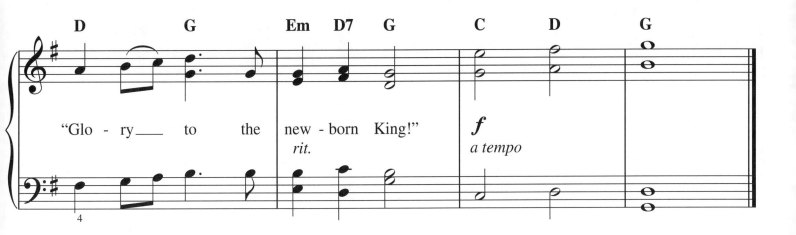

HE IS BORN, THE HOLY CHILD

(Il Est Ne, Le Divin Enfant)

Traditional French Carol

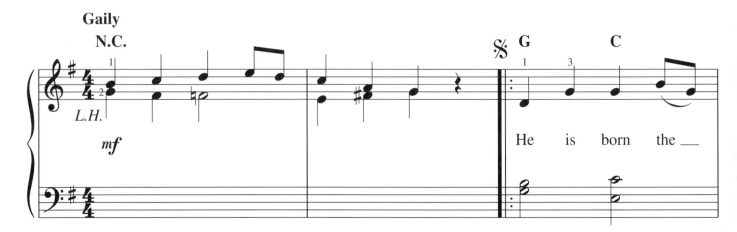

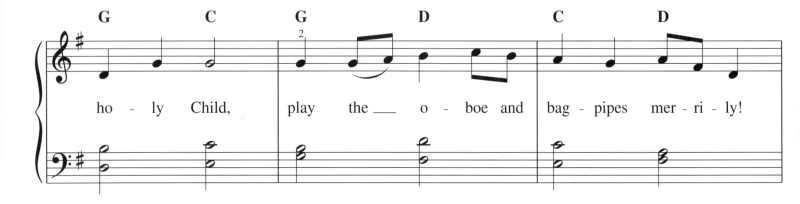

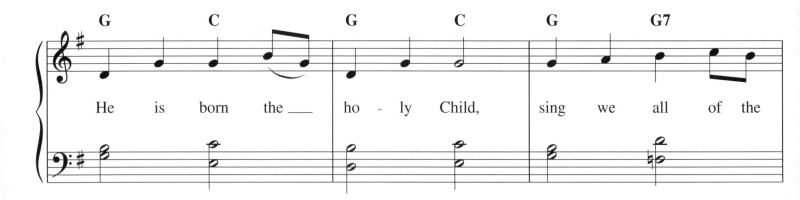

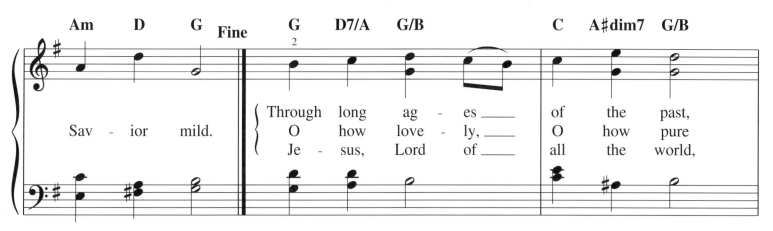

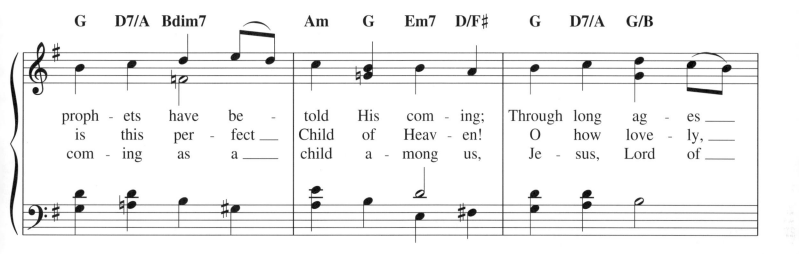

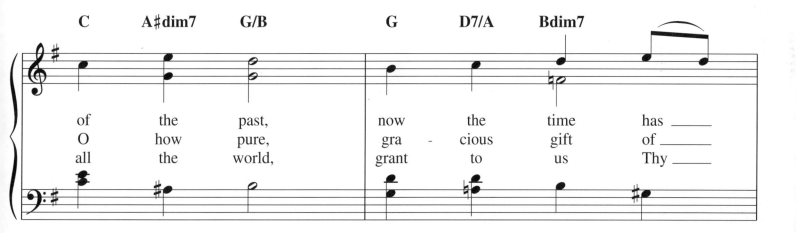

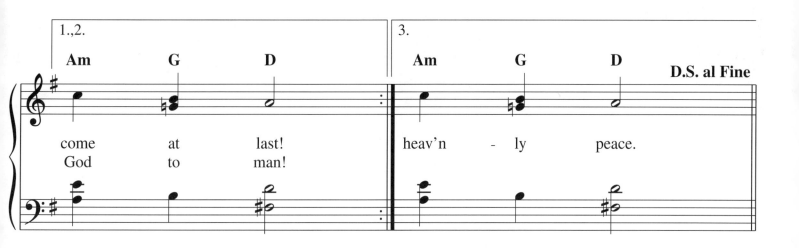

HERE WE COME A-WASSAILING

Traditional

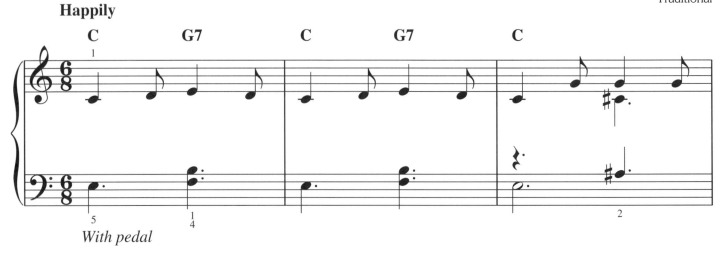

With pedal

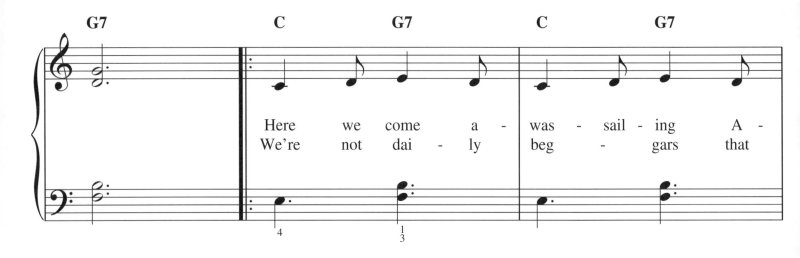

Here we come a - was - sail - ing A -
We're not dai - ly beg - gars A that

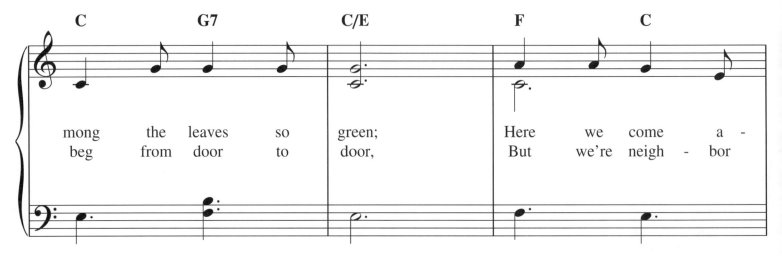

mong the leaves so green;
beg from door to door,

Here we come a -
But we're neigh - bor

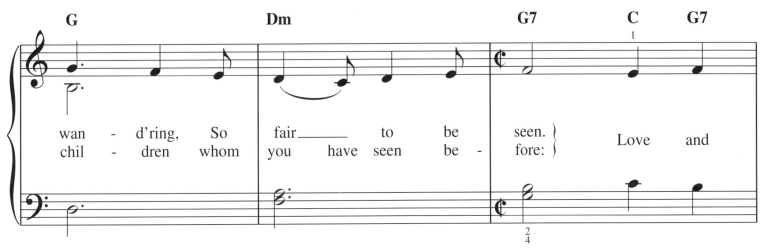

wan - d'ring, So fair___ to be seen. } Love and
chil - dren whom you have seen be - fore:

joy come to you, And to you your was - sail too; And God

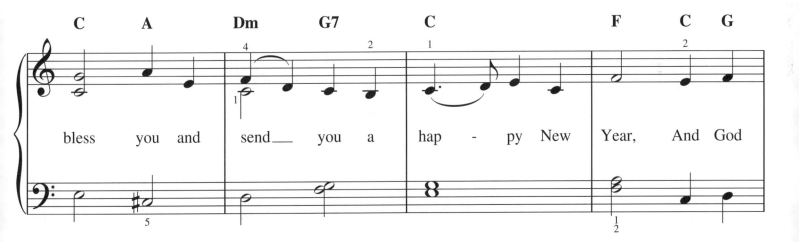

bless you and send___ you a hap - py New Year, And God

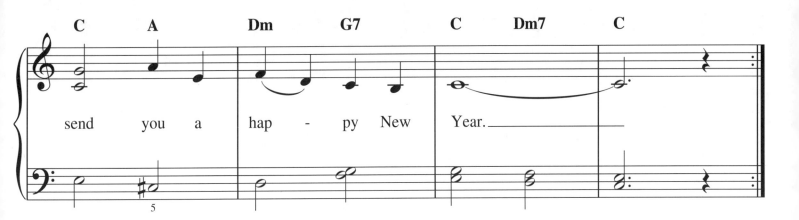

send you a hap - py New Year.___

THE HOLLY AND THE IVY

18th Century English Carol

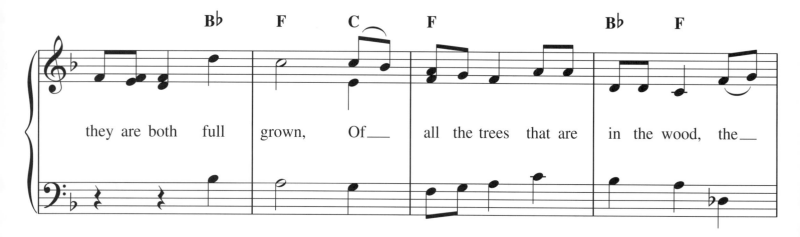

83

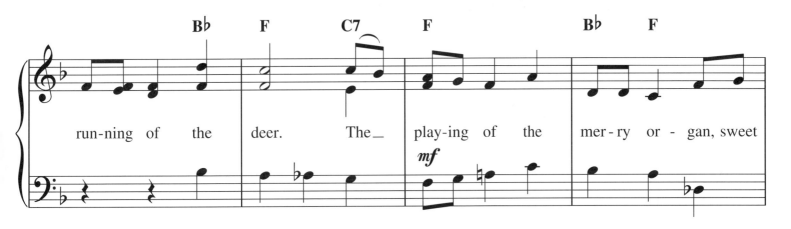

run-ning of the deer. The_ play-ing of the mer-ry or - gan, sweet

sing-ing in the choir. *cresc.* The hol - ly and the

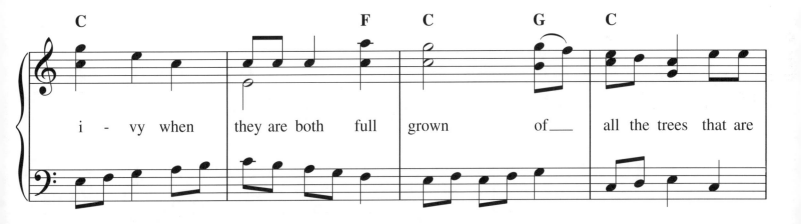

i - vy when they are both full grown of_ all the trees that are

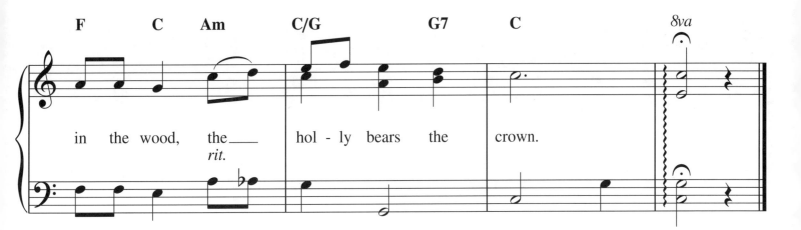

in the wood, the_ hol - ly bears the crown.

I HEARD THE BELLS
ON CHRISTMAS DAY

Words by HENRY WADSWORTH LONGFELLOW
Music by JOHN BAPTISTE CALKIN

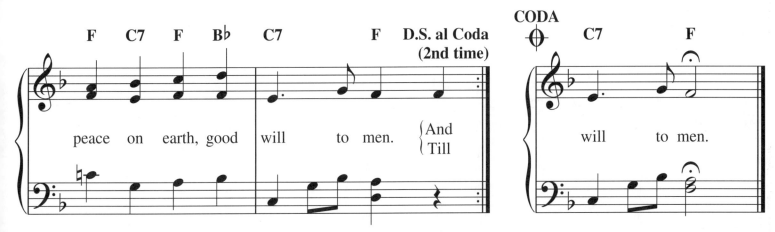

Additional Lyrics

3. And in despair I bow'd my head:
   "There is no peace on earth," I said,
   "For hate is strong, and mocks the song
   Of peace on earth, good will to men."

4. Then pealed the bells more loud and deep:
   "God is not dead, nor doth He sleep;
   The wrong shall fail, the right prevail,
   With peace on earth, good will to men."

5. Till ringing, singing on its way,
   The world revolved from night to day,
   A voice, a chime, a chant sublime,
   Of peace on earth, good will to men!

I SAW THREE SHIPS

Traditional English Carol

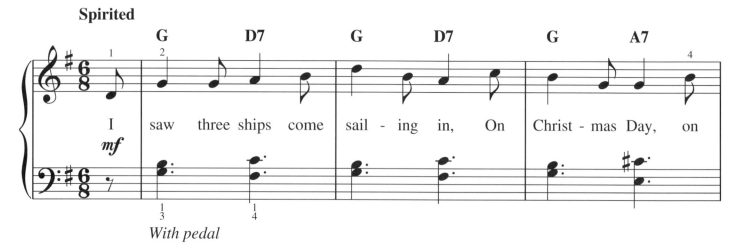

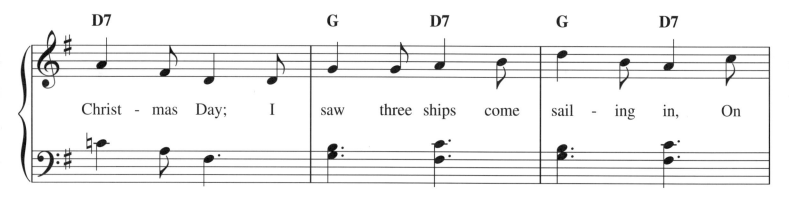

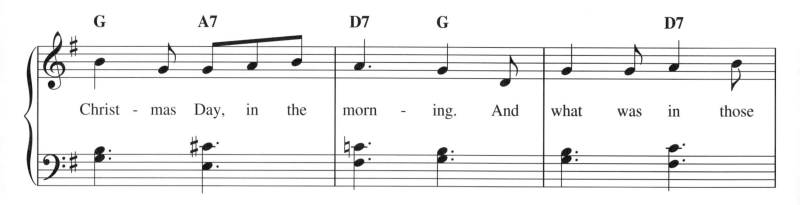

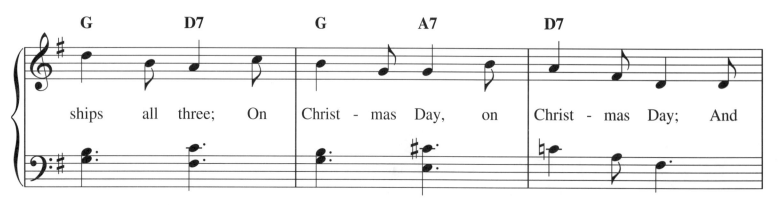

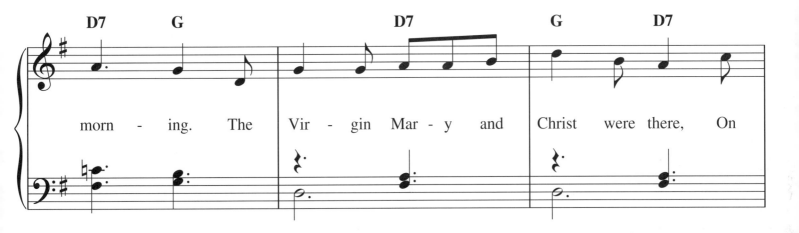

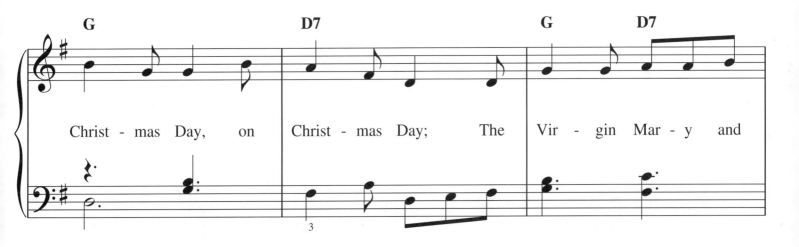

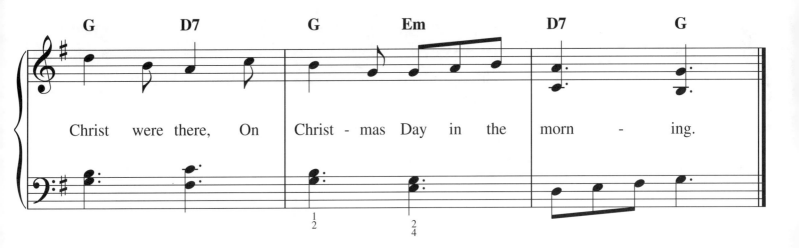

IN THE FIELD WITH
THEIR FLOCKS ABIDING

Traditional

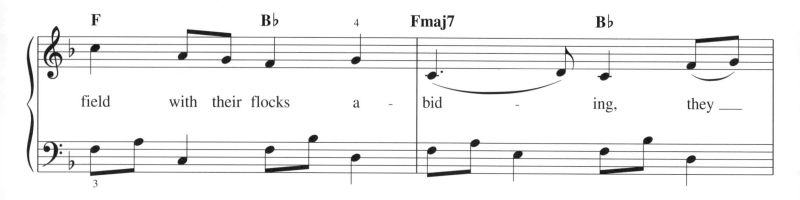

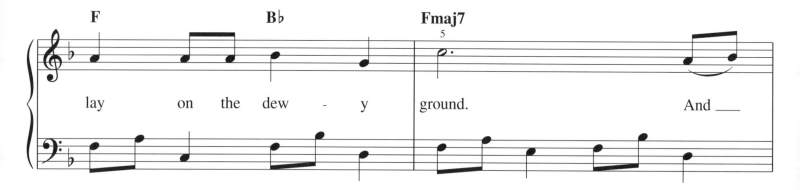

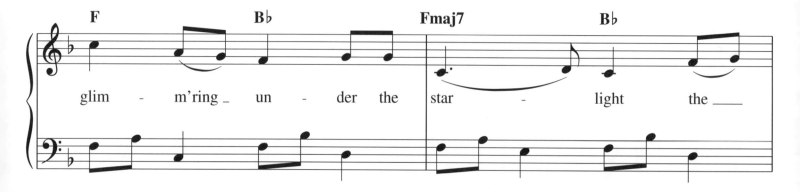

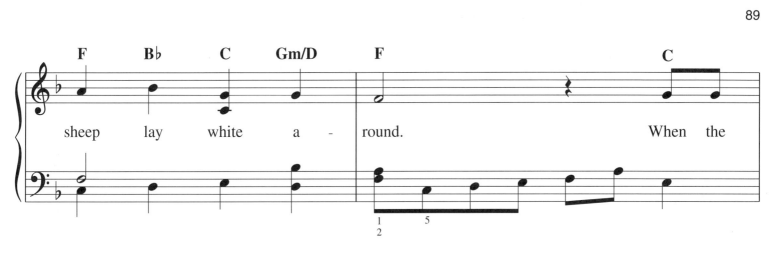

sheep lay white a - round. When the

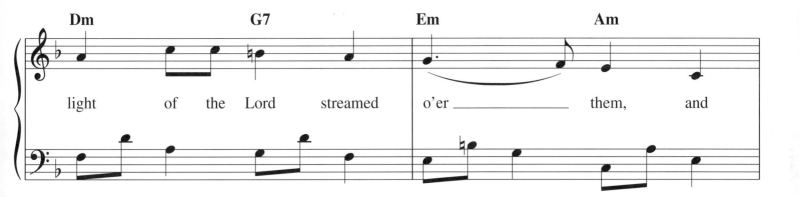

light of the Lord streamed o'er _____ them, and

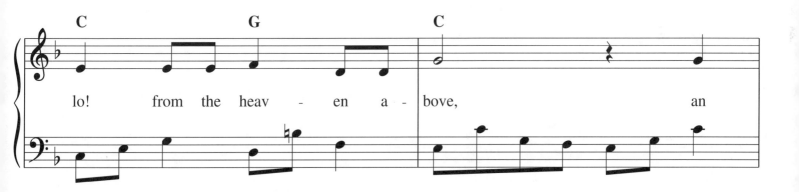

lo! from the heav - en a - bove, an

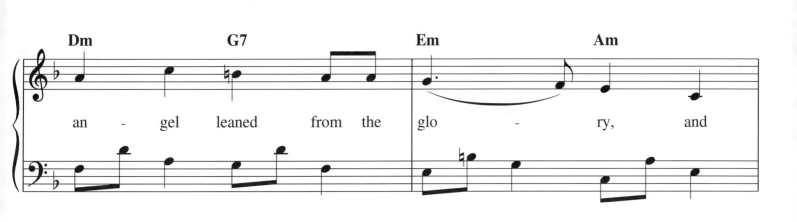

an - gel leaned from the glo - ry, and

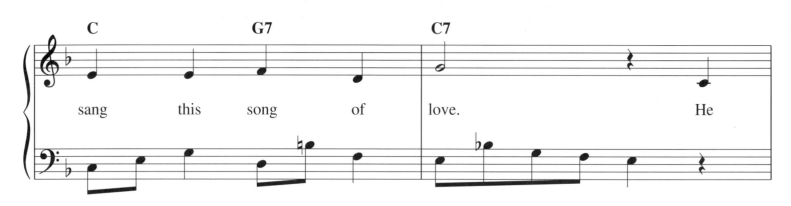

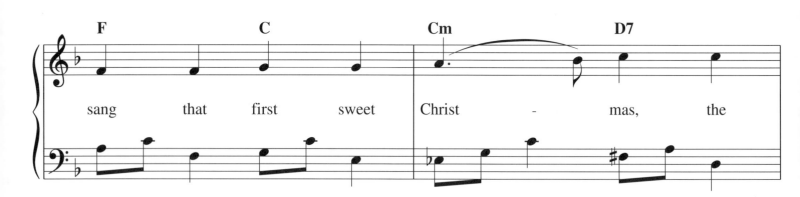

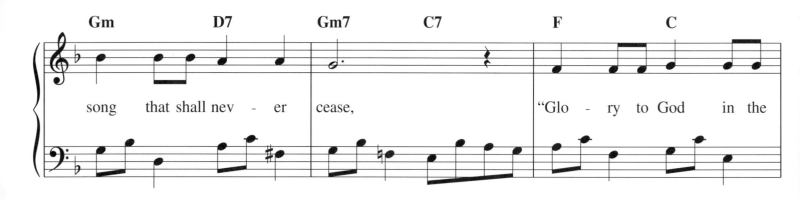

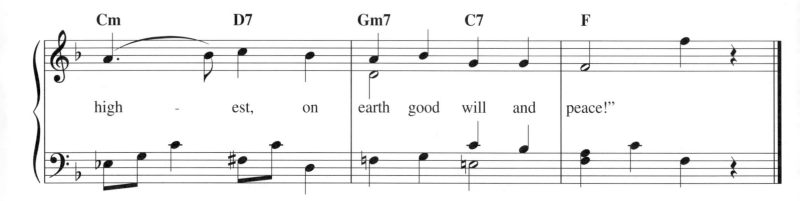

IN THE SILENCE OF THE NIGHT

Traditional Carol

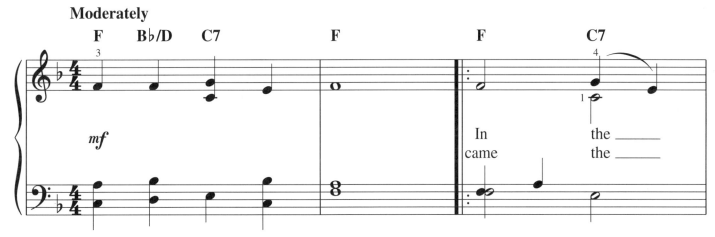

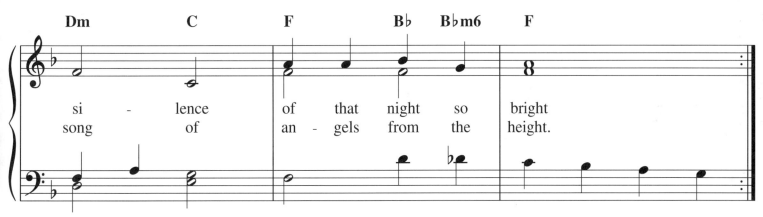

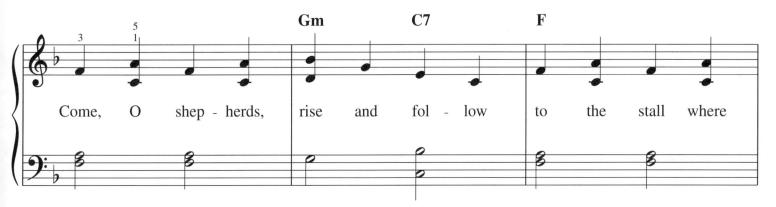

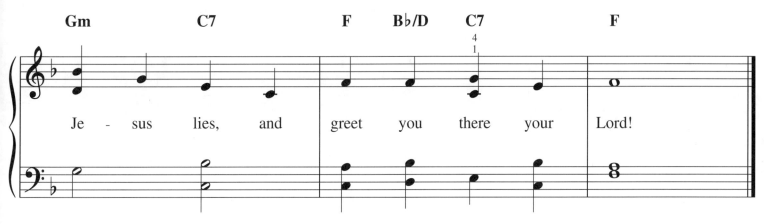

IT CAME UPON THE MIDNIGHT CLEAR

Words by EDMUND HAMILTON SEARS
Music by RICHARD STORRS WILLIS

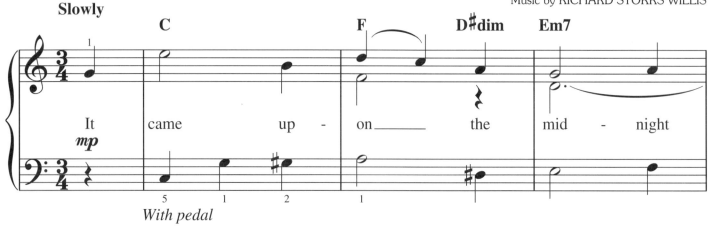

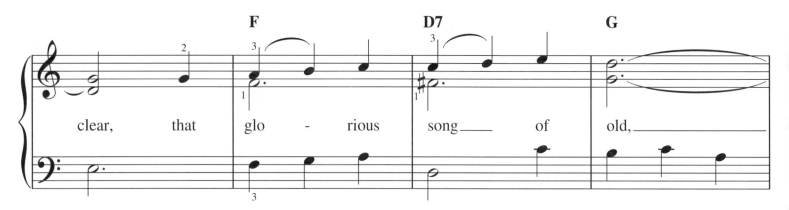

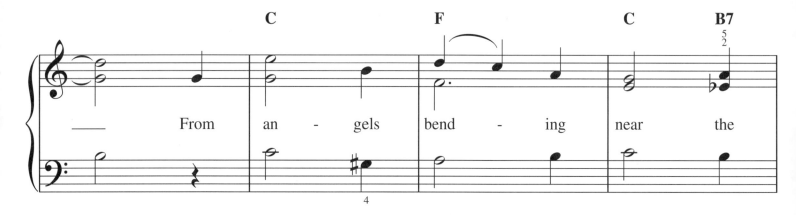

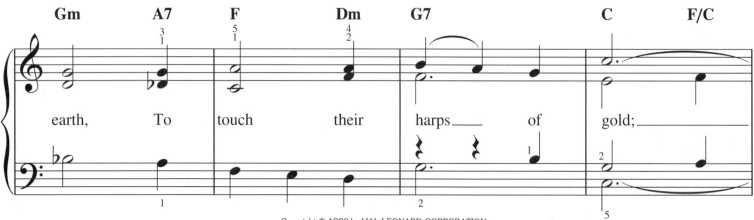

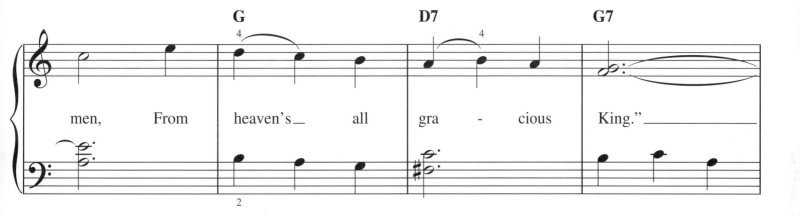

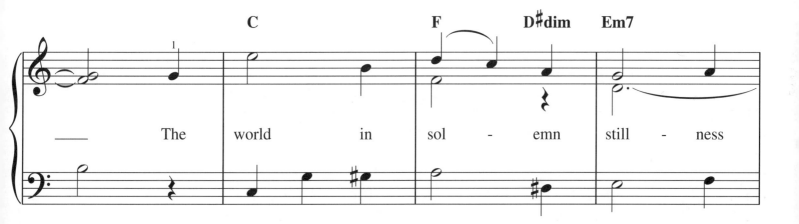

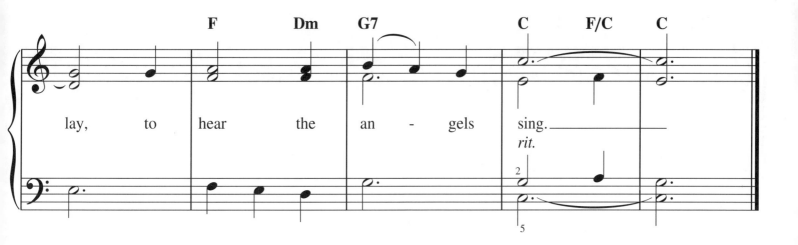

JESU, JOY OF MAN'S DESIRING

By JOHANN SEBASTIAN BACH

Slowly and evenly

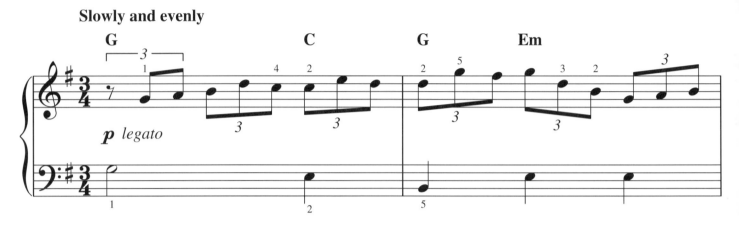

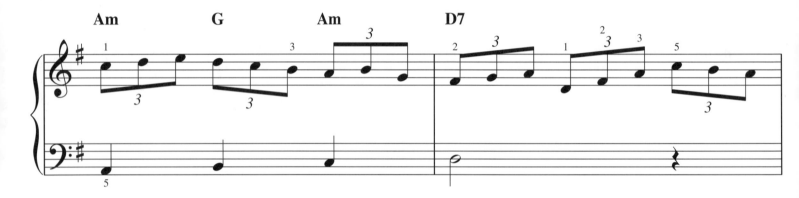

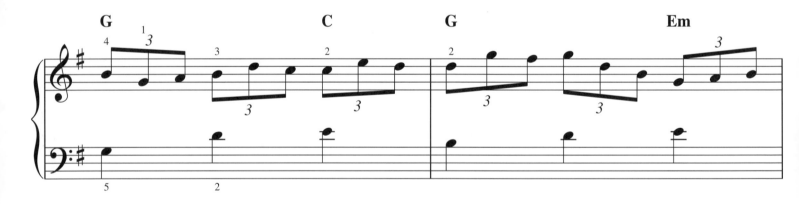

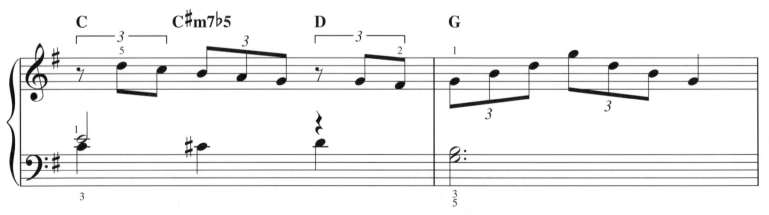

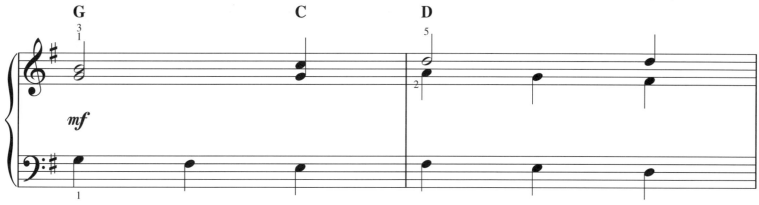

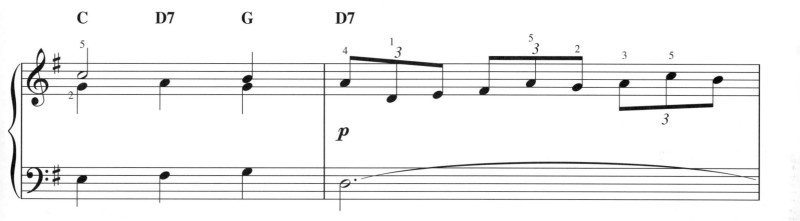

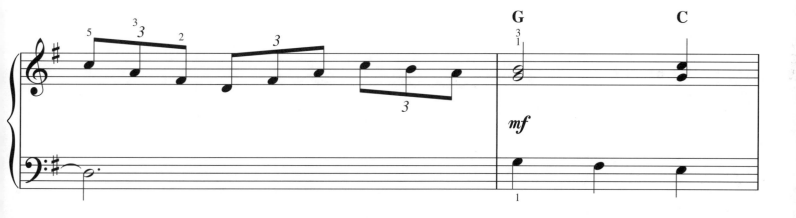

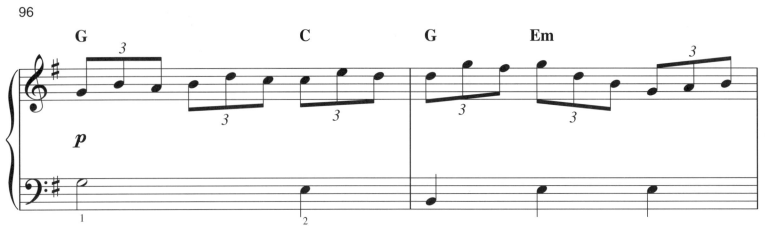

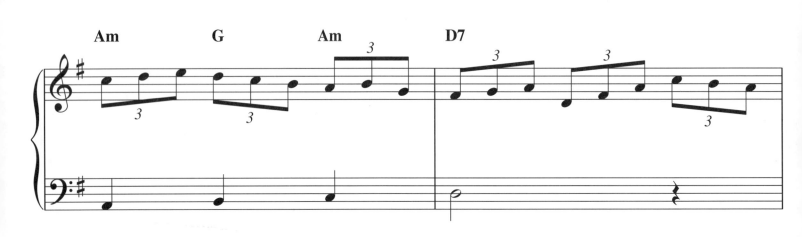

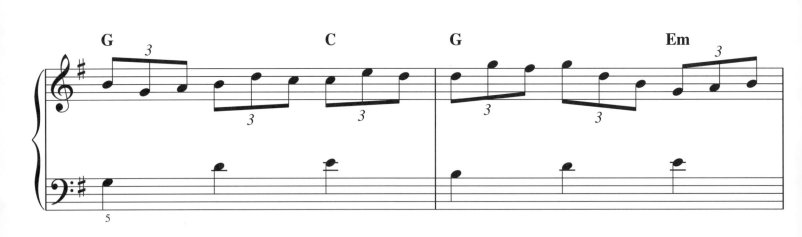

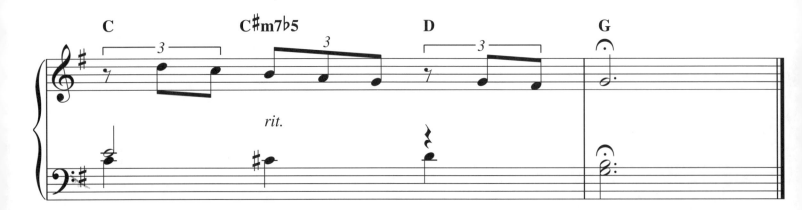

O COME AWAY, YE SHEPHERDS

18th Century French Text
Tune from Air, "Nanon Dormait"

Gaily

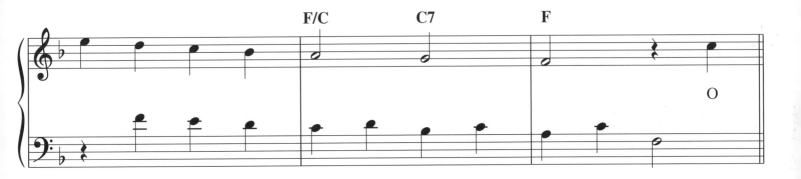

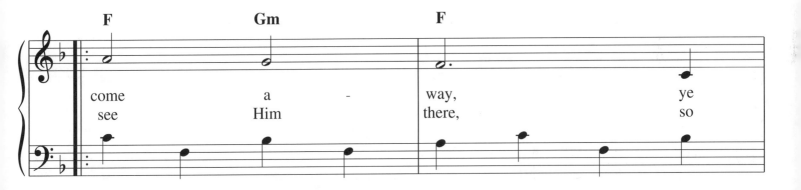

come a - way, ye
see Him there, so

shep - herds, leave your sheep! A
na - ked, weak and help - less! A

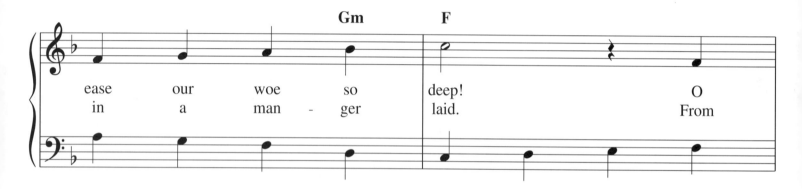

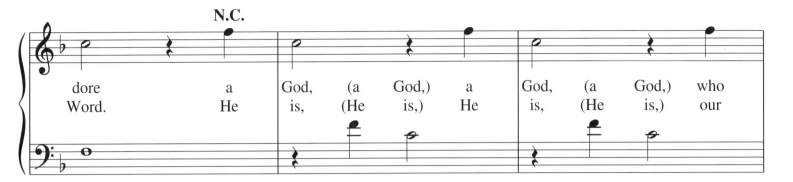

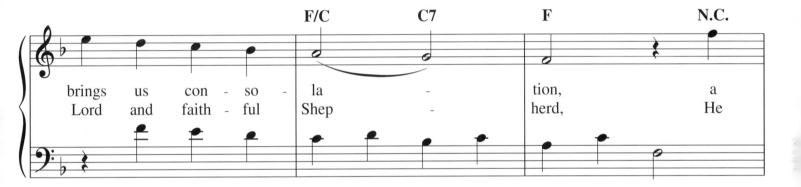

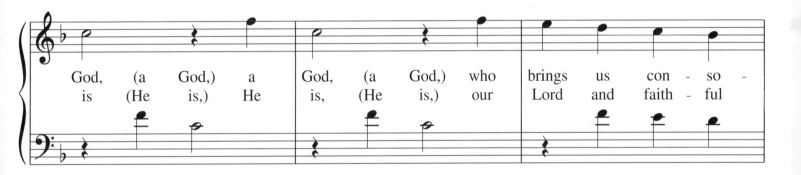

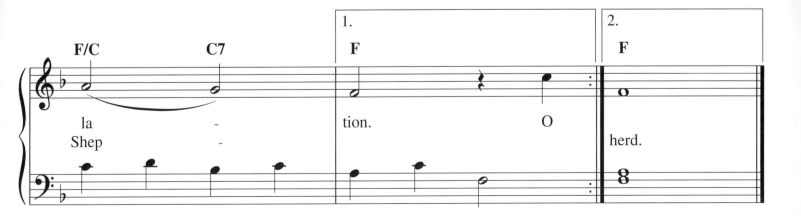

JESUS HOLY, BORN SO LOWLY

Traditional Polish

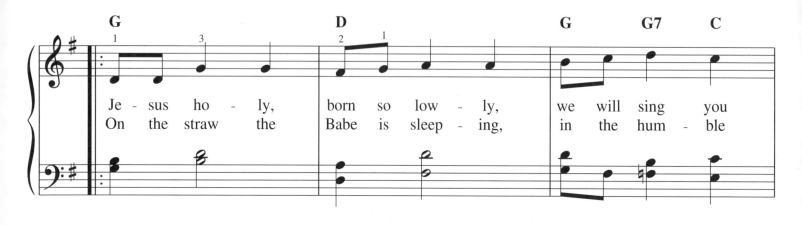

Je - sus ho - ly, born so low - ly, we will sing you
On the straw the Babe is sleep - ing, in the hum - ble

car - ols gay. Je - sus dear - est, pre - cious In - fant,
man - ger bed. Mar - y lov - ing watch is keep - ing,

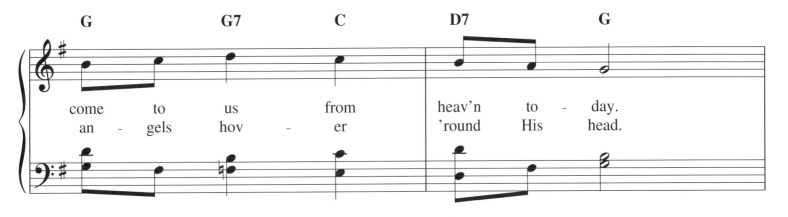

come to us from heav'n to - day.
an - gels hov - er 'round His head.

Shep - herds, join the joy - ful cho - rus,
Shep - herds, bow in a - do - ra - tion,

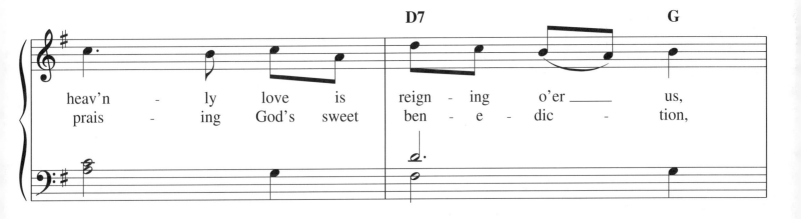

heav'n - ly love is reign - ing o'er _____ us,
prais - ing God's sweet ben - e - dic - tion,

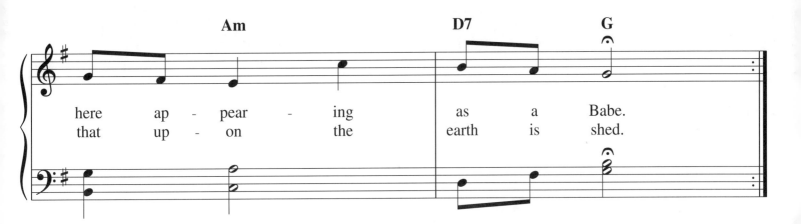

here ap - pear - ing as a Babe.
that up - on the earth is shed.

JOY TO THE WORLD

Words by ISAAC WATTS
Music by GEORGE FRIDERIC HANDEL
Arranged by LOWELL MASON

Majestically

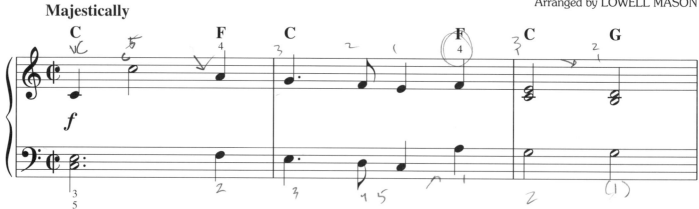

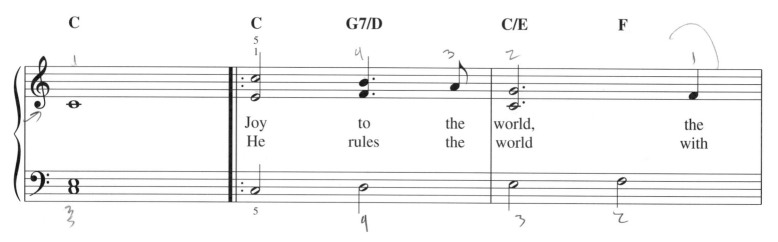

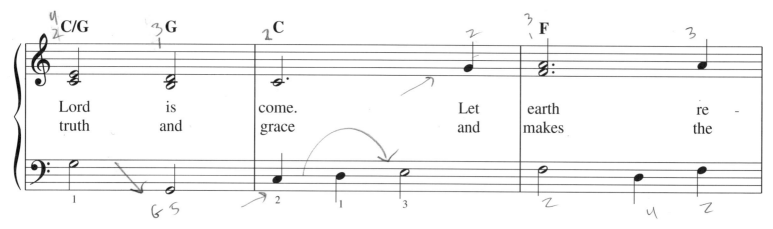

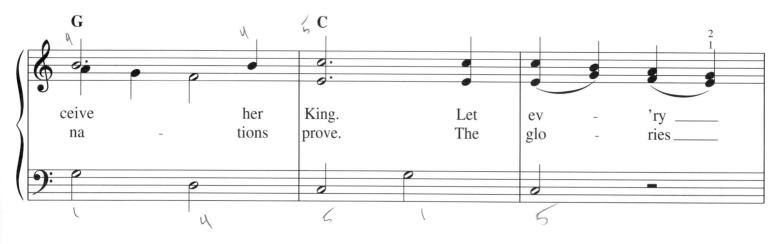

heart _____ pre - pare ___ Him ___ room, _____ And
of _____ His right - eous - ness, _____ And

heav'n and na - ture ___ sing, And ___ heav'n and na - ture ___
won - ders of His love, And ___ won - ders of His

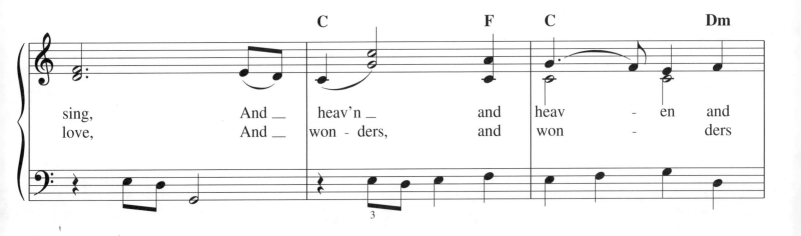

sing, And ___ heav'n ___ and heav - en and
love, And ___ won - ders, and won - ders

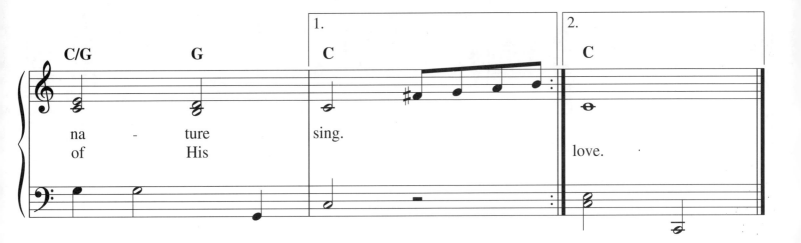

na - ture sing. love.
of His

LO, HOW A ROSE E'ER BLOOMING

15th Century German Carol
Translated by Theodre Baker
Music from Alte Catholische Geistliche Kirchengesang

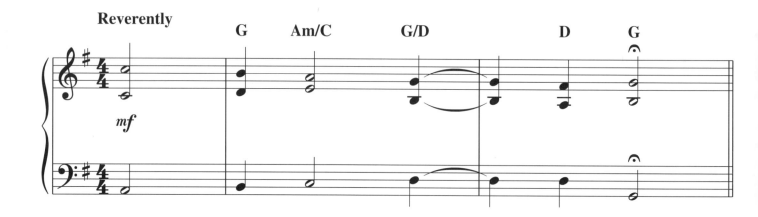

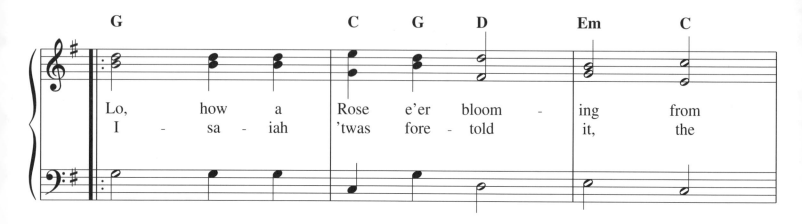

Lo, how a Rose e'er bloom - ing, from
I - sa - iah 'twas fore - told it, from the

ten - der stem hath sprung! Of Jes - se's
Rose I have in mind; with Mar - y

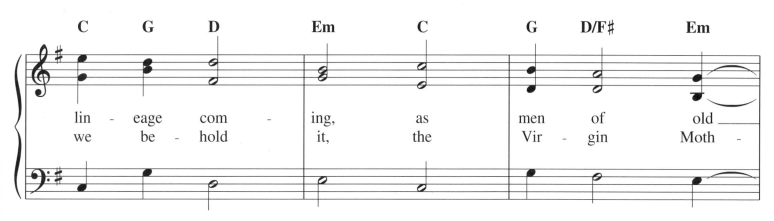

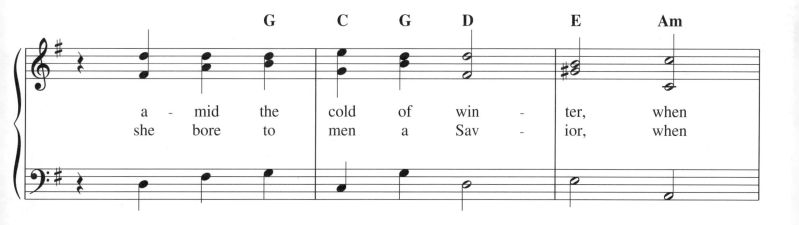

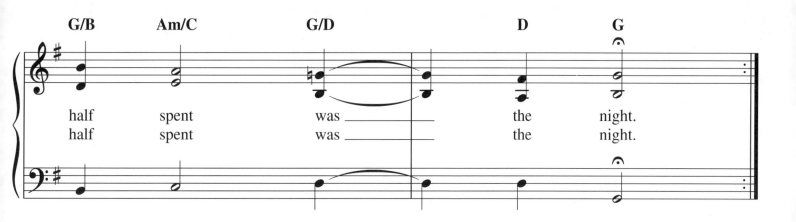

MASTERS IN THIS HALL

Traditional English

Vigorously

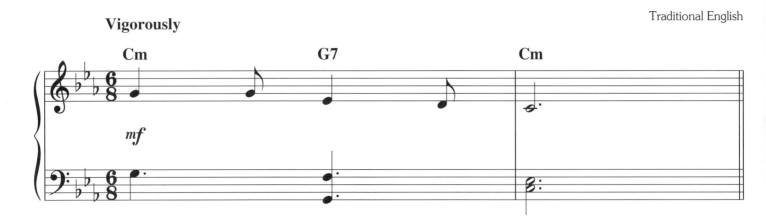

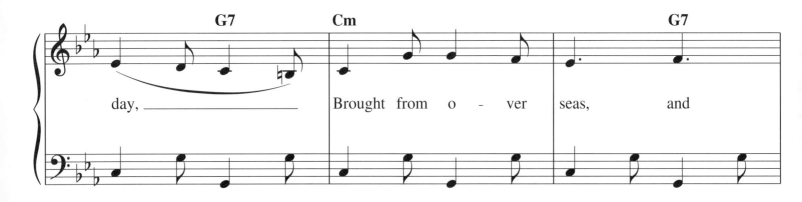

Mas - ters in this hall, _____ Hear ye news to -

day, _____ Brought from o - ver seas, and

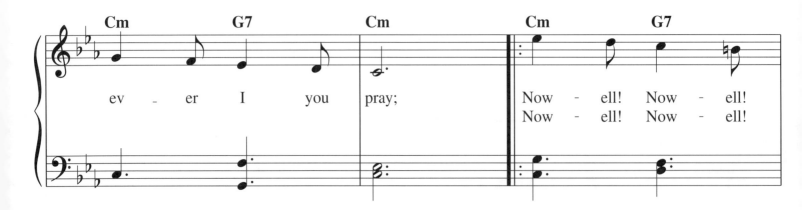

ev - er I you pray; Now - ell! Now - ell!
Now - ell! Now - ell!

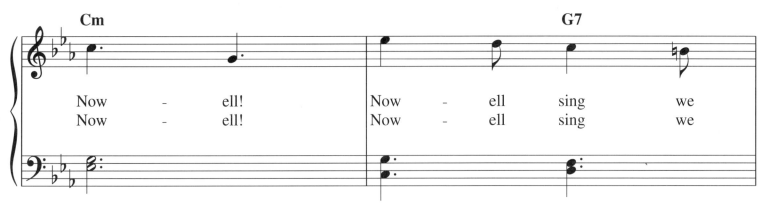

Now - ell!   Now - ell sing we
Now - ell!   Now - ell sing we

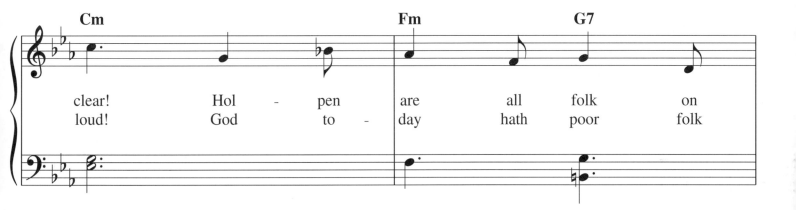

clear!   Hol - pen   are   all   folk   on
loud!   God   to - day   hath   poor   on   folk

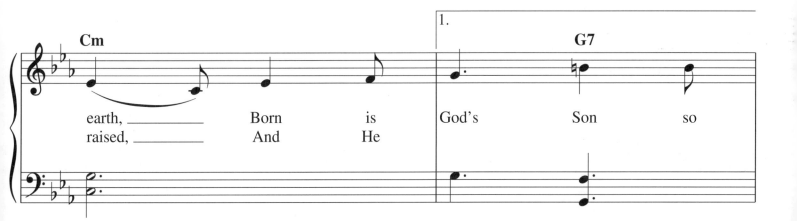

earth, _____ Born   is   God's   Son   so
raised, _____ And   is   He

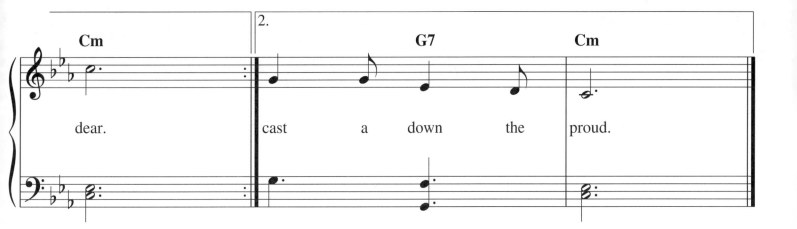

dear.   cast   a   down   the   proud.

NEIGHBOR, WHAT HAS YOU SO EXCITED?

Traditional French

Flowing simply

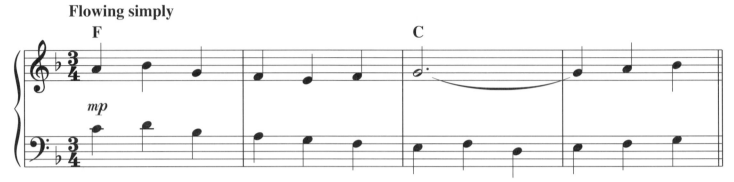

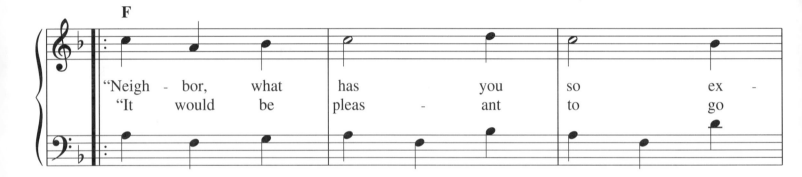

"Neigh - bor, what has you so ex -
"It would what be pleas - ant to go

cit - ed? Do tell me, please."
with you, like - ly I'll go.

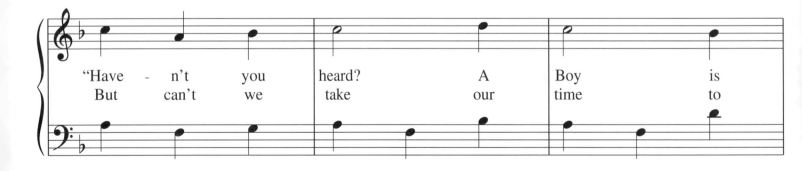

"Have - n't you heard? A Boy is
But can't we take our time to

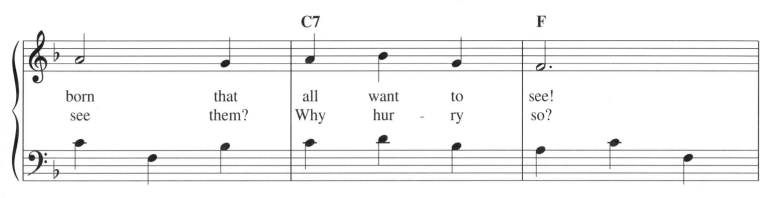

born   that   all   want   to   see!
see   them?   Why   hur -   ry   so?

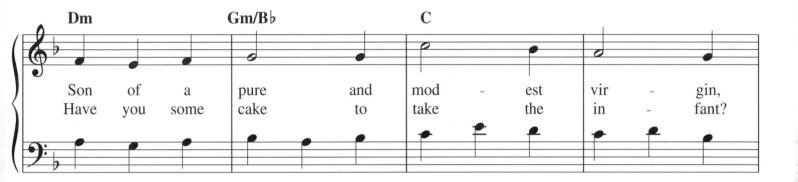

Son   of   a   pure   and   mod -   est   vir -   gin,
Have   you   some   cake   to   take   the   in -   fant?

Mar -   y's   her   name;   They   say   her   Ba -   by
Sug -   ar - plums   too?   I'm   sure   that   Mar -   y's

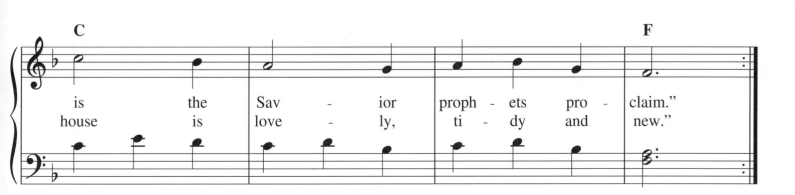

is   the   Sav -   ior   proph - ets   pro -   claim."
house   is   love -   ly,   ti -   dy   and   new."

NOËL! NOËL!

French-English Carol

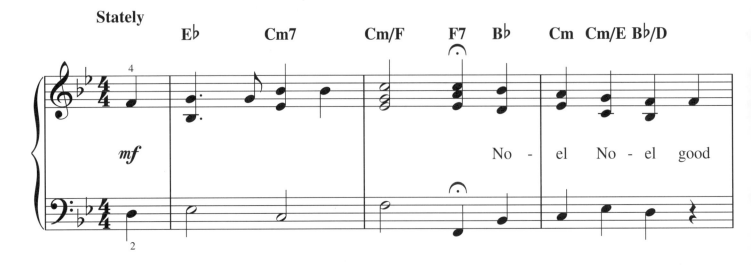

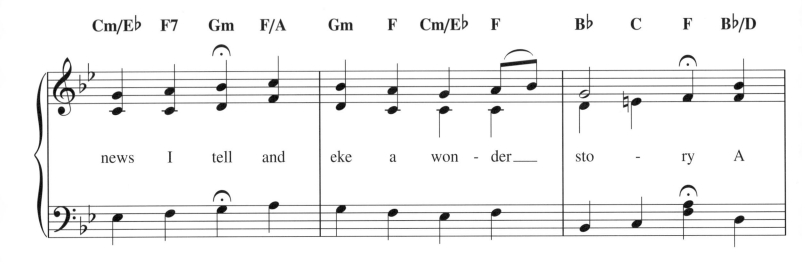

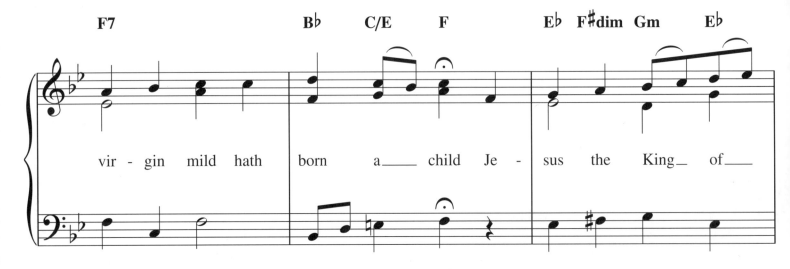

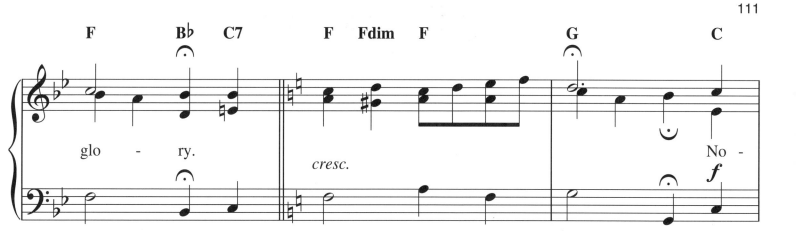

glo - ry. *cresc.* No -

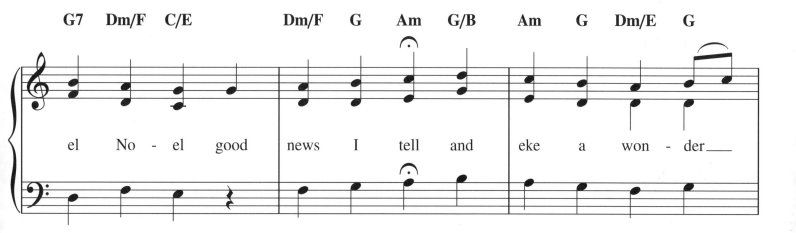

el No - el good news I tell and eke a won - der

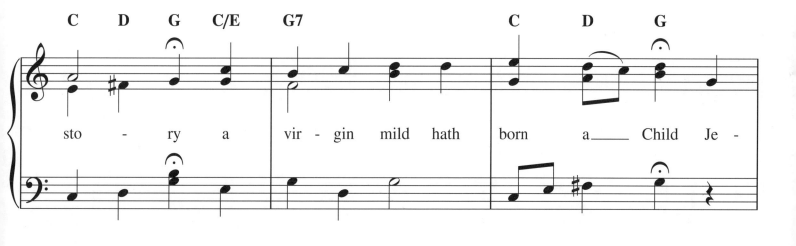

sto - ry a vir - gin mild hath born a____ Child Je -

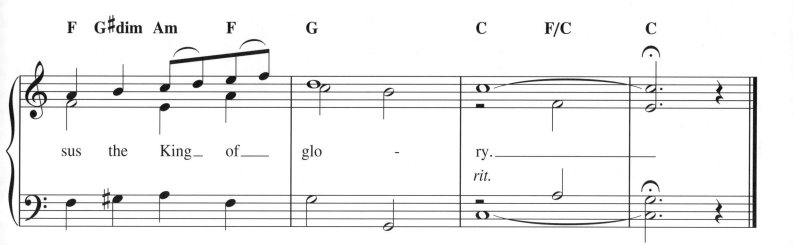

sus the King__ of____ glo - ry.____ *rit.*

O BETHLEHEM

Traditional Spanish

Expressively

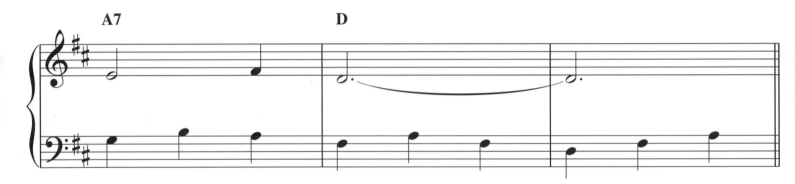

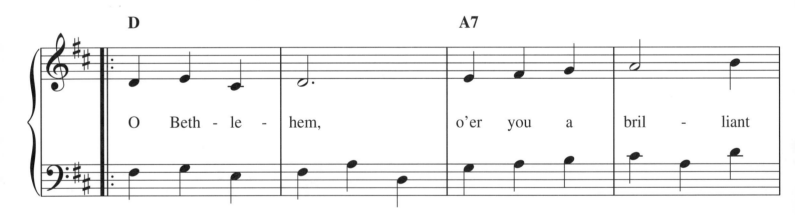

O Beth - le - hem,   o'er you a   bril - liant

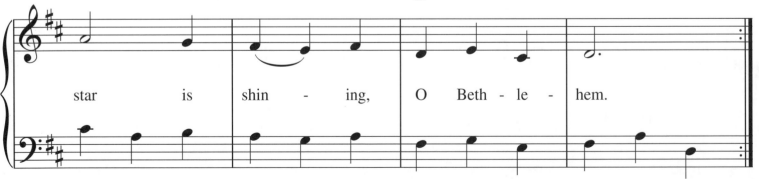

star   is   shin - ing,   O   Beth - le - hem.

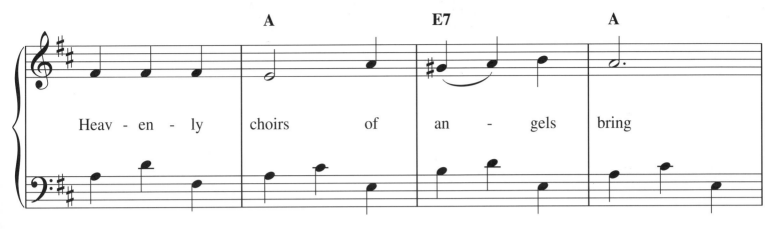

Heav - en - ly   choirs   of   an - gels   bring

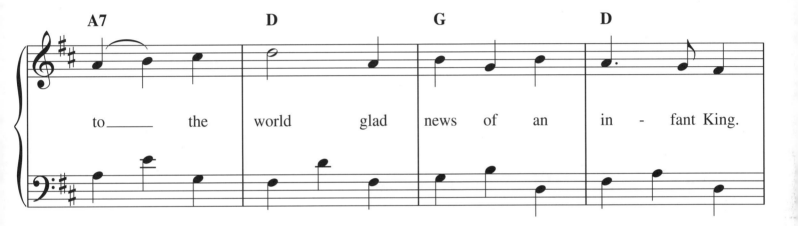

to____ the   world   glad   news   of   an   in - fant King.

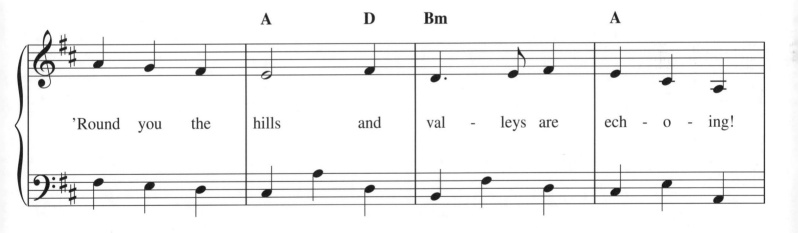

'Round you the   hills   and   val - leys are   ech - o - ing!

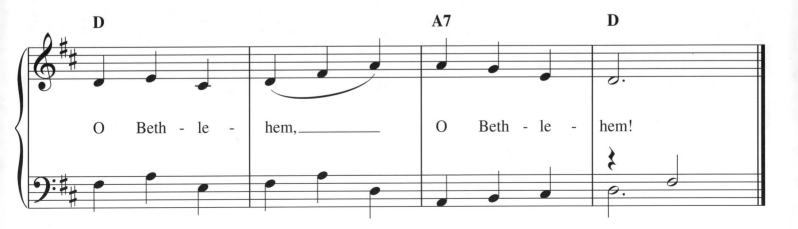

O Beth - le -   hem,_____   O Beth - le - hem!

O CHRISTMAS TREE

Traditional German Carol

Moderately

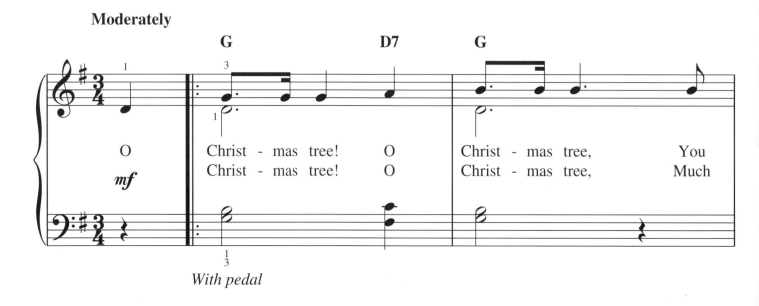

With pedal

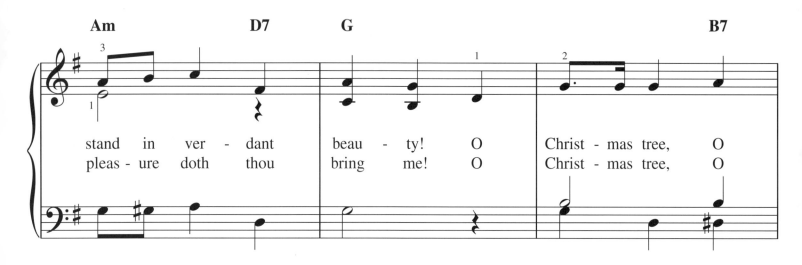

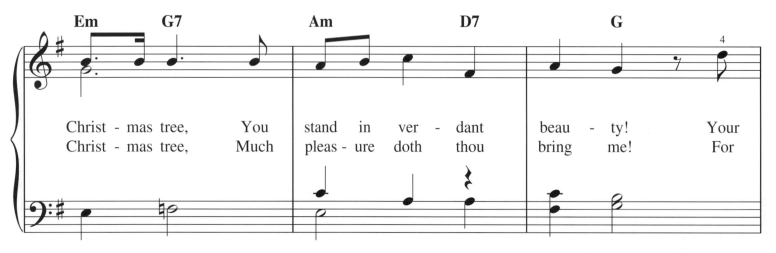

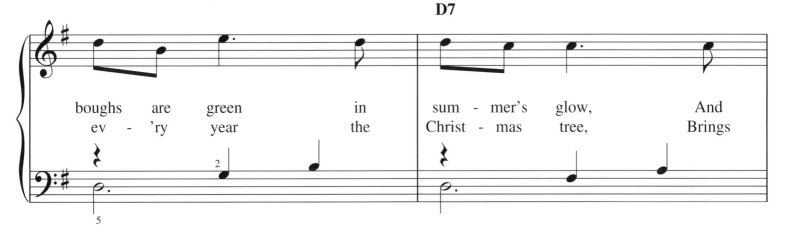

boughs are green in sum - mer's glow, And
ev - 'ry year in the Christ - mas tree, Brings

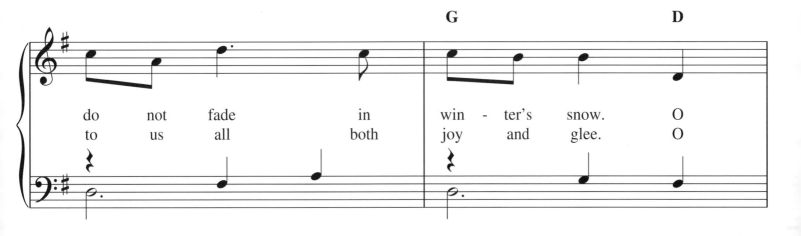

do not fade in win - ter's snow. O
to us all both joy and glee. O

G   F   E7

Christ - mas tree, O Christ - mas tree, You
Christ - mas tree, O Christ - mas tree, Much

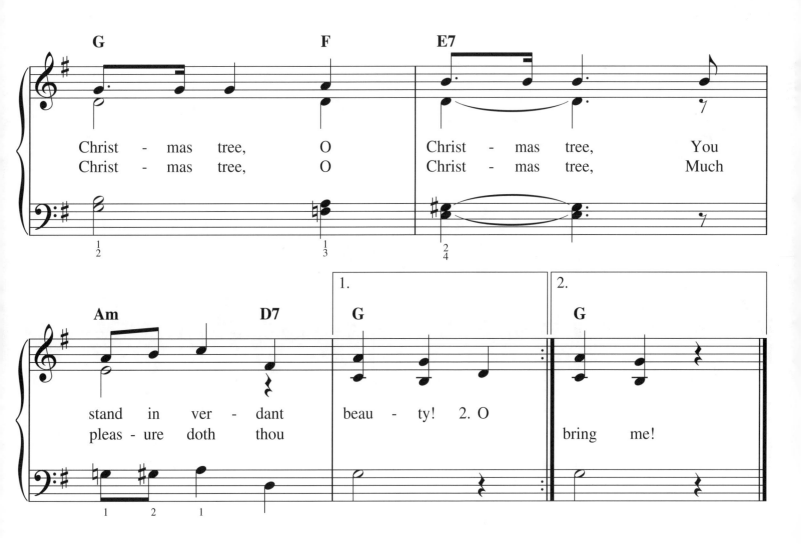

Am   D7   1. G   2. G

stand in ver - dant beau - ty! 2. O
plea - sure doth thou bring me!

O COME, ALL YE FAITHFUL
(Adeste Fideles)

Words and Music by JOHN FRANCIS WADE
Latin Words Translated by FREDERICK OAKELEY

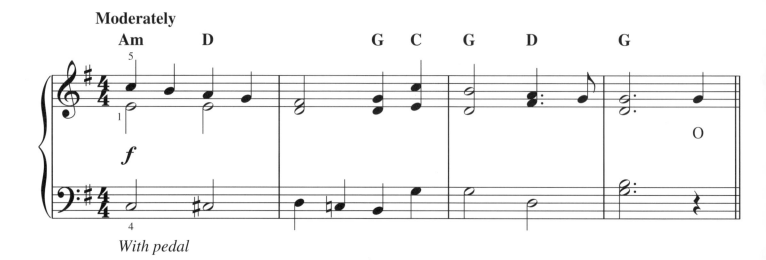

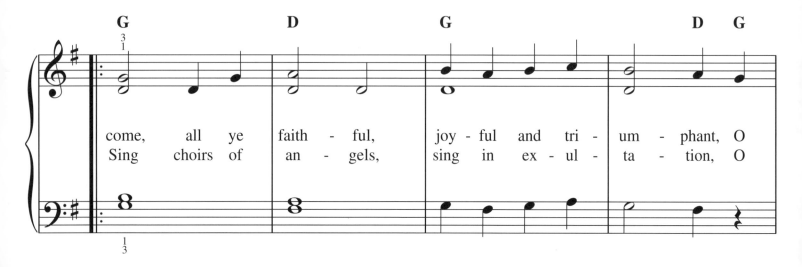

come, all ye faith - ful, joy - ful and tri - um - phant, O
Sing choirs of an - gels, sing in ex - ul - ta - tion, O

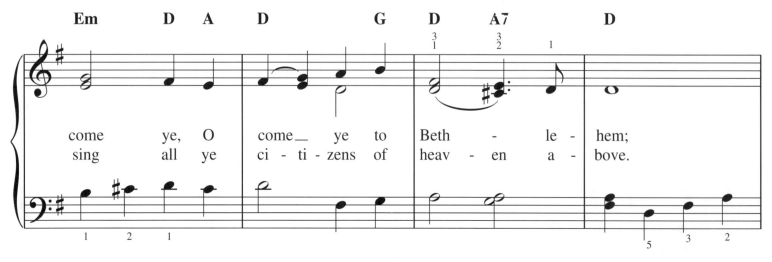

come ye, O come__ ye to Beth - le - hem;
sing all ye ci - ti - zens of heav - en a - bove.

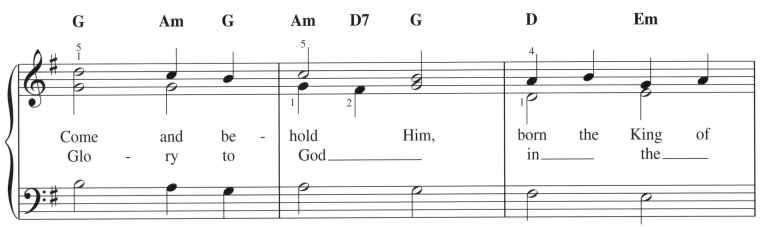

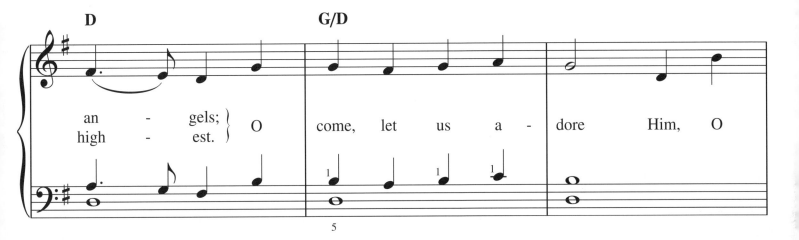

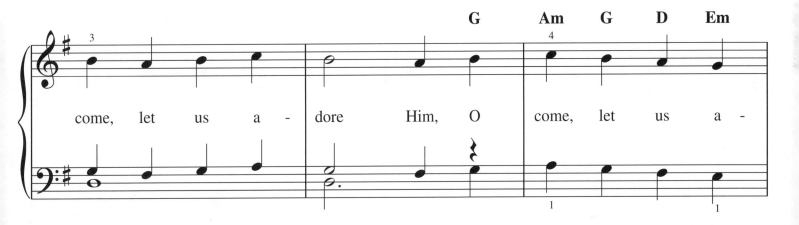

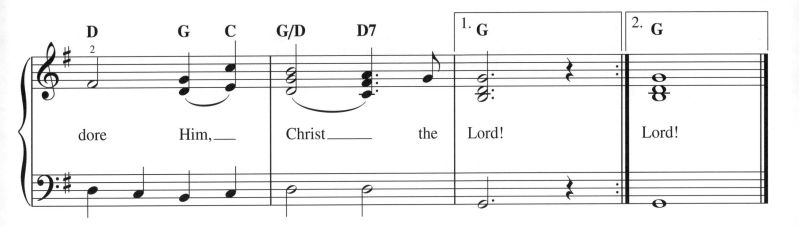

O COME, LITTLE CHILDREN

Words by C. von SCHMIDT
Music by J.P.A. SCHULZ

Moderately fast

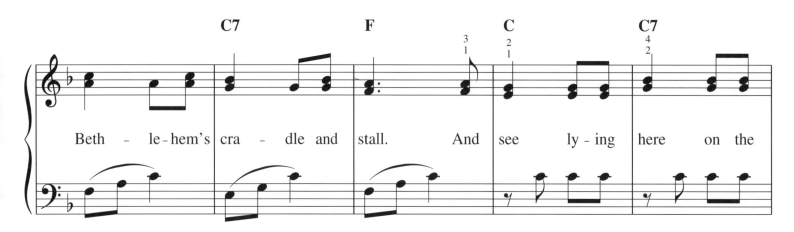

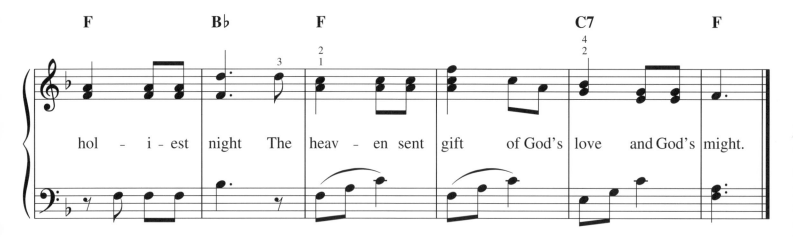

Additional Lyrics

2. The Baby lies here on the straw and the hay,
   While Joseph and Mary are kneeling to pray;
   The shepherds have hastened to worship their King,
   And angels in chorus right cheerfully sing.

3. We too would be humble and worship the Child
   With shepherds and Joseph and Mary so mild.
   Let voices ring out – for how could we be sad?
   Rejoice with the angels for tidings so glad.

O SANCTISSIMA

Sicilian Carol

Moderately fast, with spirit

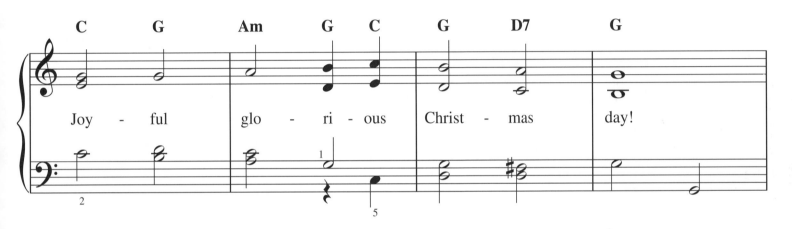

Day of ho - li - ness, __ peace and hap - pi - ness, __

Joy - ful glo - ri - ous Christ - mas day!

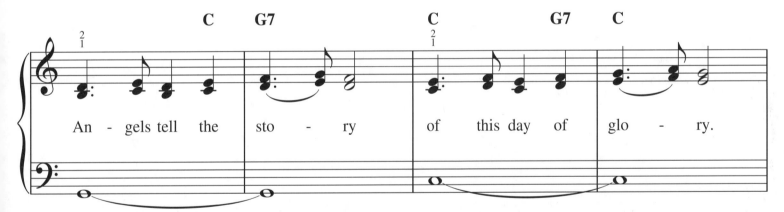

An - gels tell the sto - ry of this day of glo - ry.

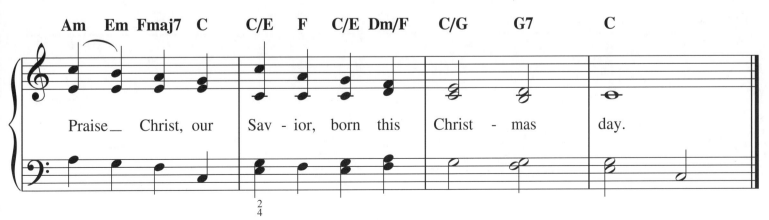

Praise __ Christ, our Sav - ior, born this Christ - mas day.

O COME, O COME IMMANUEL

Plainsong, 13th Century
Words translated by JOHN M. NEALE
and HENRY S. COFFIN

Like an old plainsong

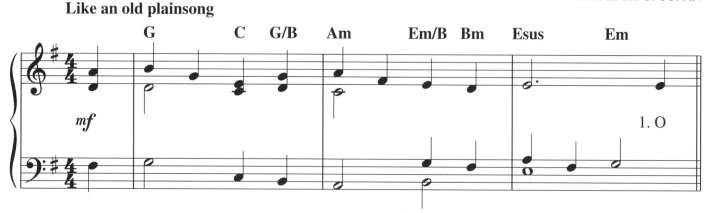

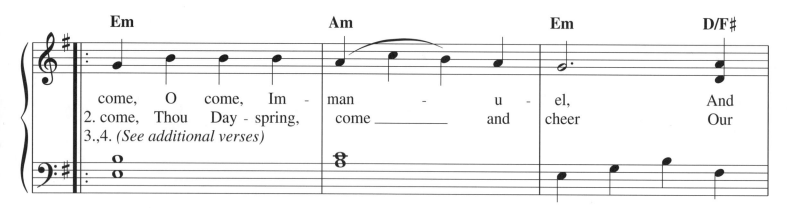

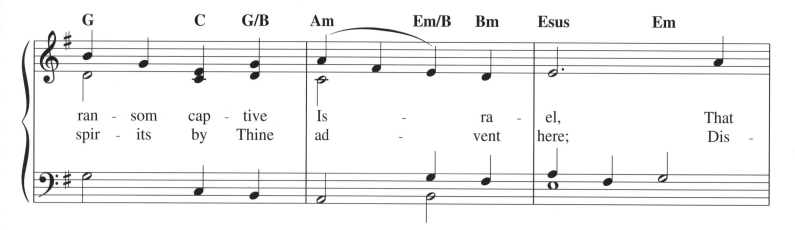

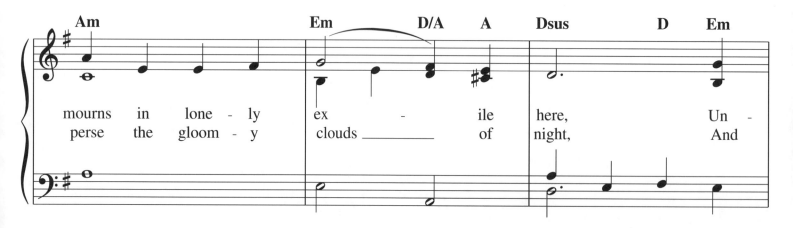

til the Son of God _____ ap - pear.
death's dark shad - ows put _____ to flight. }

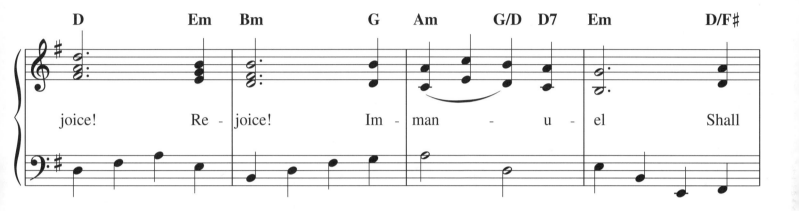

joice! Re - joice! Im - man - u - el Shall

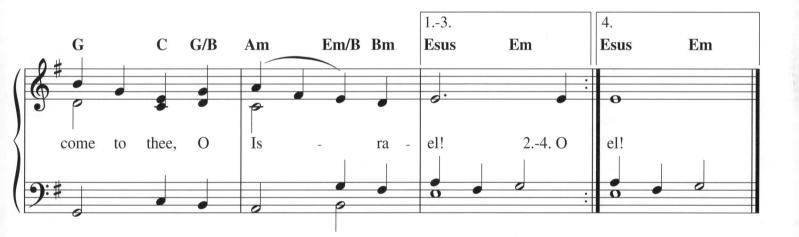

come to thee, O Is - ra - el! 2.-4. O el!

Additional Verses

3. O come, Thou wisdom from on high,
And order all things, far and nigh;
To us the path of knowledge show,
And cause us in her ways to go.
Refrain

4. O come, Desire of nations, bind
All peoples in one heart and mind;
Bid envy, strife and quarrels cease,
Fill all the world with heaven's peace.
Refrain

O COME REJOICING

Traditional Polish Carol

Gaily

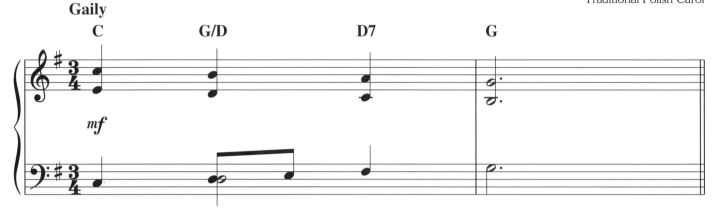

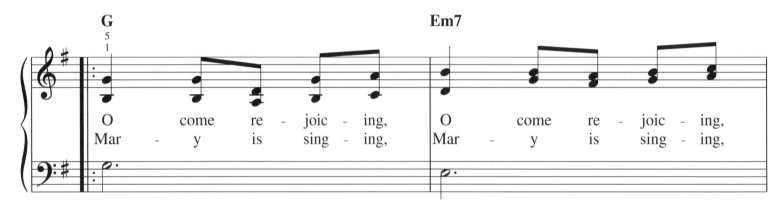

O come re-joic-ing,　O come re-joic-ing,
Mar-y is sing-ing,　Mar-y is sing-ing,

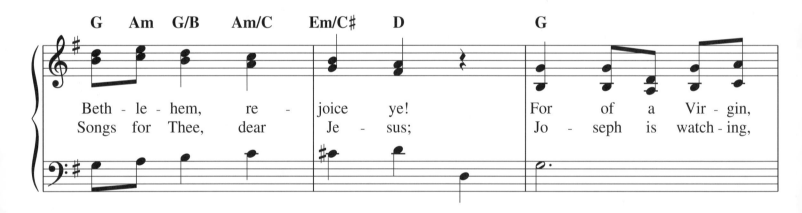

Beth-le-hem, re-joice ye!　For of a Vir-gin,
Songs for Thee, dear Je-sus;　Jo-seph is watch-ing,

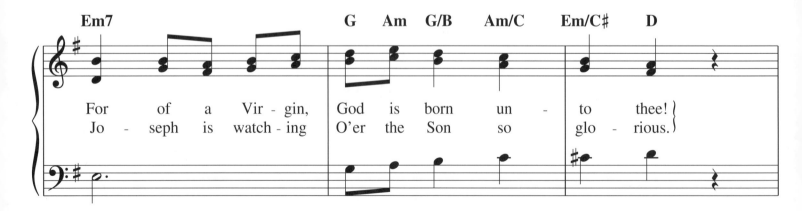

For of a Vir-gin,　God is born un-to thee! }
Jo-seph is watch-ing　O'er the Son so glo-rious. }

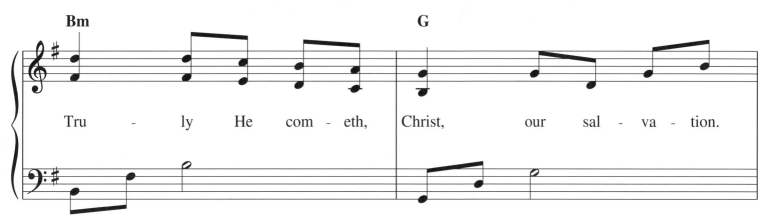

Tru - ly He com - eth, Christ, our sal - va - tion.

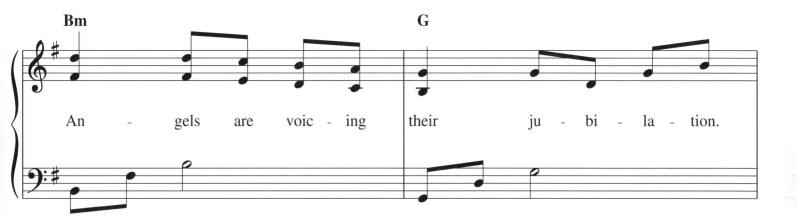

An - gels are voic - ing their ju - bi - la - tion.

Shep - herds come to praise Him, Ox - en kneel be - fore Him.

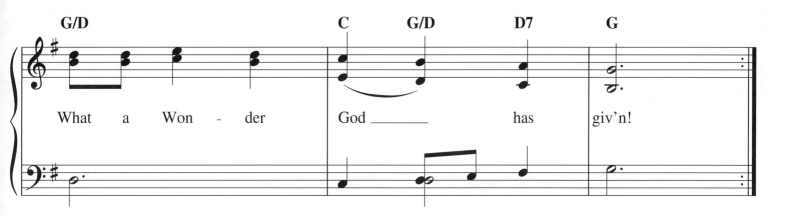

What a Won - der God _____ has giv'n!

O HOLY NIGHT

French Words by PLACIDE CAPPEAU
English Words by JOHN S. DWIGHT
Music by ADOLPHE ADAM

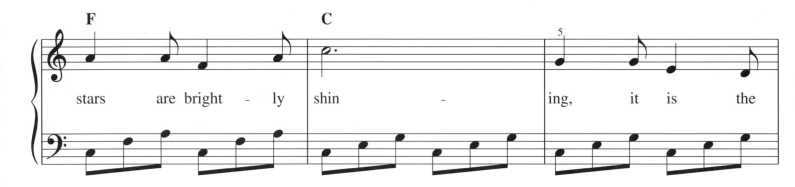

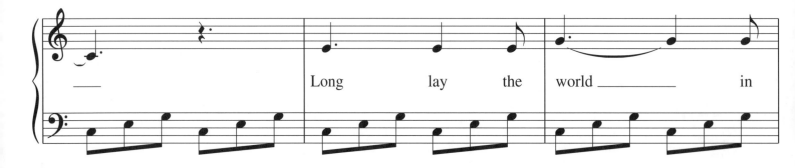

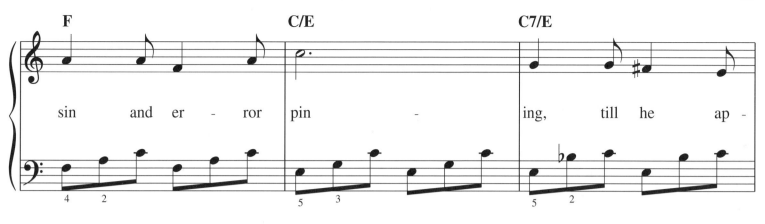

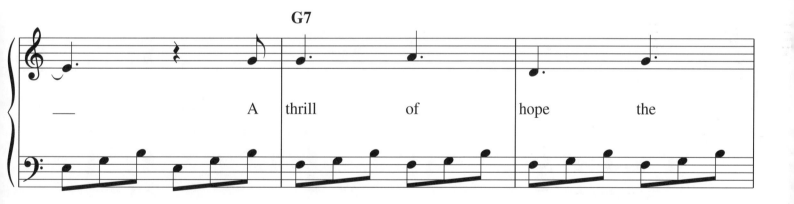

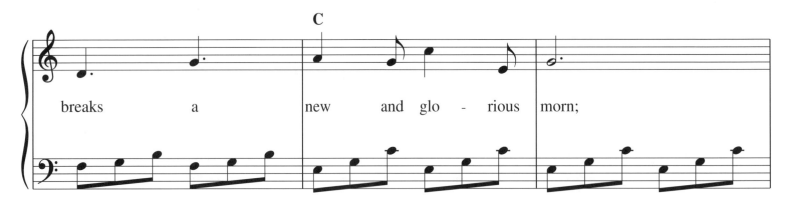

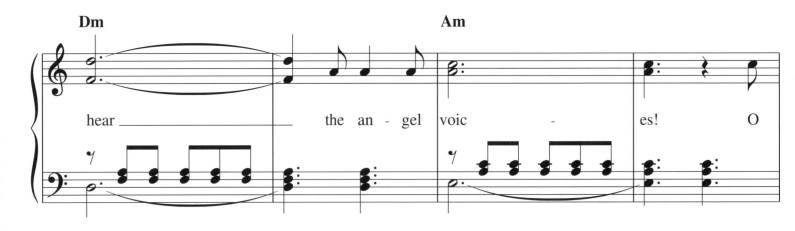

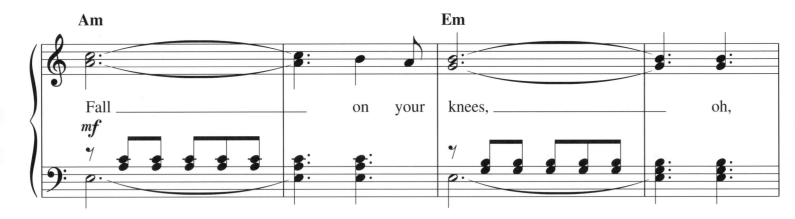

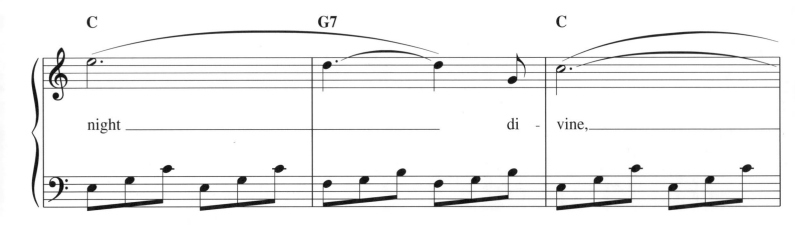

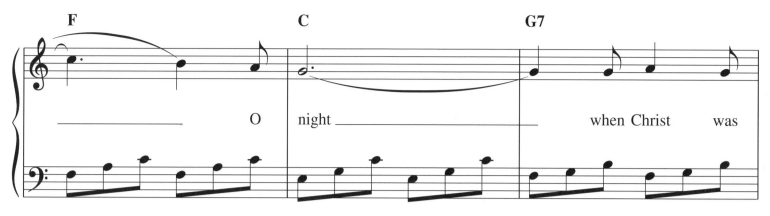

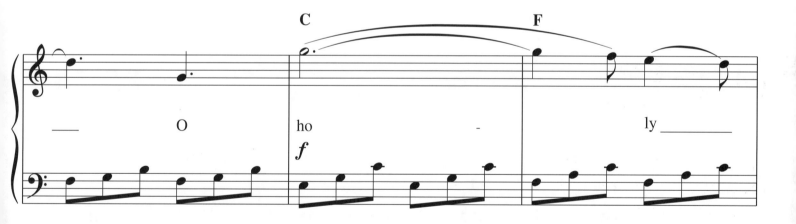
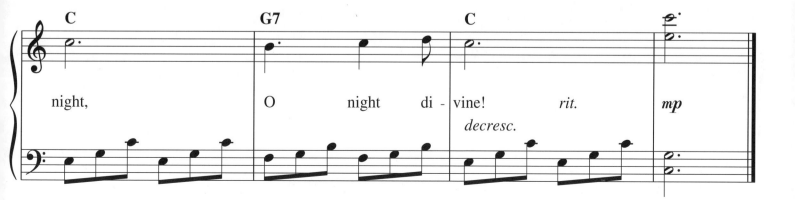

O LET US ALL BE GLAD TODAY

Words and Music by
MARTIN LUTHER

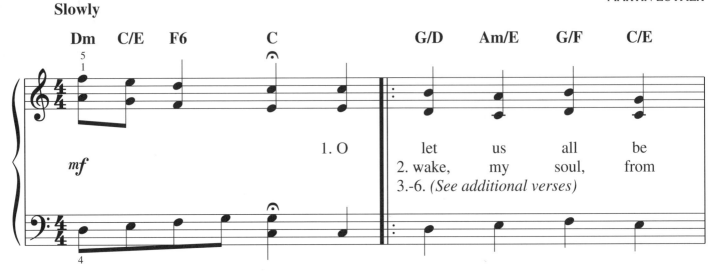

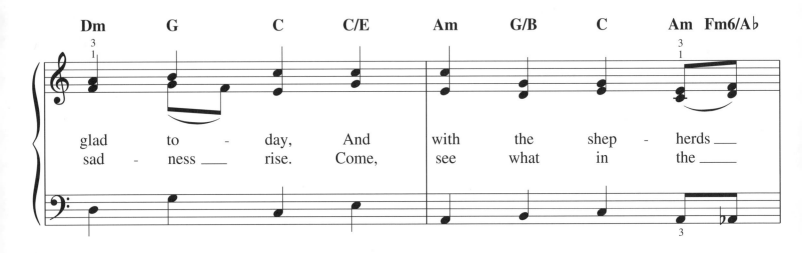

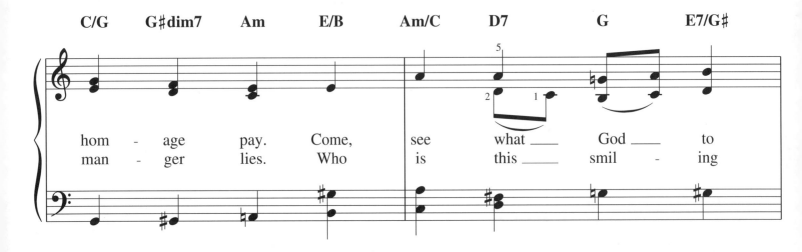

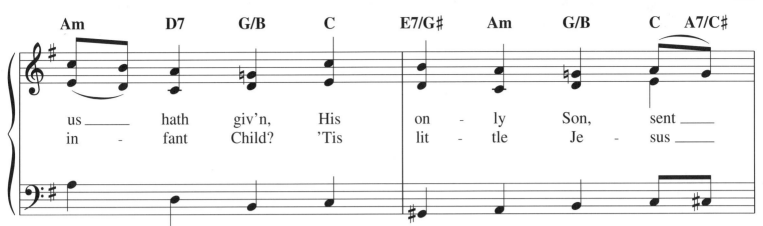

us _____ hath giv'n, His on — ly Son, sent _____
in - fant Child? 'Tis lit - tle Je - sus _____

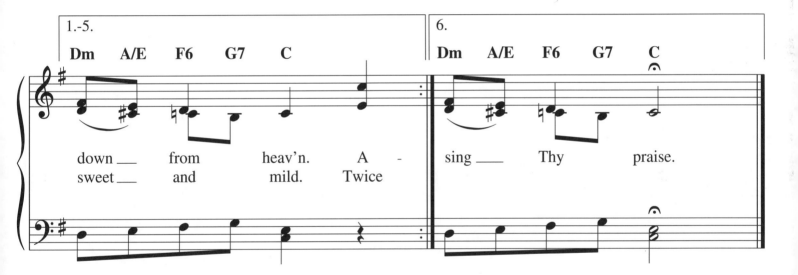

1.-5.

down _____ from heav'n. A -
sweet _____ and mild. Twice

6.

sing _____ Thy praise.

Additional Verses

3. Twice welcome, O thou heavenly guest,
   To save a world with sin distressed;
   Com'st Thou in lowly guise for me?
   What homage shall I give to Thee?

4. Ah! Lord eternal heavenly King,
   Hast Thou become so mean a thing?
   And hast Thou left Thy blissful seat,
   To rest where colts and oxen eat?

5. Jesus, my Savior, come to me,
   Make here a little crib for Thee;
   A bed make in this heart of mine,
   That I may ay remember Thine.

6. Then from my soul glad songs shall ring;
   Of Thee each day I'll gladly sing;
   Then glad hosannas will I raise,
   From heart that loves to sing Thy praise.

O LITTLE TOWN OF BETHLEHEM

Words by PHILLIPS BROOKS
Music by LEWIS H. REDNER

Slowly

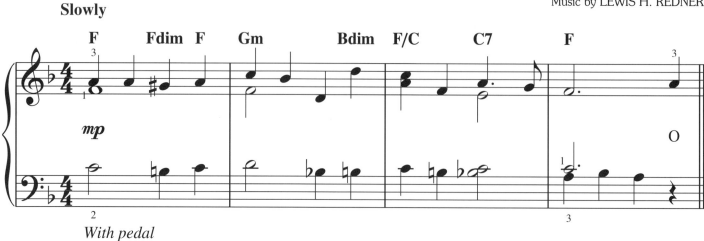

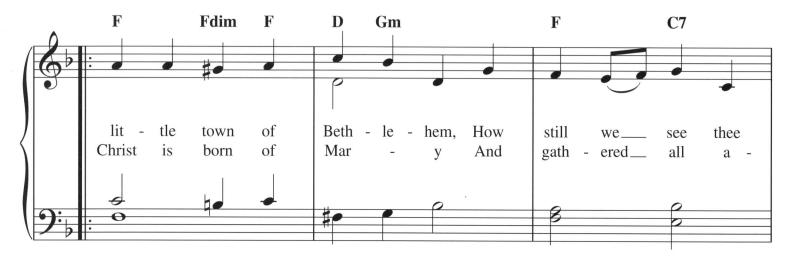

lit - tle town of Beth - le - hem, How still we___ see thee
Christ is born of Mar - y And gath - ered___ all a -

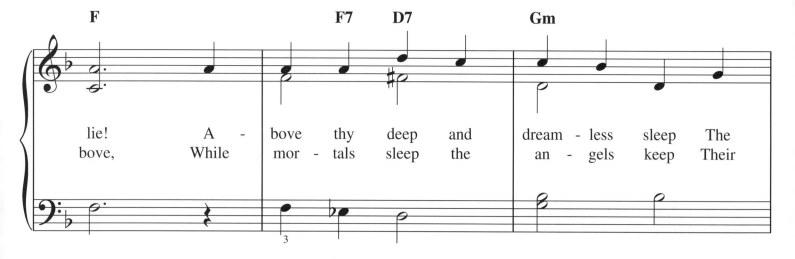

lie! A - bove thy deep and dream - less sleep The
bove, While mor - tals sleep the an - gels keep Their

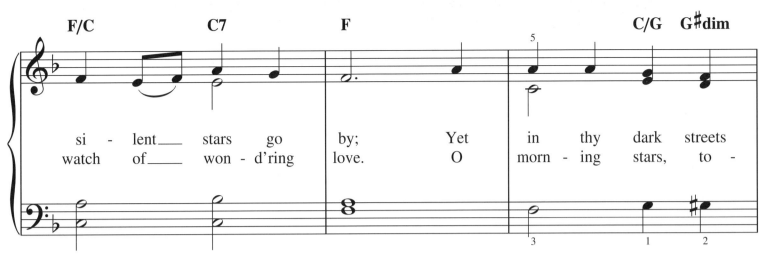

si - lent___ stars go by; Yet in thy dark streets
watch of___ won - d'ring love. O morn - ing stars, to -

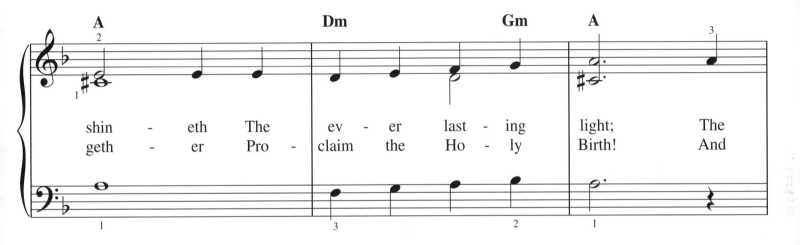

shin - eth The ev - er last - ing light; The
geth - er Pro - claim the Ho - ly Birth! And

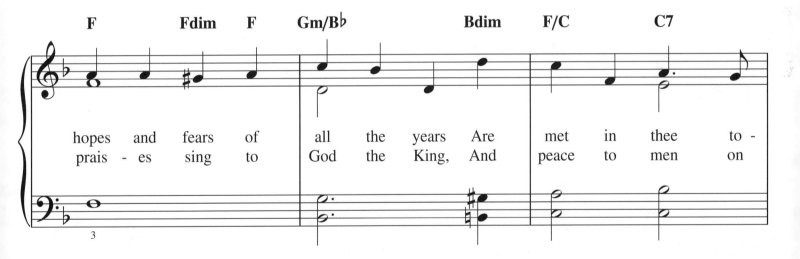

hopes and fears of all the years Are met in thee to -
prais - es sing to God the King, And peace to men on

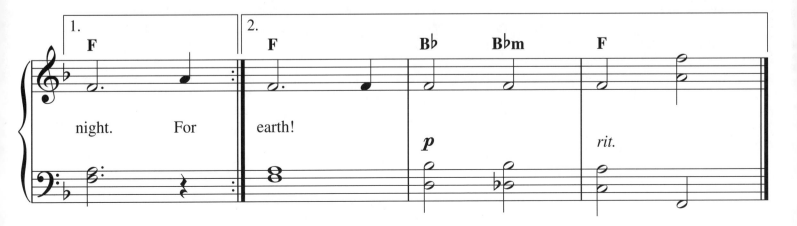

night. For earth!

OF THE FATHER'S LOVE BEGOTTEN

Words by AURELIUS C. PRUDENTIUS
Translated by JOHN M. NEALE
and HENRY W. BAKER
13th Century Plainsong
Arranged by C. WINFRED DOUGLAS

Of the Fa-ther's love be-got - ten,
O ye heights of heav'n, a-dore Him;
Christ, to Thee with God the Fa - ther,

Ere the worlds be-gan to be,
An - gel hosts, His prais - es sing;
And, O Ho - ly Ghost, to Thee,

He is Al - pha and O - me - ga,
Pow'rs do - min - ions, how be - fore Him
Hymn and chant and high thanks-giv - ing,

In keeping with the tradition of this song, no time signature is indicated.

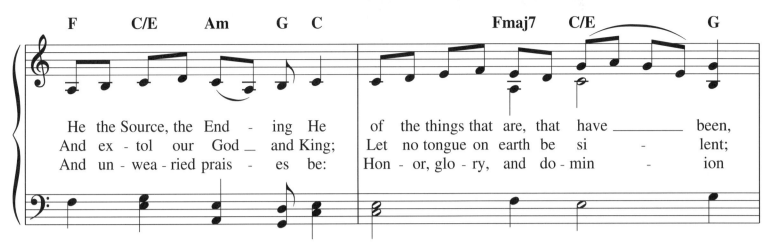

He the Source, the End - ing He
And ex - tol our God __ and King;
And un - wea - ried prais - es be:

of the things that are, that have _____ been,
Let no tongue on earth be si - lent;
Hon - or, glo - ry, and do - min - ion

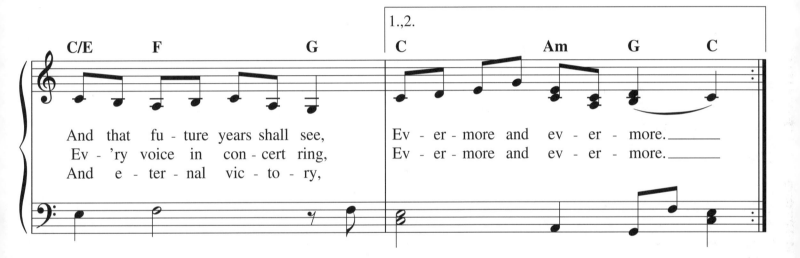

1.,2.

And that fu - ture years shall see,
Ev - 'ry voice in con - cert ring,
And e - ter - nal vic - to - ry,

Ev - er - more and ev - er - more. _____
Ev - er - more and ev - er - more. _____

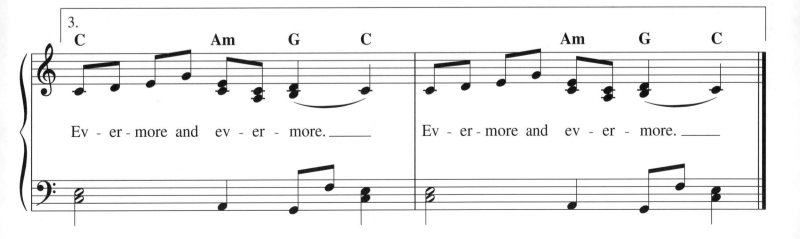

3.

Ev - er - more and ev - er - more. _____

Ev - er - more and ev - er - more. _____

ON CHRISTMAS NIGHT

Sussex Carol

Joyfully

f

With pedal

1. On Christ-mas night true Chris - tians sing, To The
2. King of Kings to us ___ is giv'n, The
3.,4. *(See additional verses)*

hear the news ___ the an - gels bring, On The
Lord of earth ___ and King of Heav'n.

Christ - mas night true Chris - tians sing, To The
King of Kings to us ___ is giv'n,

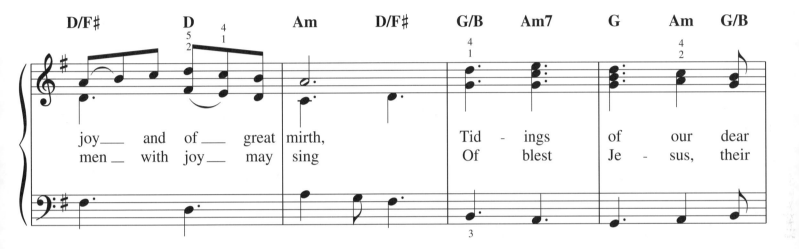

Additional Verses

3. So how on earth can men be sad,
   When Jesus comes to make us glad?
   So how on earth can men be sad,
   When Jesus comes to make us glad?
   From all our sins to set us free,
   Buying for us our liberty.

4. From out the darkness have we light,
   Which makes the angels sing this night:
   From out the darkness have we light,
   Which makes the angels sing this night:
   "Glory to God, his peace to men,
   And good will, evermore! Amen."

ONCE IN ROYAL DAVID'S CITY

Words by CECIL F. ALEXANDER
Music by HENRY J. GAUNTLETT

Gently

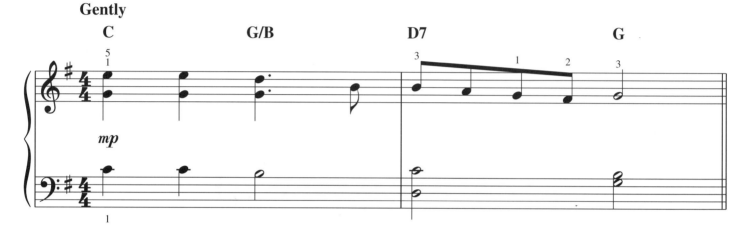

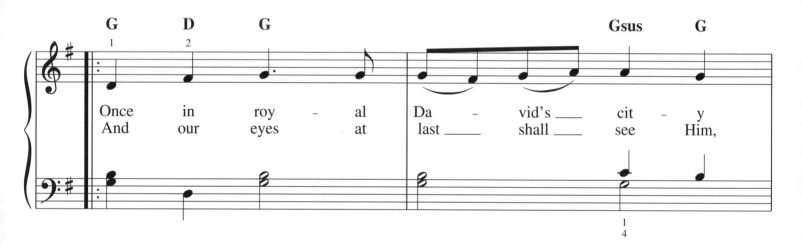

Once in roy - al Da - vid's ___ cit - y
And in our eyes at last ___ shall ___ see Him,

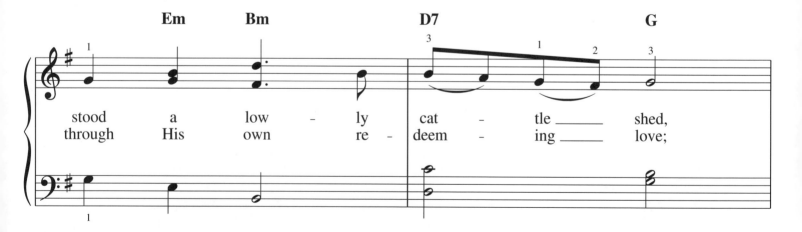

stood a low - ly cat - tle ___ shed,
through His own re - deem - ing ___ love;

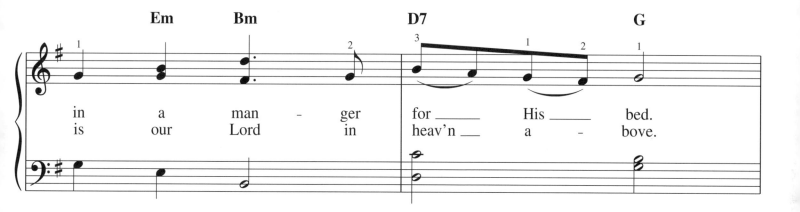

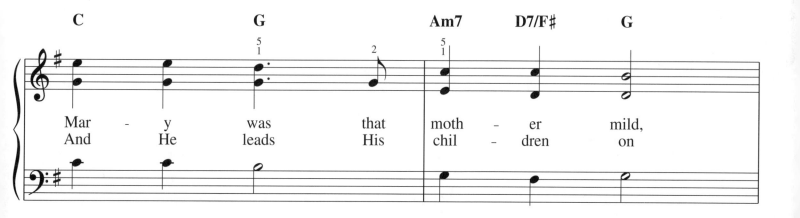

PAT-A-PAN
(Willie, Take Your Little Drum)

Words and Music by
BERNARD de la MONNOYE

March Tempo

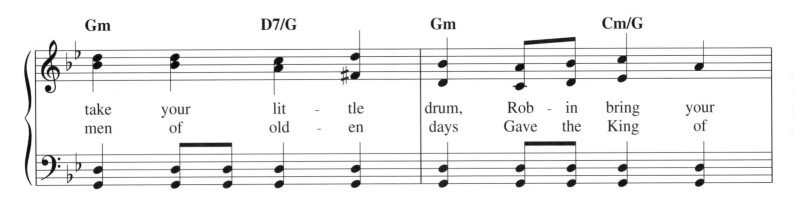

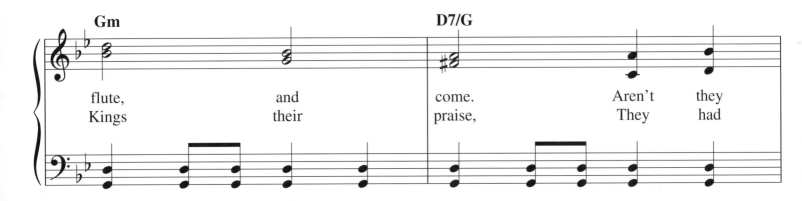

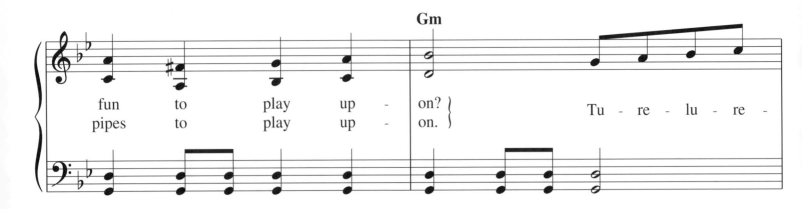

lu,   Pat - a - pat - a - pan;   {When   you   play   your   fife   and
                                         {And   al - so   the   drums   they'd

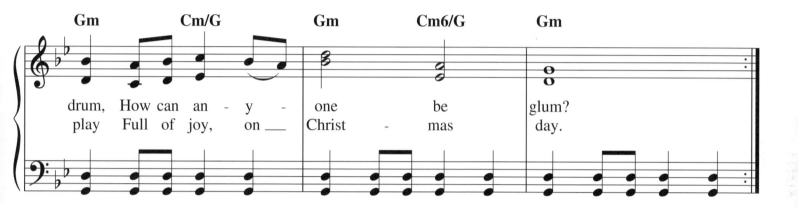

drum, How can an - y - one   be   glum?
play   Full of joy,   on ___ Christ - mas   day.

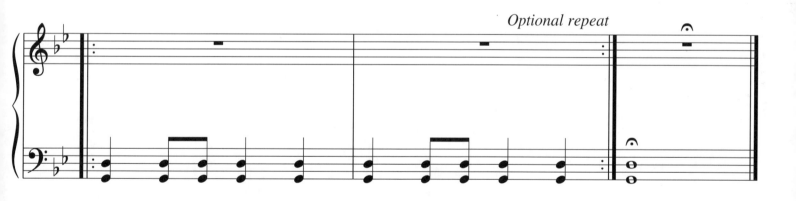

Optional repeat

Additional Verse

3. God and man today become
    Closely joined as flute and drum.
    Let the joyous tune play on!
    As the instruments you play,
    We will sing, this Christmas day.

REJOICE AND BE MERRY

Gallery Carol

RING OUT, YE WILD AND MERRY BELLS

Words and Music by
C. MAITLAND

Brightly

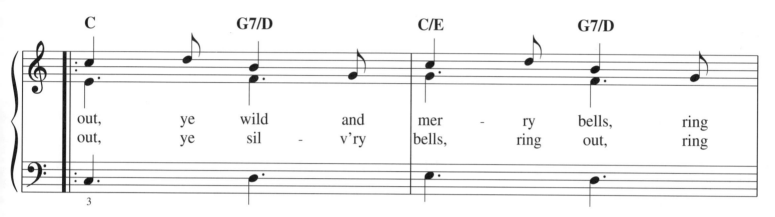

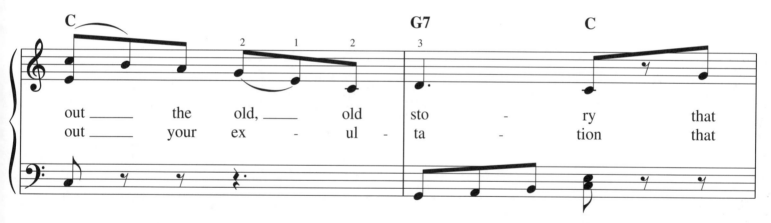

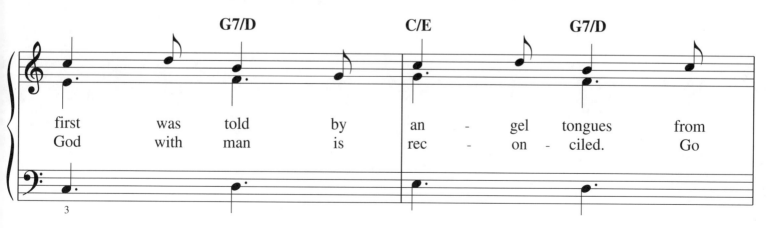

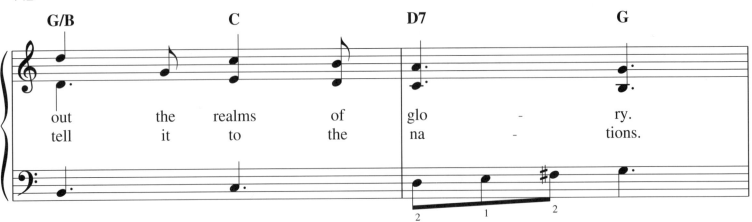

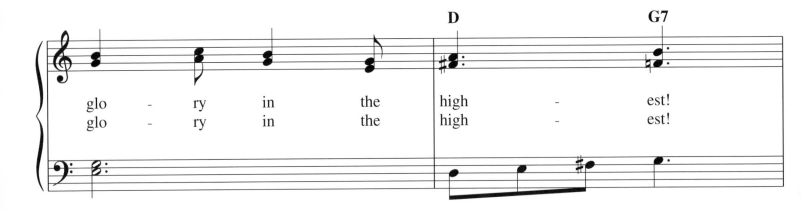

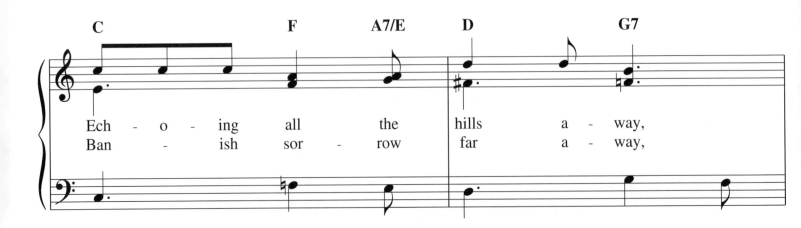

glo - ry in the high - est!}
glo - ry in the high - est!}

Ring, sweet bells, ring ev - er - more, peal from ev - 'ry

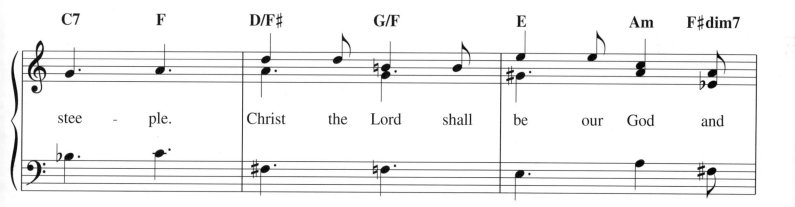

stee - ple. Christ the Lord shall be our God and

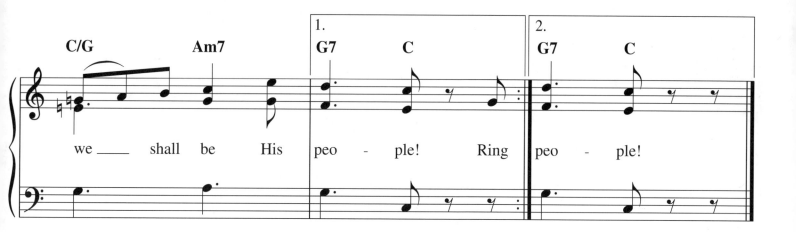

we ___ shall be His peo - ple! Ring peo - ple!

RISE UP, SHEPHERD, AND FOLLOW

African-American Spiritual

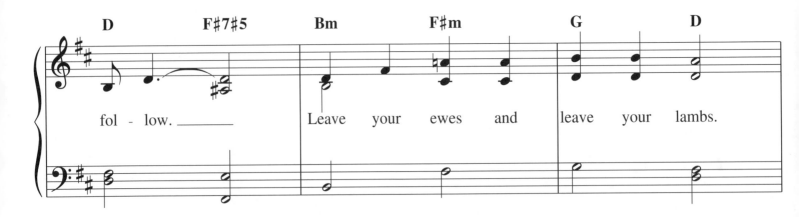

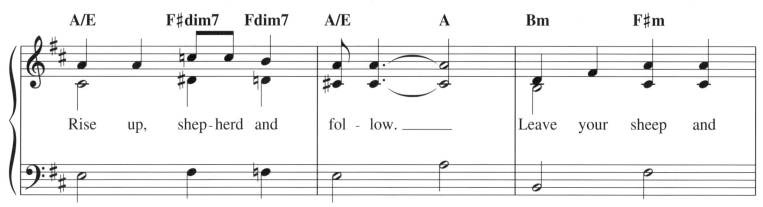

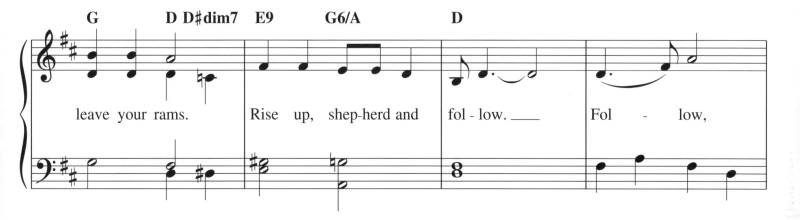

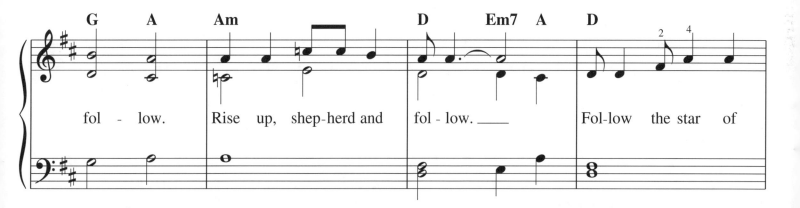

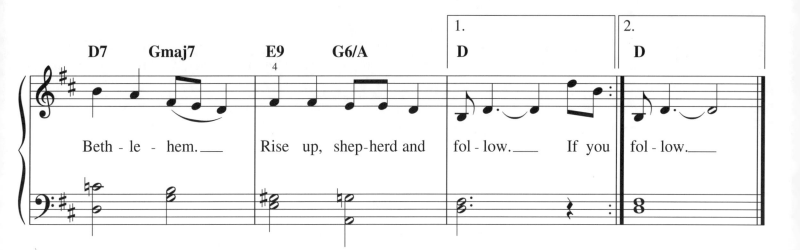

SHEPHERD! SHAKE OFF YOUR DROWSY SLEEP

Traditional French Carol

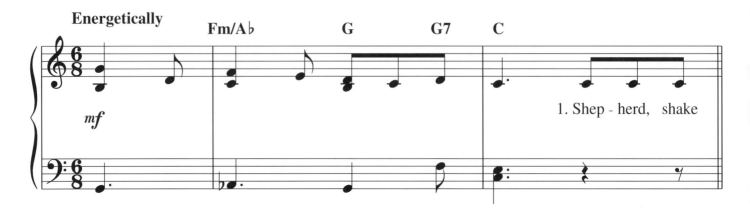

1. Shep - herd, shake

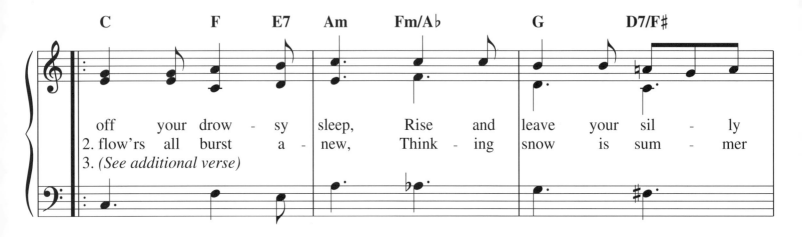

off your drow - sy sleep, Rise and leave your sil - ly
2. flow'rs all burst a - new, Think - ing snow is sum - mer
3. *(See additional verse)*

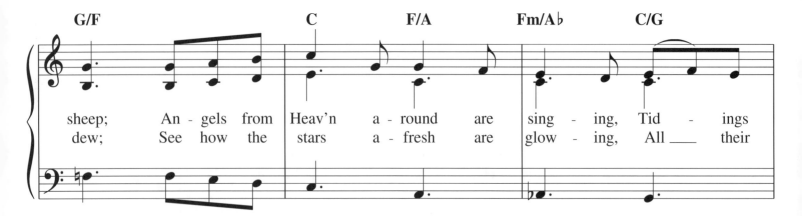

sheep; An - gels from Heav'n a - round are sing - ing, Tid - ings
dew; See how the stars a - fresh are glow - ing, All ___ their

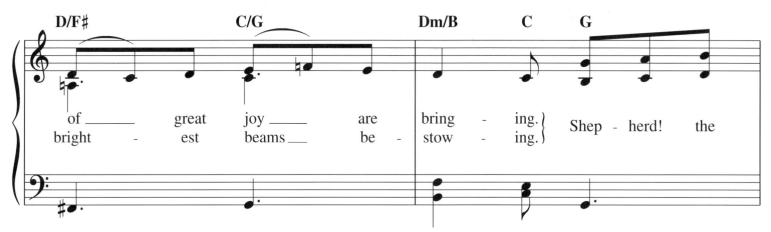

of _____ great joy _____ are bring - ing.

bright - est beams ___ be - stow - ing.

Shep - herd! the

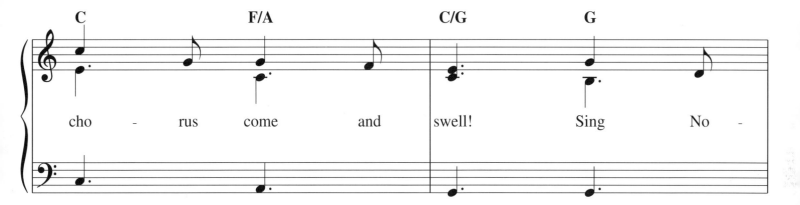

cho - rus come and swell! Sing No -

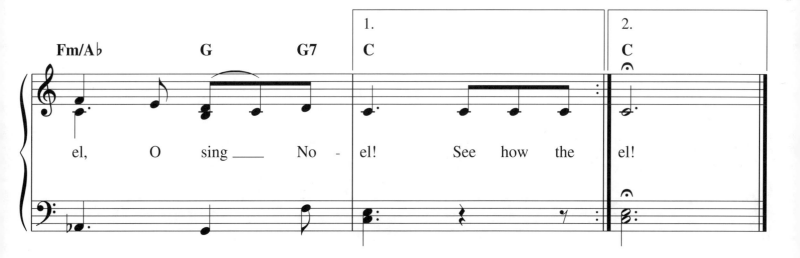

el, O sing ___ No - el! See how the el!

Additional Verse

3. Shepherd, then up and quick away!
   Seek the Babe ere break of day.
   He is the hope of ev'ry nation,
   All in Him shall find salvation.

SHEPHERD'S CRADLE SONG

Words and Music by
C.D. SCHUBERT

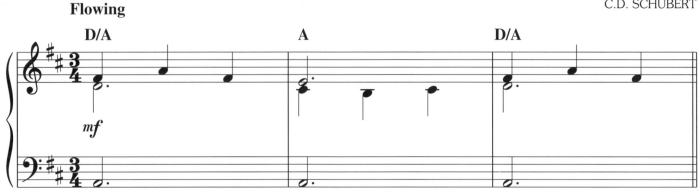

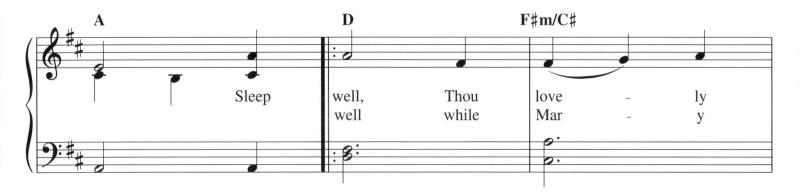

Sleep | well, | Thou | love - | ly
well | while | Mar - | y

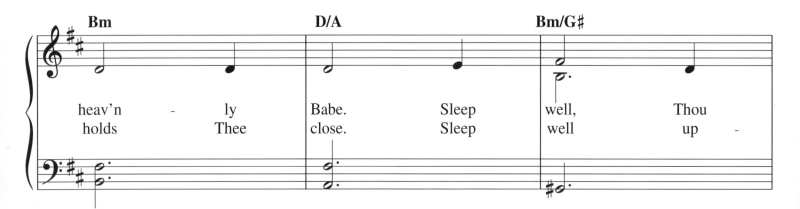

heav'n - | ly | Babe. | Sleep | well, | Thou
holds | Thee | close. | Sleep | well | up -

sweet - | est | Child, _____ | While
on _____ | her | breast, _____ | Dear

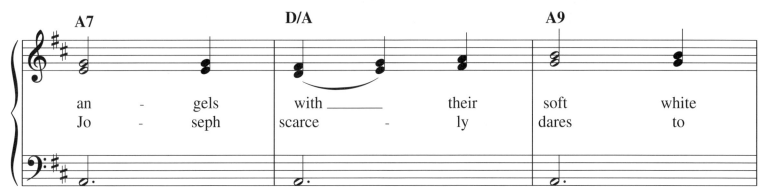

an - gels with _____ their soft white
Jo - seph scarce - ly dares to

wings Stir breez - es, cool _____ and
breathes; He's not dis - turb _____ Thy

D   A   A7

mild. We shep - herds
rest! The lambs stand

A9/C♯

poor will sing to Thee A
mute a - bout the stall As

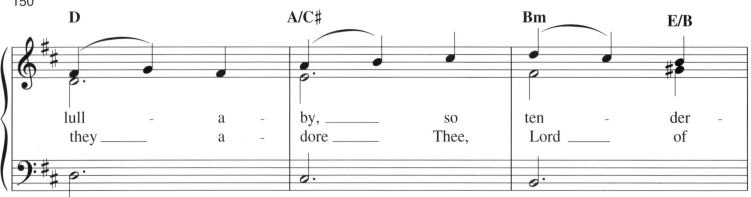

lull - a - by, _____ so ten - der -
they _____ a - dore _____ Thee, Lord _____ of

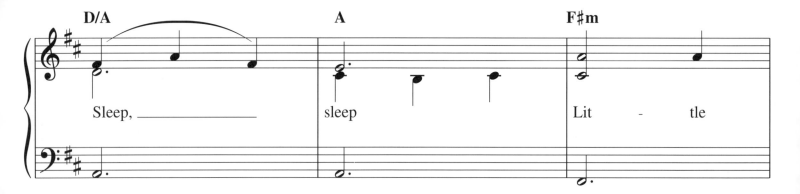

ly; }
all! }
Sleep, _____ sleep

Sleep, _____ sleep Lit - tle

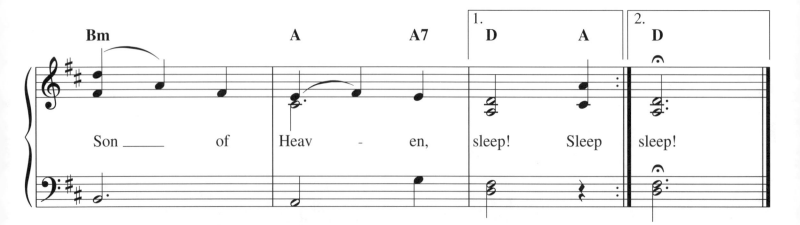

Son _____ of Heav - en, sleep! Sleep sleep!

STAR OF THE EAST

Words by GEORGE COOPER
Music by AMANDA KENNEDY

Flowing Waltz

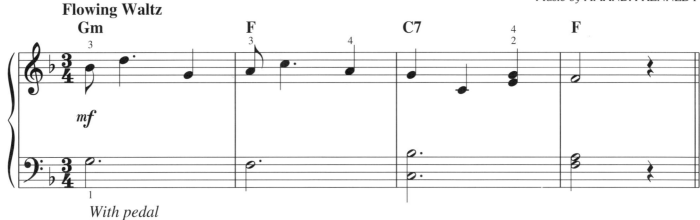

With pedal

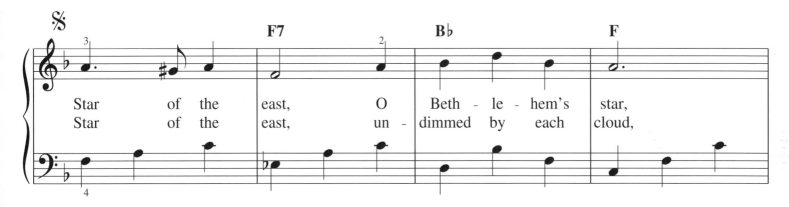

Star of the east, O Beth-le-hem's star,
Star of the east, un-dimmed by each cloud,

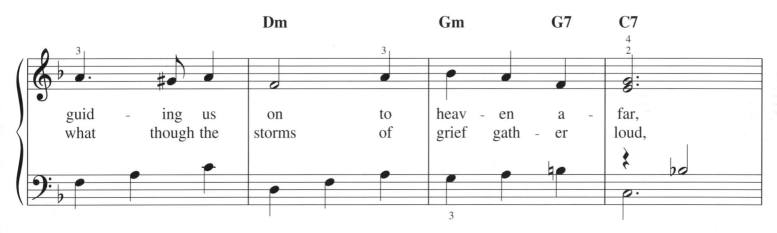

guid-ing us on to heav-en a-far,
what though the storms of grief gath-er loud,

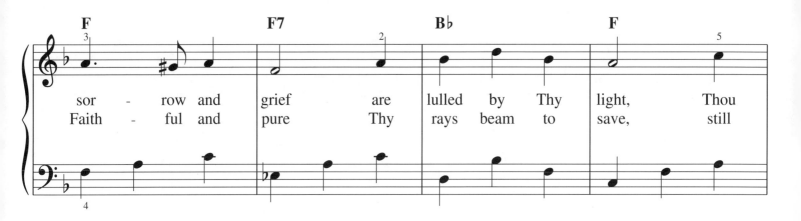

sor-row and grief are lulled by Thy light, Thou
Faith-ful and pure are Thy rays beam to save, still

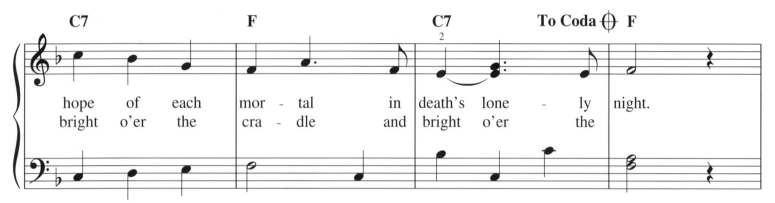

hope   of   each   mor - tal   in   death's   lone - ly   night.
bright   o'er   the   cra - dle   and   bright   o'er   the

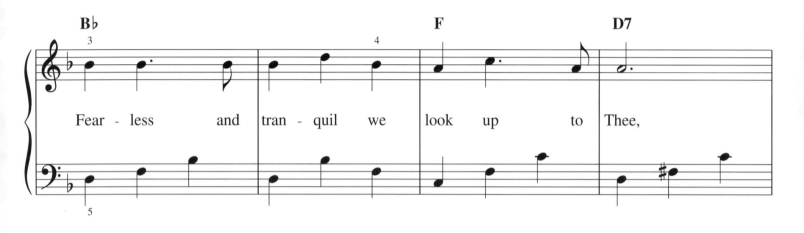

Fear - less   and   tran - quil   we   look   up   to   Thee,

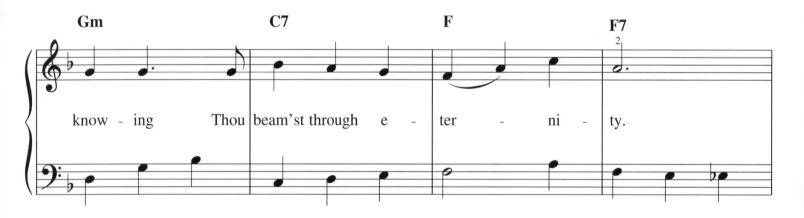

know - ing   Thou   beam'st through   e - ter - ni - ty.

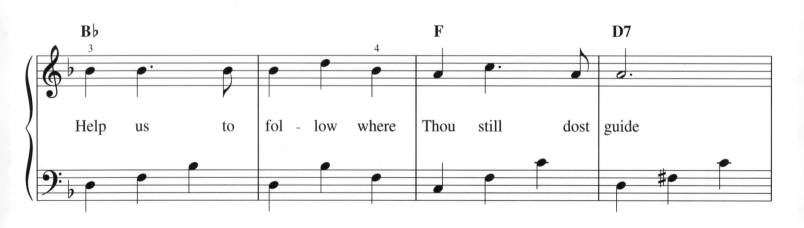

Help   us   to   fol - low   where   Thou   still   dost   guide

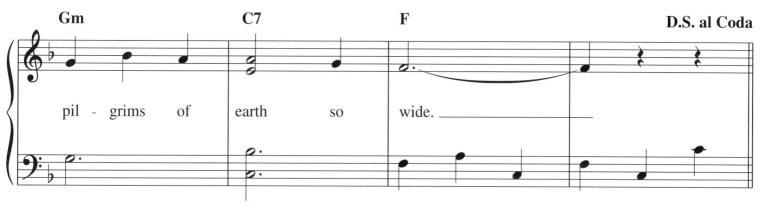

Gm   C7   F   D.S. al Coda

pil - grims   of   earth   so   wide. _____

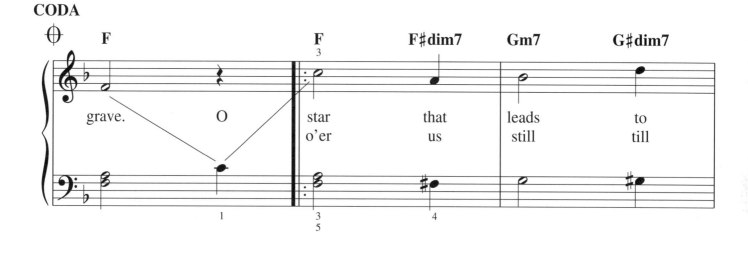

CODA

F   F   F♯dim7   Gm7   G♯dim7

grave.   O   star   that   leads   to
o'er   us   still   till

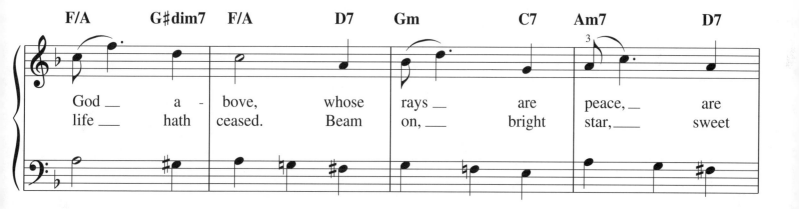

F/A   G♯dim7   F/A   D7   Gm   C7   Am7   D7

God __   a - bove,   whose rays __   are   peace, __   are
life __ hath ceased. Beam on, __   bright star, __   sweet

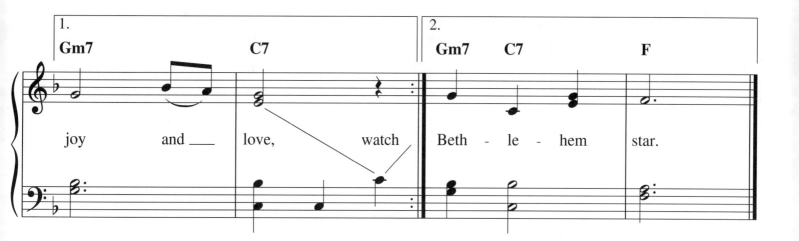

1.
Gm7   C7   2.
Gm7   C7   F

joy   and __   love,   watch   Beth - le - hem   star.

SHOUT THE GLAD TIDINGS

Traditional

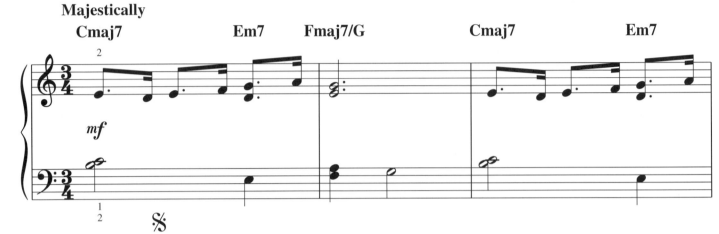

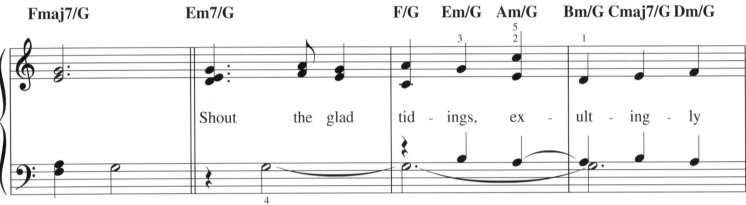

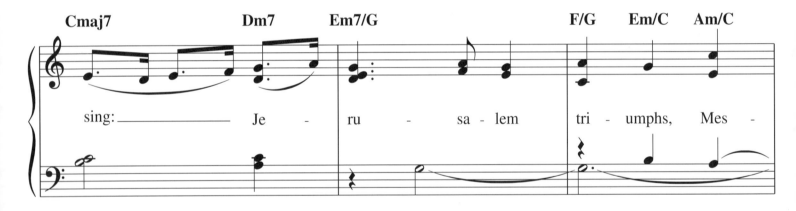

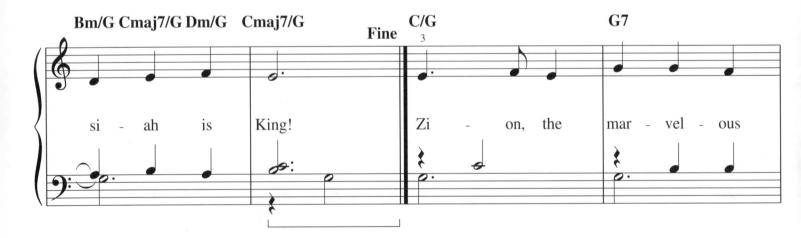

155

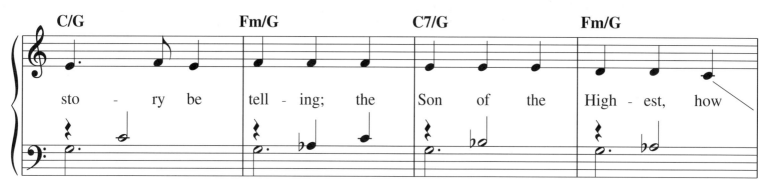

C/G　　Fm/G　　C7/G　　Fm/G

sto - ry be tell - ing; the Son of the High - est, how

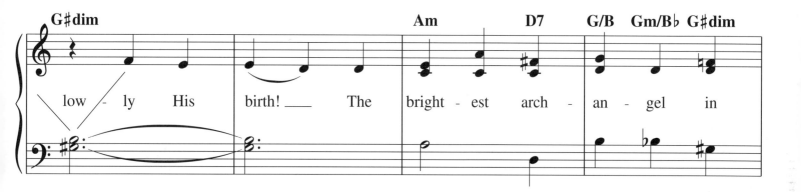

G♯dim　　Am　D7　G/B　Gm/B♭　G♯dim

low - ly His birth! ___ The bright - est arch - an - gel in

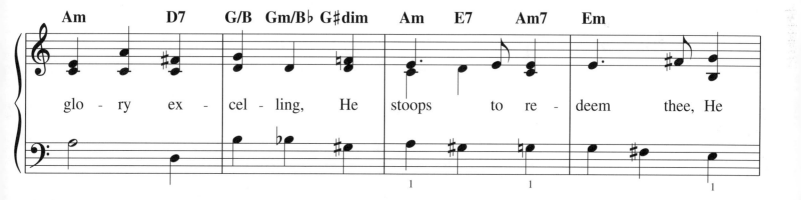

Am　D7　G/B　Gm/B♭　G♯dim　Am　E7　Am7　Em

glo - ry ex - cel - ling, He stoops to re - deem thee, He

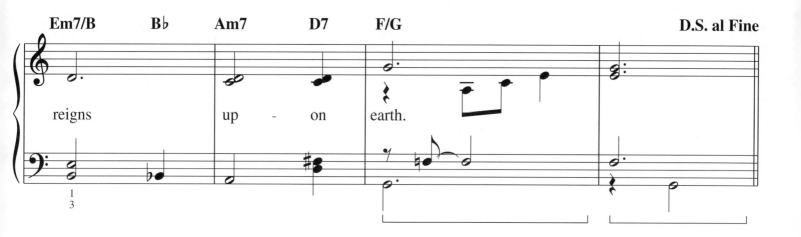

Em7/B　B♭　Am7　D7　F/G　　D.S. al Fine

reigns up - on earth.

SILENT NIGHT

Words by JOSEPH MOHR
Translated by JOHN F. YOUNG
Music by FRANZ X. GRUBER

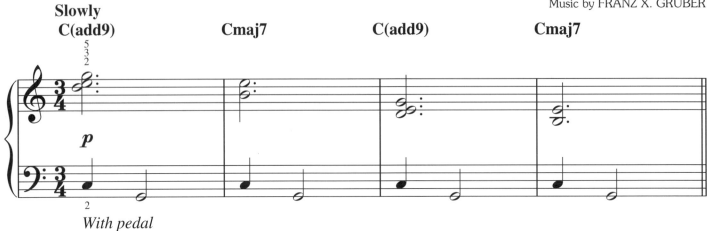

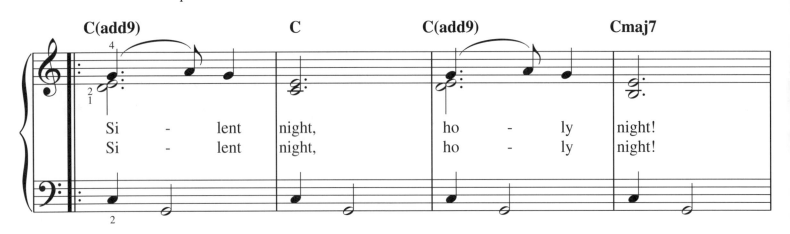

Si - lent night, ho - ly night!
Si - lent night, ho - ly night!

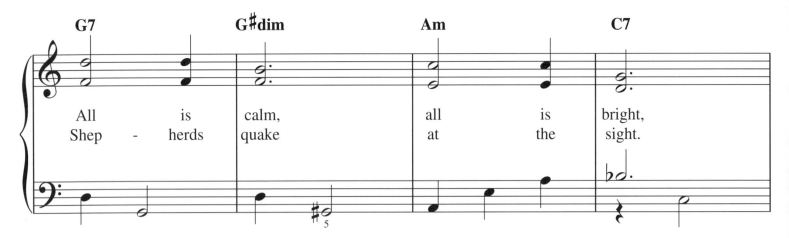

All is calm, all is bright,
Shep - herds quake at the sight.

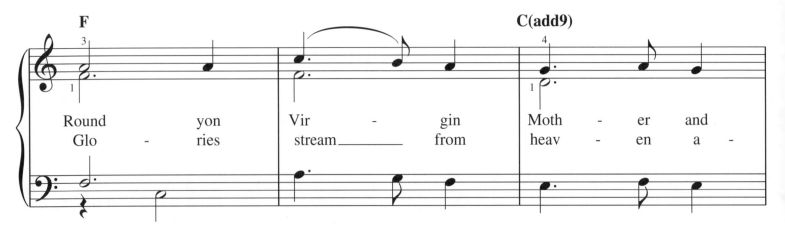

Round yon Vir - gin Moth - er and
Glo - ries stream from heav - en a -

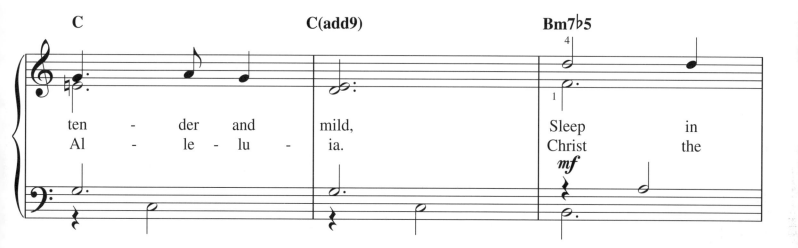

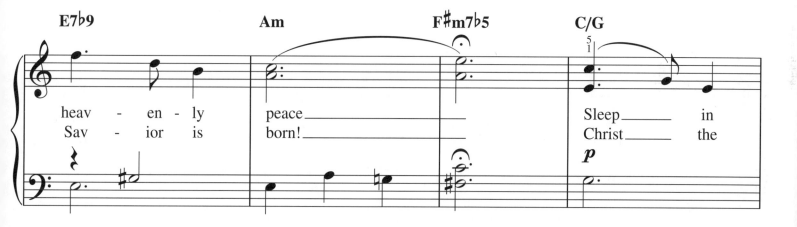

THE SIMPLE BIRTH

Traditional Flemish Carol

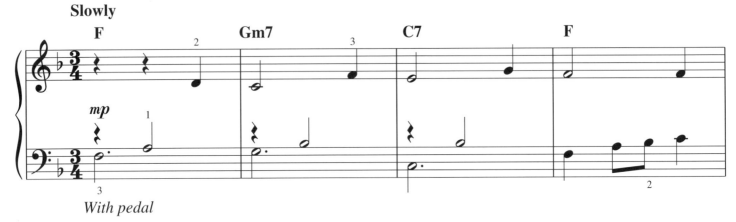

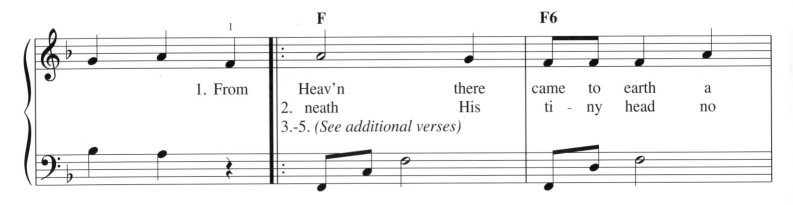

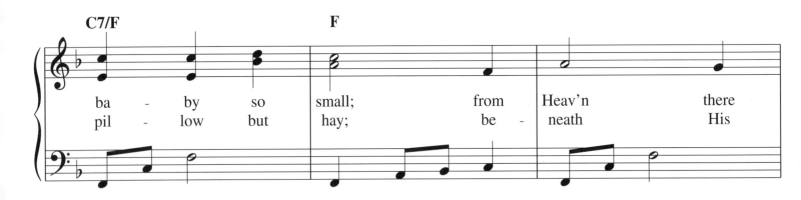

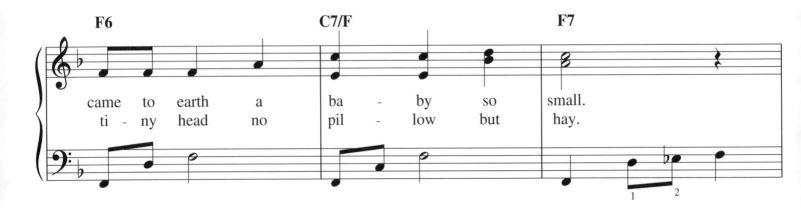

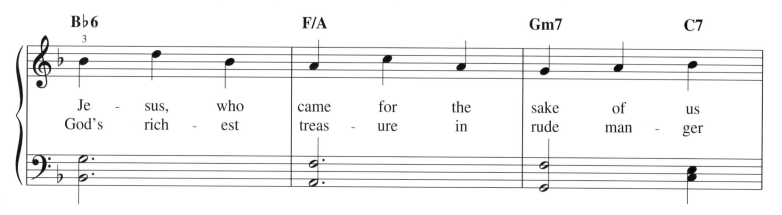

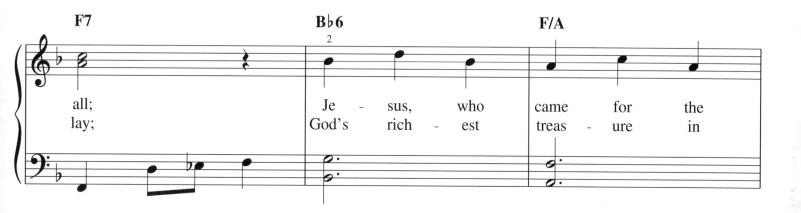

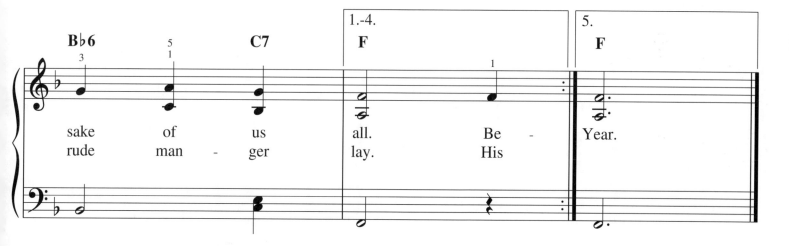

Additional Verses

3. His eyes of blackest jet were sparkling with light; *(2x)*
   Rosy cheeks bloomed on His face fair and bright. *(2x)*

4. And from His lovely mouth the laughter did swell, *(2x)*
   When He saw Mary, whom He loved so well. *(2x)*

5. He came to weary earth, so dark and so drear, *(2x)*
   To wish to mankind a blessed New Year. *(2x)*

SING, O SING, THIS BLESSED MORN

Words by CHRISTOPHER WORDSWORTH
Traditional German Tune

Moderately

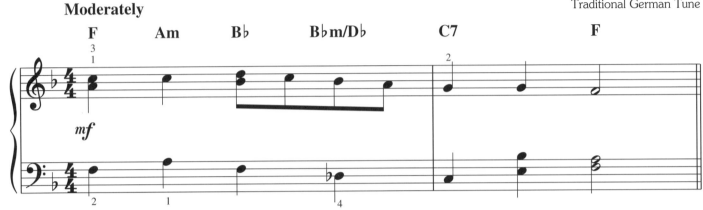

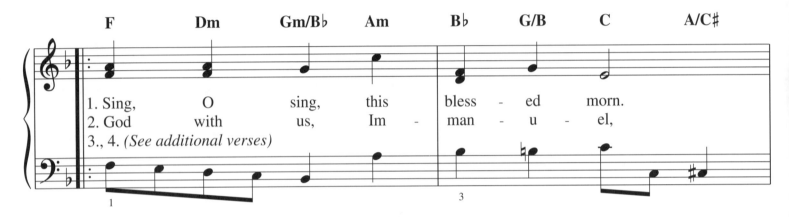

1. Sing, O sing, this bless - ed morn.
2. God with us, Im - man - u - el,
3., 4. *(See additional verses)*

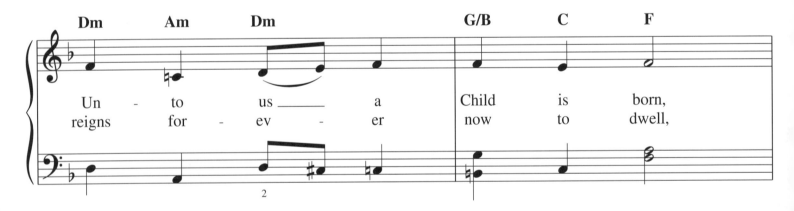

Un - to us _____ a Child is born,
reigns for - ev - er now to dwell,

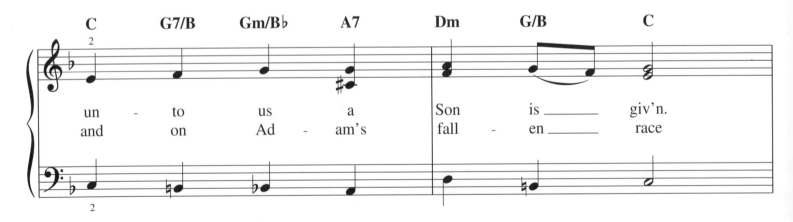

un - to us a Son is _____ giv'n.
and on Ad - am's fall - en _____ race

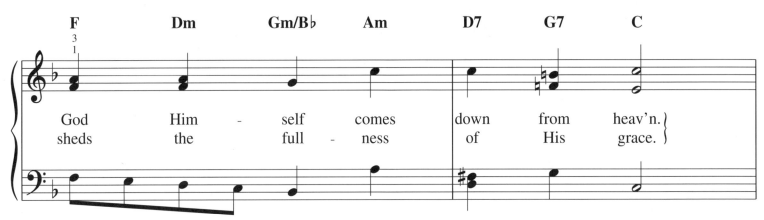

God   Him - self   comes   down   from   heav'n.
sheds   the   full - ness   of   His   grace.

Refrain

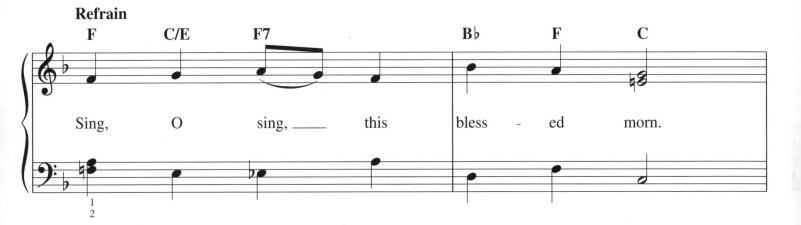

Sing,   O   sing, ____ this   bless - ed   morn.

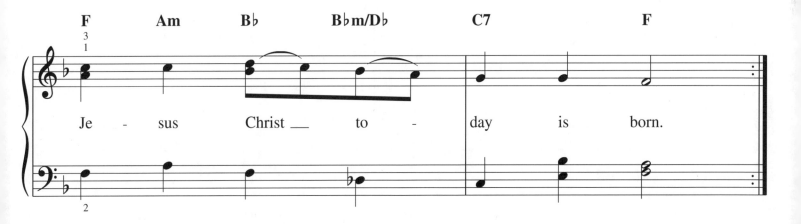

Je - sus   Christ ___ to - day   is   born.

Additional Verses

3. God comes down that man may rise,
   Lifted by Him to the skies.
   Christ is Son of man that we
   Son of God in Him may be.
   Refrain

4. O renew us, Lord, we pray,
   With Thy spirit day by day,
   That we ever one may be
   With the Father and with Thee.
   Refrain

SING WE NOW OF CHRISTMAS

Traditional

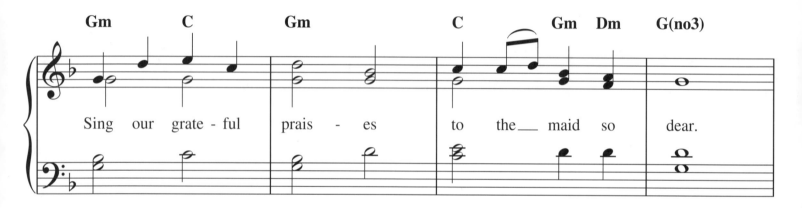

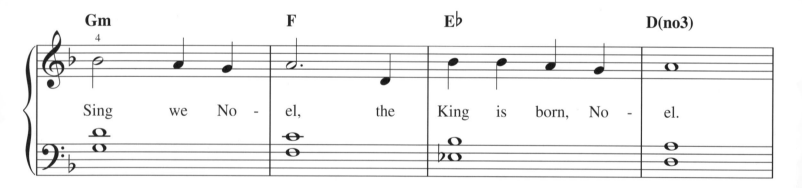

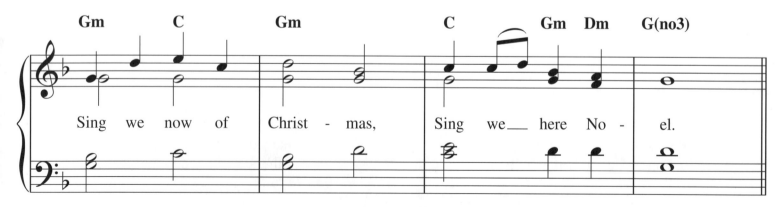

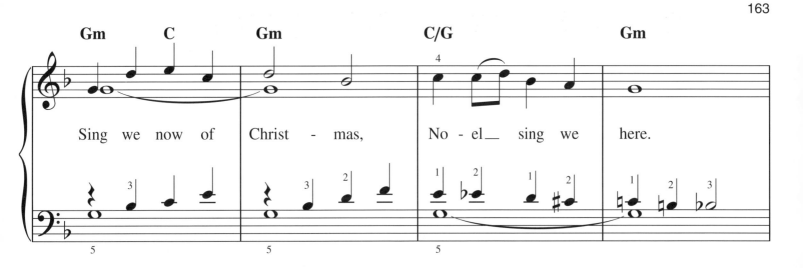

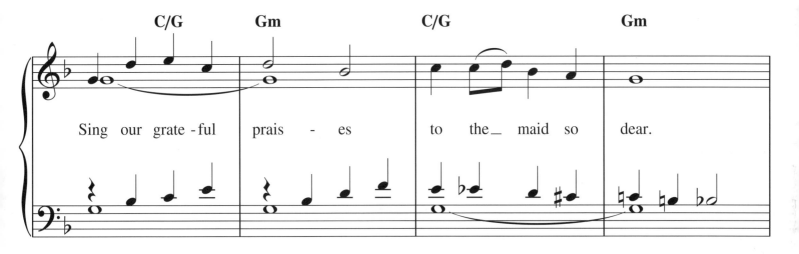

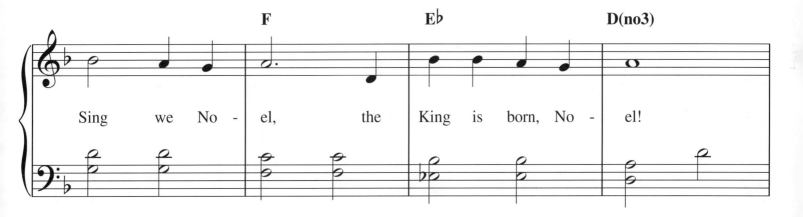

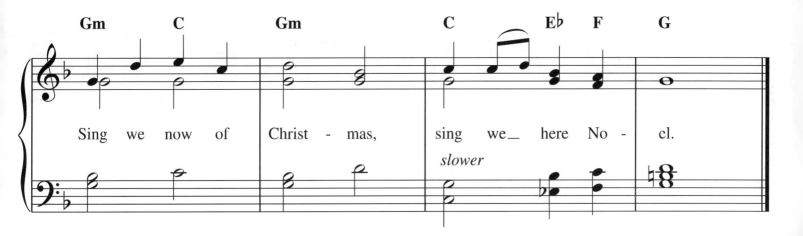

SLEEP, HOLY BABE

Words by EDWARD CASWELL
Music by J.B. DYKES

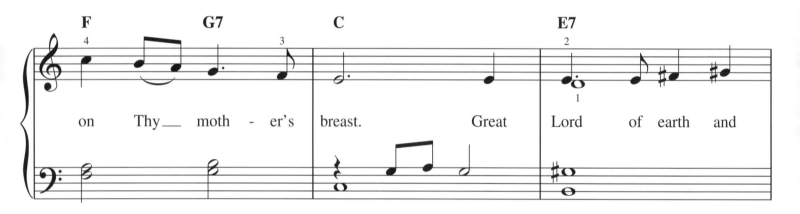

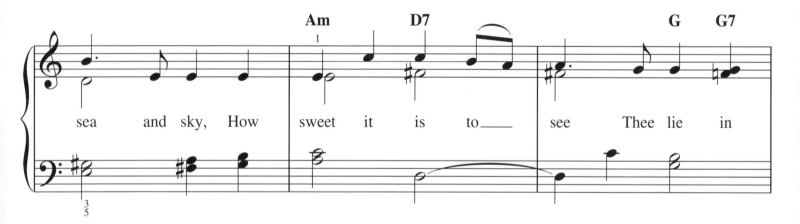

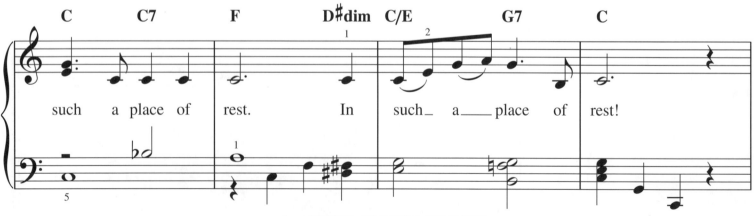

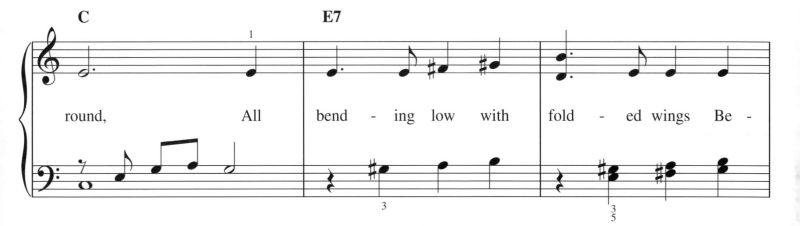

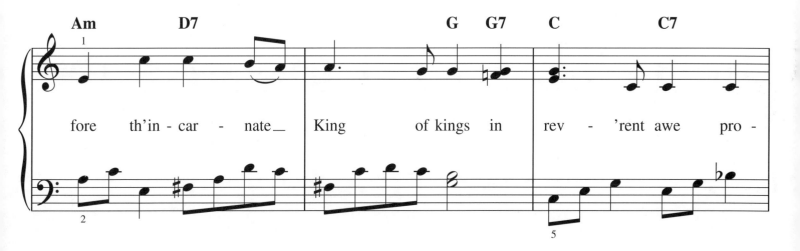

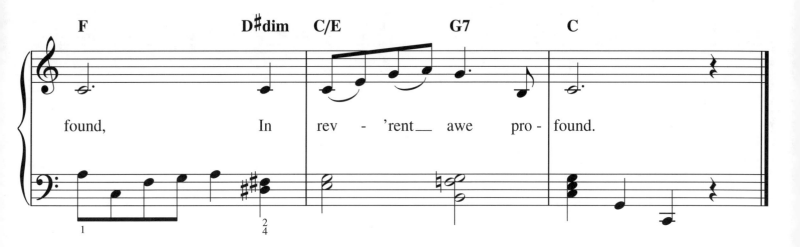

SLEEP, O SLEEP, MY PRECIOUS CHILD

Traditional Italian Carol

Moderately fast

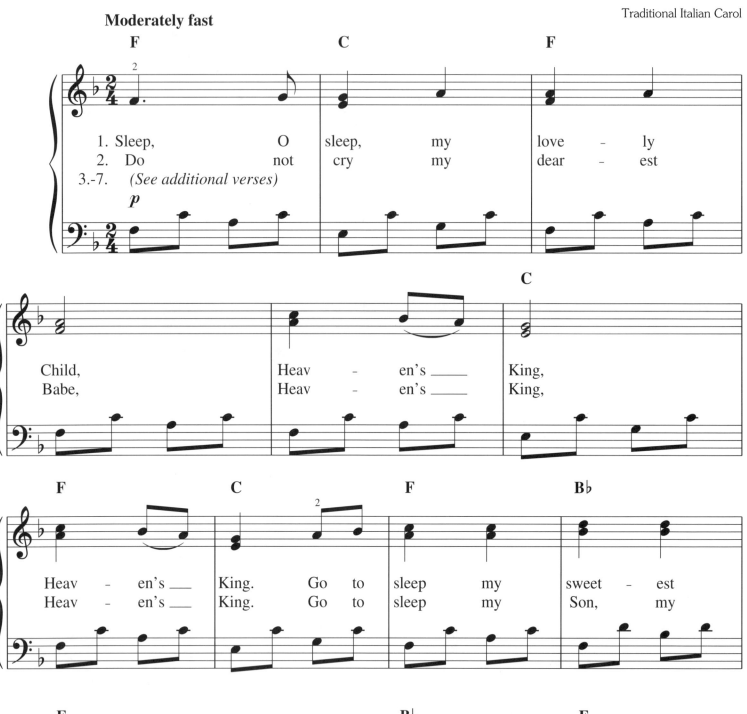

1. Sleep, O sleep, my love - ly
2. Do not cry my dear - est
3.-7. *(See additional verses)*

Child, Heav - en's _____ King,
Babe, Heav - en's _____ King,

Heav - en's _____ King. Go to sleep my sweet - est
Heav - en's _____ King. Go to sleep my Son, my

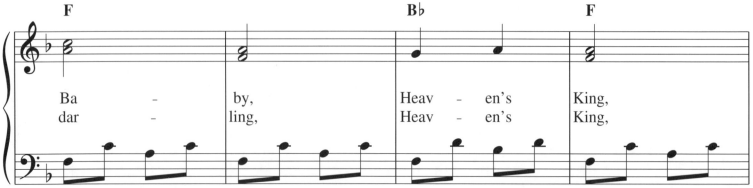

Ba - by, Heav - en's King,
dar - ling, Heav - en's King,

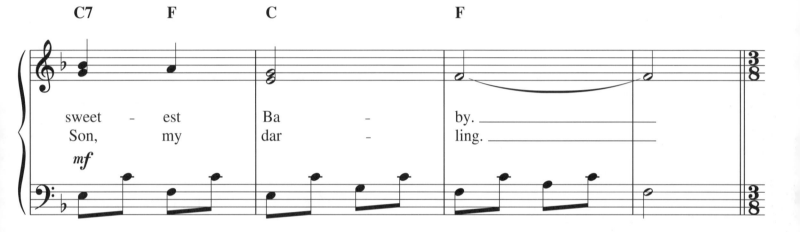

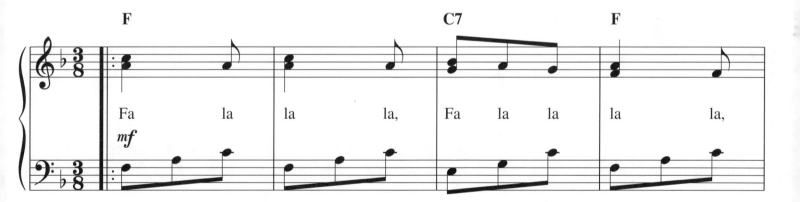

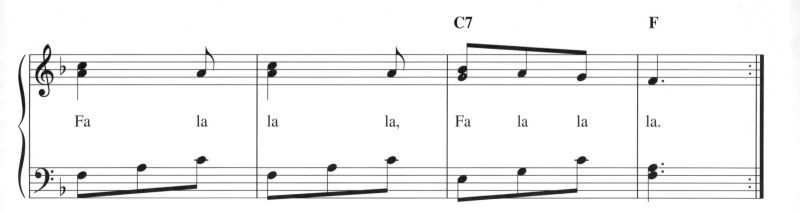

THE SNOW LAY ON THE GROUND

Traditional Irish Carol

Moderately slow

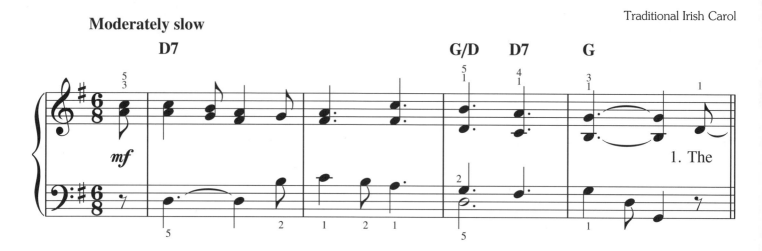

1. The

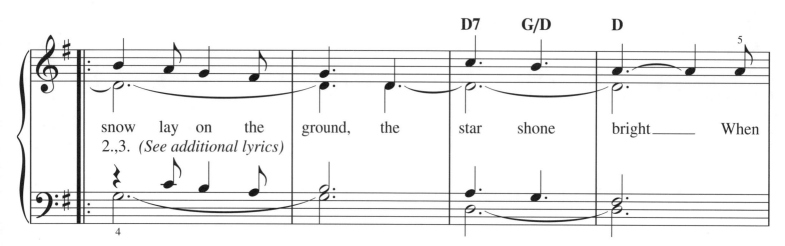

snow lay on the ground, the star shone bright____ When
2.,3. *(See additional lyrics)*

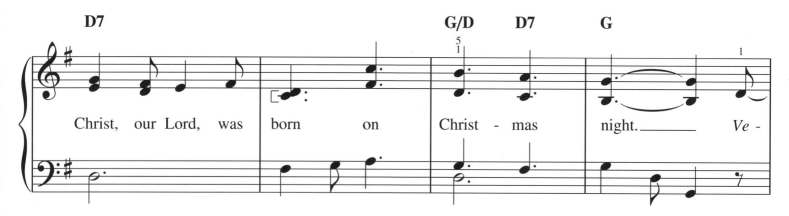

Christ, our Lord, was born on Christ - mas night.____ Ve -

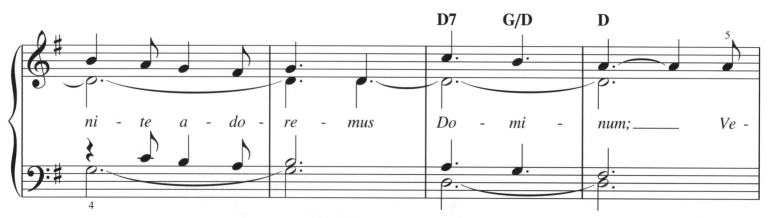

ni - te a - do - re - mus Do - mi - num;____ Ve -

ni - te a - do - re - mus, Do - mi - num._____ Ve -

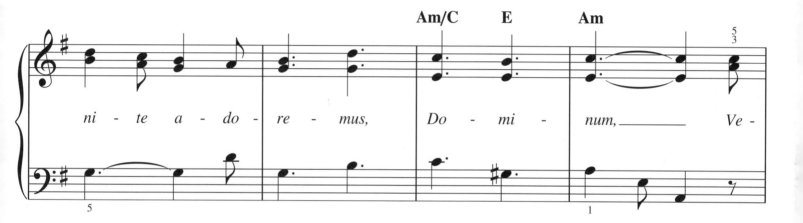

ni - te a - do - re - mus, Do - mi - num,_____ Ve -

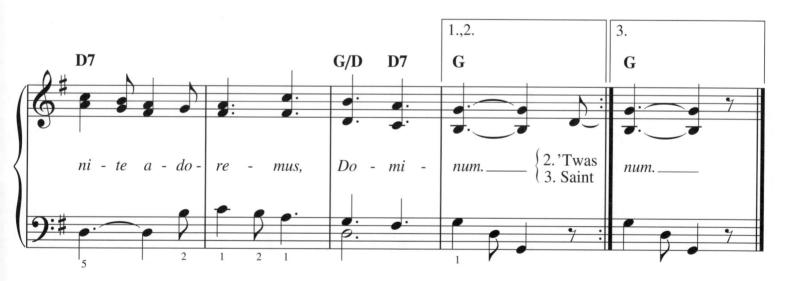

ni - te a - do - re - mus, Do - mi - num._____ { 2.'Twas   num._____
{ 3. Saint

Additional Lyrics

2. 'Twas Mary, Virgin pure, of holy Anne,
   That brought into this world the God made man.
   She laid Him in a stall at Bethlehem,
   The ass and oxen share the roof with them.

3. Saint Joseph, too, was by to tend the Child;
   To guard Him and protect His Mother mild;
   The angels hovered round, and sang this song;
   Venite adoremus Dominum.

THE STAR OF CHRISTMAS MORNING

Traditional

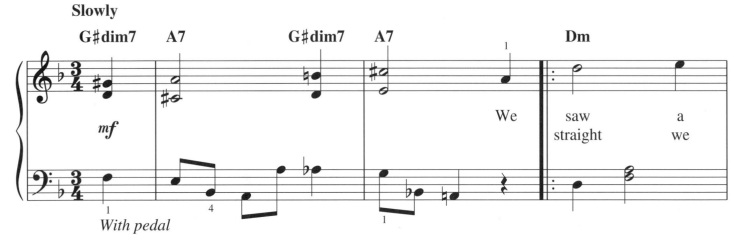

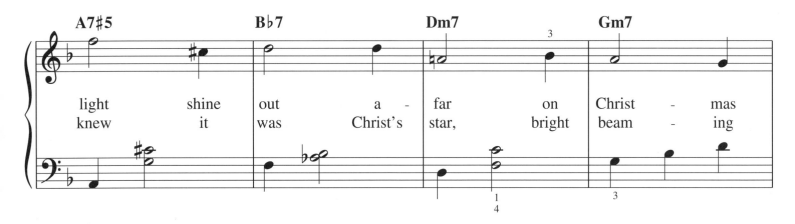

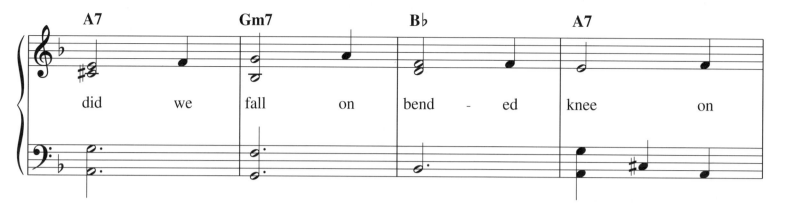

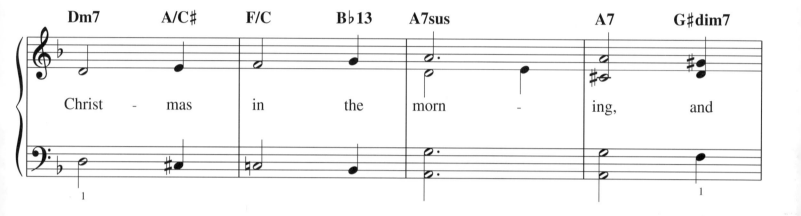

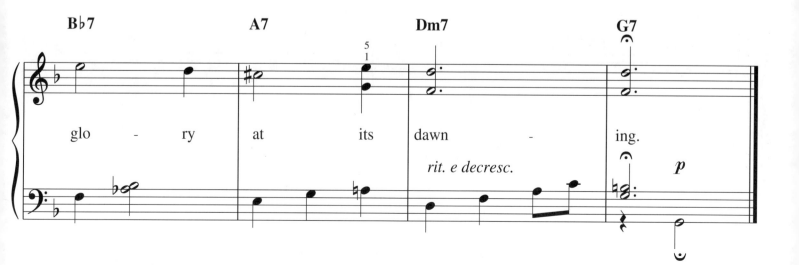

STILL, STILL, STILL

Salzburg Melody, c.1819
Traditional Austrian Text

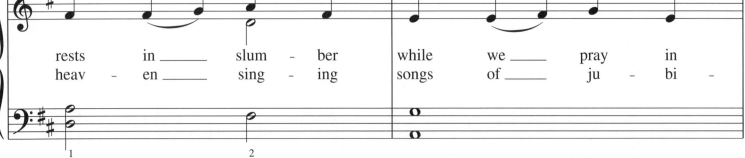

Still, ___ still, ___ still, to ___
Sleep, ___ sleep, ___ sleep, while ___

sleep is ___ now His will. On Mar - y's ___ breast He
we Thy ___ vig - il keep. And an - gels ___ come from

rests in ___ slum - ber while we ___ pray in
heav - en ___ sing - ing songs of ___ ju - bi -

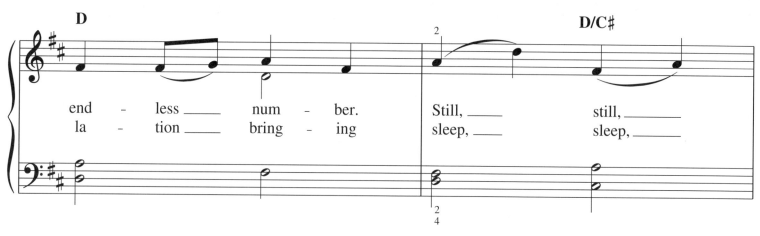

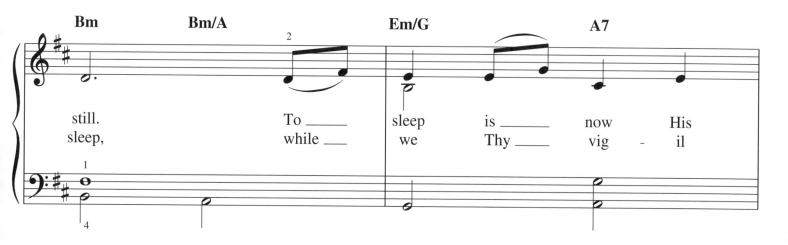

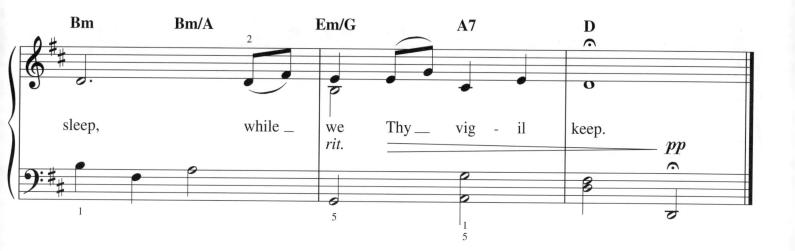

THERE'S A SONG IN THE AIR

Words and Music by JOSIAH G. HOLLAND
and KARL P. HARRINGTON

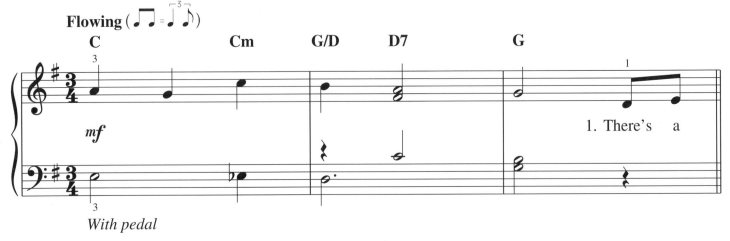

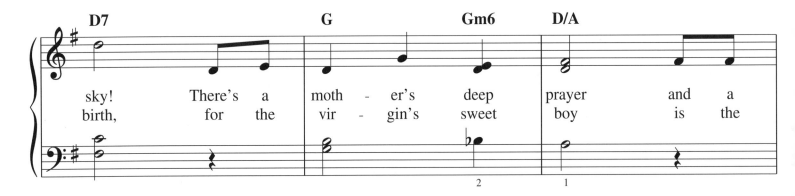

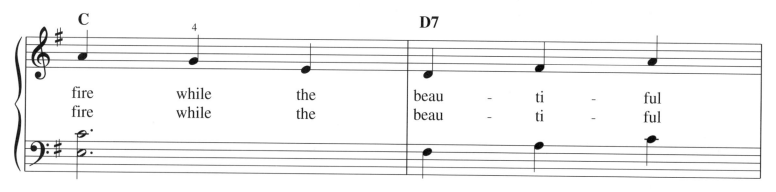

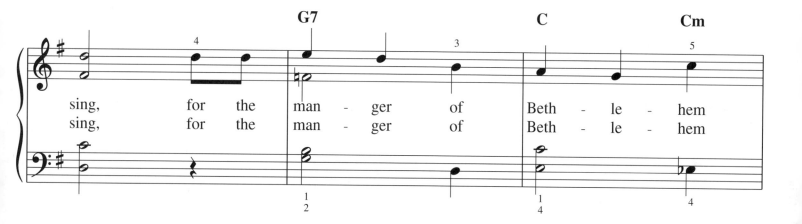

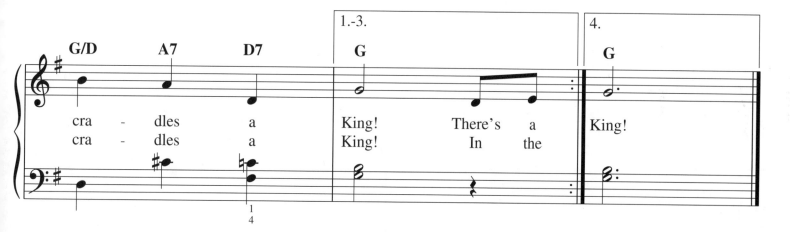

Additional Verses

3. In the light of that star
   Lie the ages impearled,
   And that song from afar
   Has swept over the world.
   Ev'ry hearth is aflame, and the angels sing
   In the homes of the nations that Jesus is King!

4. We rejoice in the light
   And we echo the song
   That comes down through the night
   From the heavenly throng.
   Ay! we shout to the lovely evangel they bring
   And we greet in His cradle our Savior and King!

TOYLAND

Words by GLEN MacDONOUGH
Music by VICTOR HERBERT

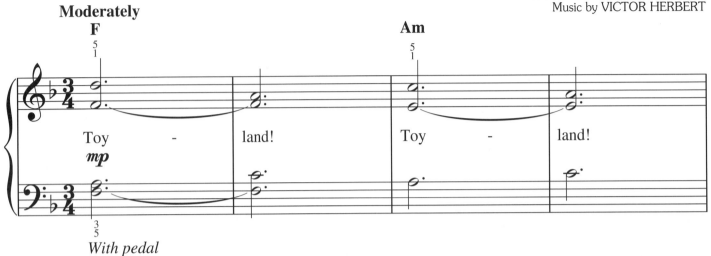

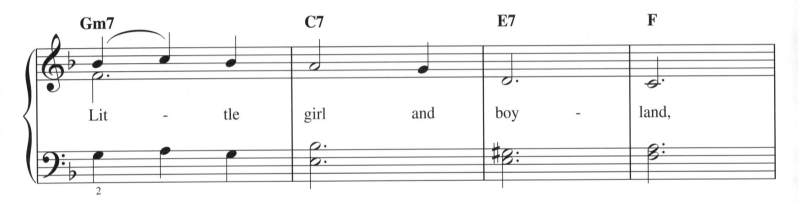

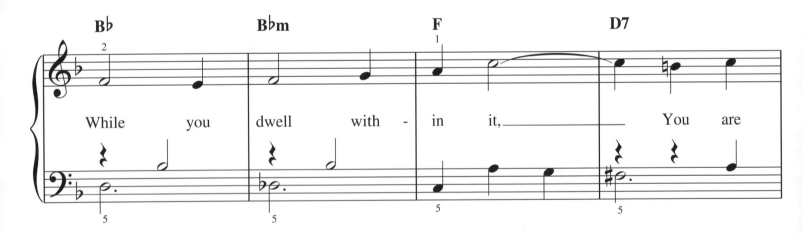

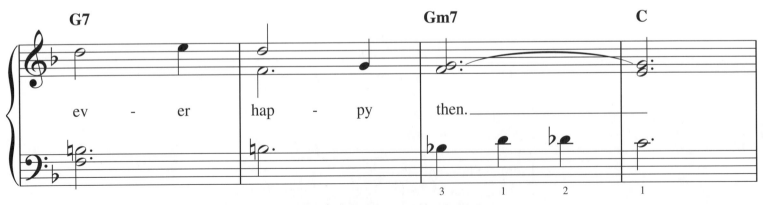

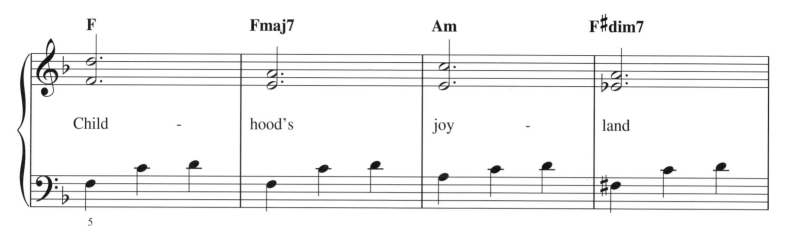

Child - hood's joy - land

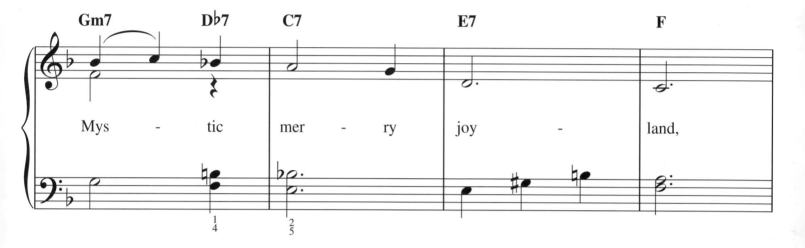

Mys - tic mer - ry joy - land,

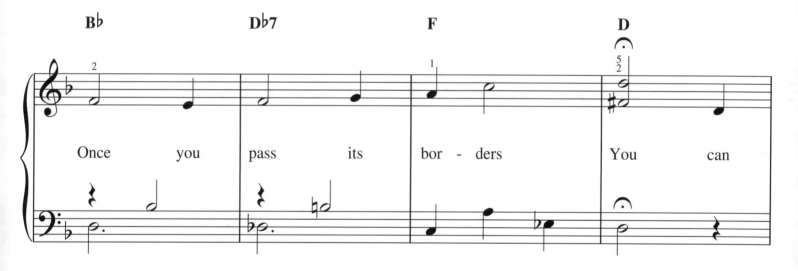

Once you pass its bor - ders You can

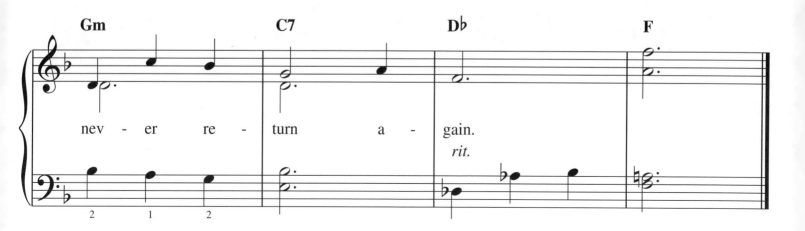

nev - er re - turn a - gain.

rit.

THE TWELVE DAYS OF CHRISTMAS

Traditional English Carol

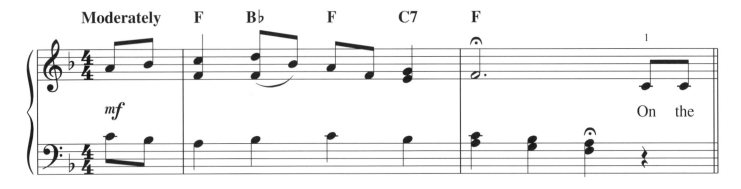

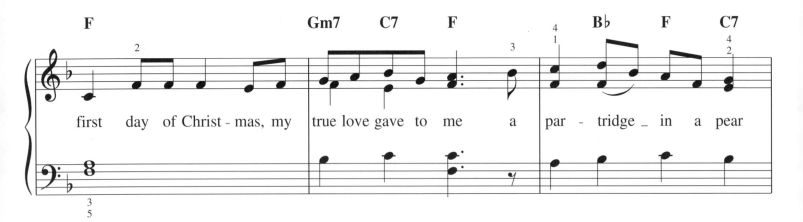

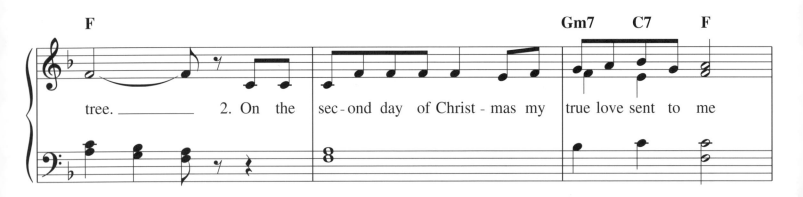

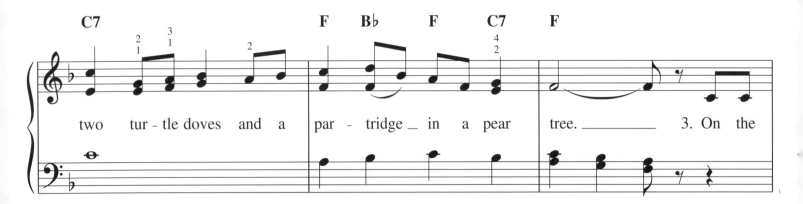

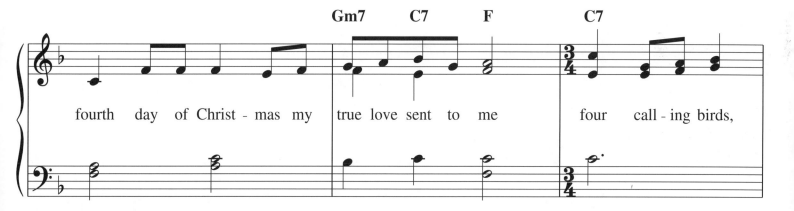

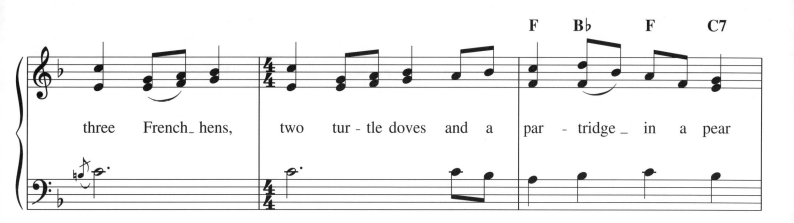

F   **Gm7**   **C7**   **F**

tree. _____ 5. On the fifth day of Christ - mas my true love sent to me

Slow and broad   **Tempo Primo**

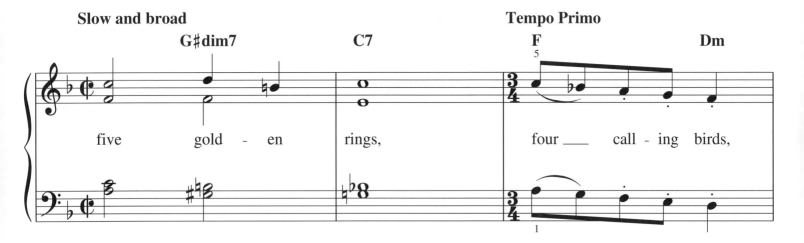

G♯dim7   **C7**   **F**   **Dm**

five gold - en rings, four __ call - ing birds,

B♭   **C7**   **F**   **B♭**   **F**   **C7**

three French hens, two __ tur - tle doves and a par - tridge _ in a pear

F   **F**   **Gm7**   **C7**   **F**

tree. _____ 6. On the sixth day of Christ - mas my true love sent to me

7.-12. *(See additional verses)*

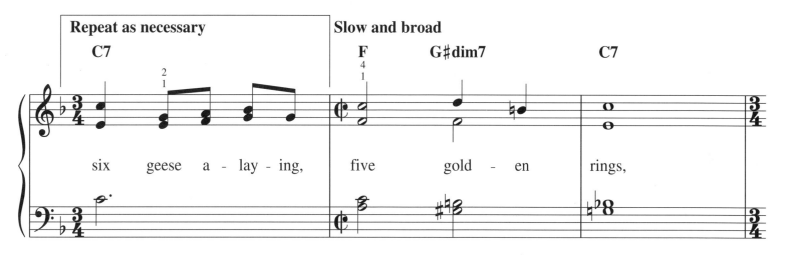

Repeat as necessary — C7

six geese a - lay - ing,

Slow and broad — F G♯dim7 C7

five gold - en rings,

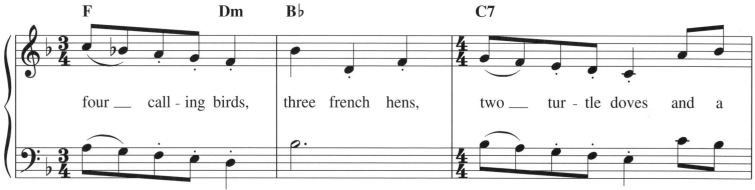

Tempo Primo — F Dm B♭ C7

four ___ call - ing birds, three french hens, two ___ tur - tle doves and a

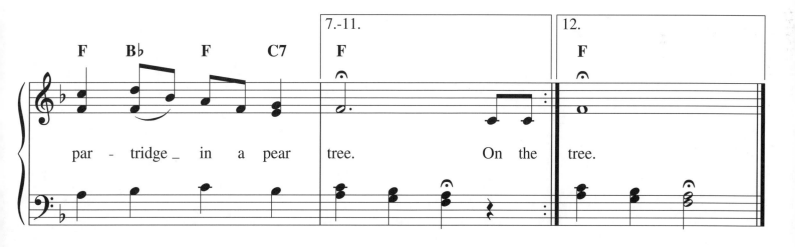

F B♭ F C7 | 7.-11. F | 12. F

par - tridge ___ in a pear tree. On the tree.

Additional Verses

Seven swans a-swimming
Eight maids a-milking
Nine ladies dancing
Ten lords a-leaping
Eleven pipers piping
Twelve drummers drumming

A VIRGIN UNSPOTTED

Traditional English Carol

1. A ___

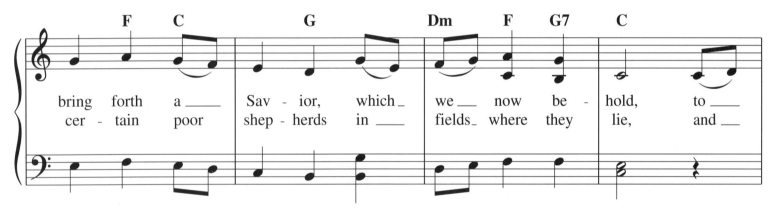

vir - gin un - spot - ted, the ___ proph - et fore - told, should ___
2. God sent an ___ an - gel from ___ Heav - en so high to ___
3., 4. *(See additional verses)*

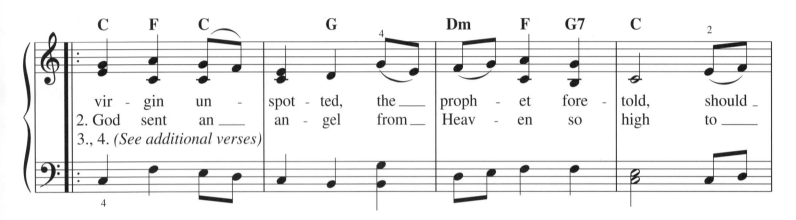

bring forth a ___ Sav - ior, which ___ we ___ now be - hold, to ___
cer - tain poor shep - herds in ___ fields ___ where they lie, and ___

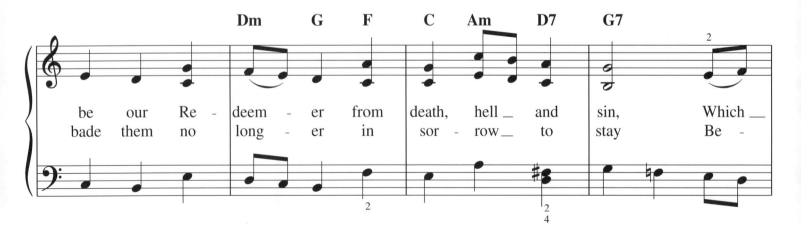

be our Re - deem - er from death, hell ___ and sin, Which ___
bade them no long - er in sor - row ___ to stay Be -

183

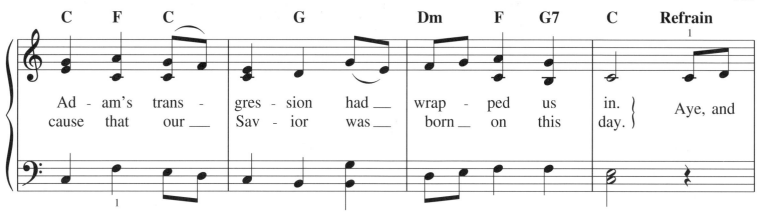

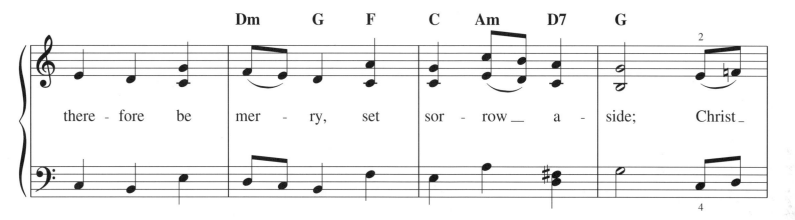

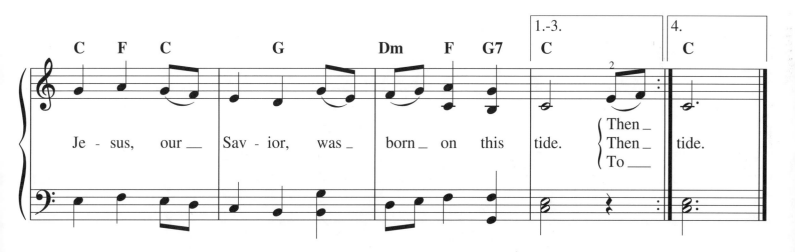

Additional Verses

3. Then presently after, the shepherds did spy
   Vast numbers of angels to stand in the sky.
   They joyfully talked and sweetly did sing:
   "To God be all glory, our heavenly King."
   Refrain

4. To teach us humility all this was done,
   And learn we from thence haught pride for to shun;
   A manger His cradle who came from above,
   The great God of mercy, of peace and of love.
   Refrain

WATCHMAN, TELL US OF THE NIGHT

Traditional

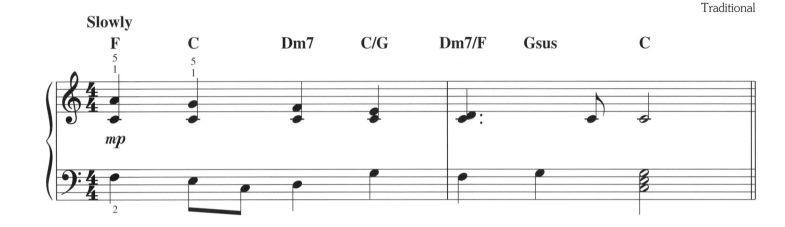

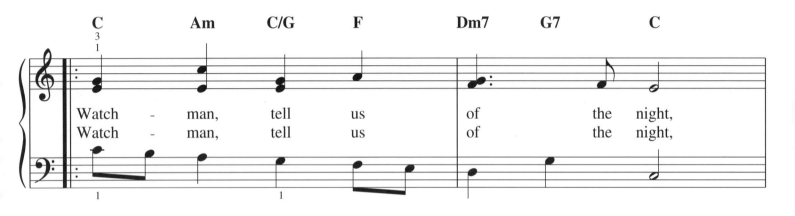

Watch - man, tell us of the night,
Watch - man, tell us of the night,

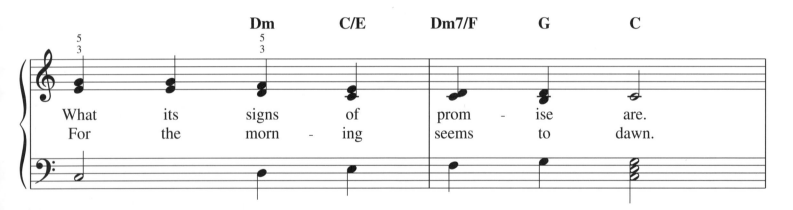

What its signs of prom - ise are.
For the morn - ing seems to dawn.

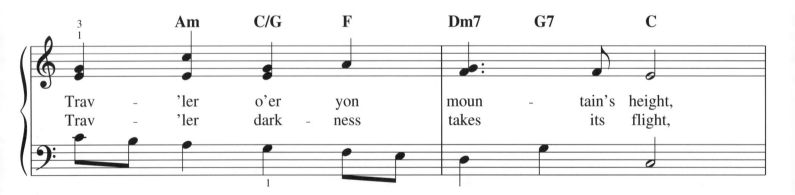

Trav - 'ler o'er yon moun - tain's height,
Trav - 'ler dark - ness takes its flight,

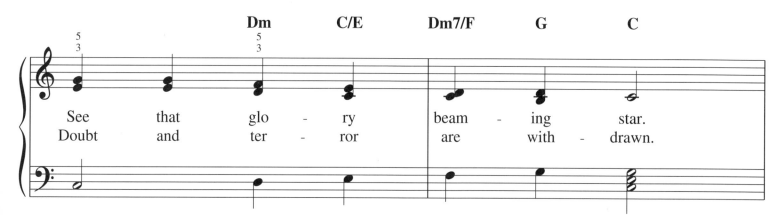

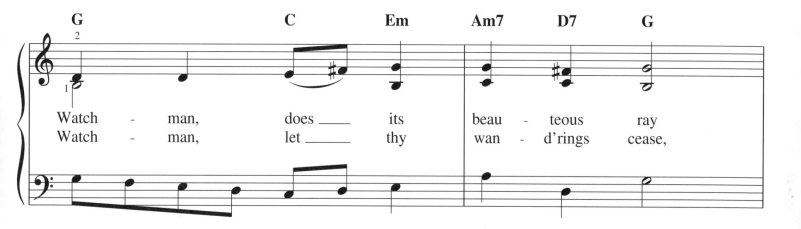

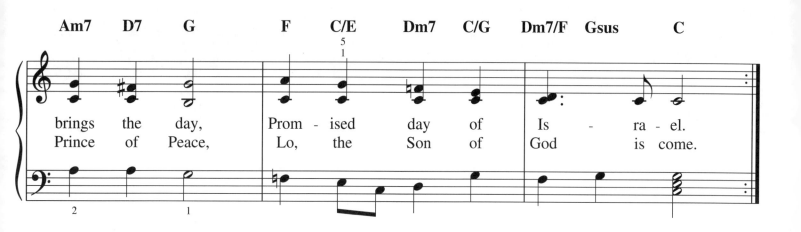

WE THREE KINGS OF ORIENT ARE

Words and Music by
JOHN H. HOPKINS, JR.

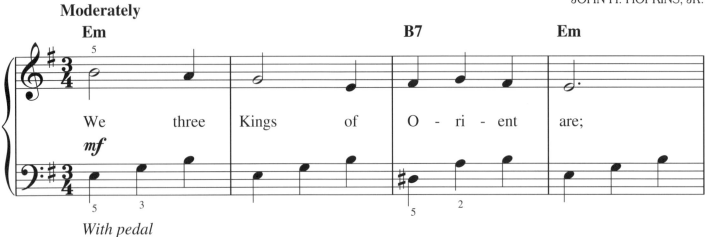

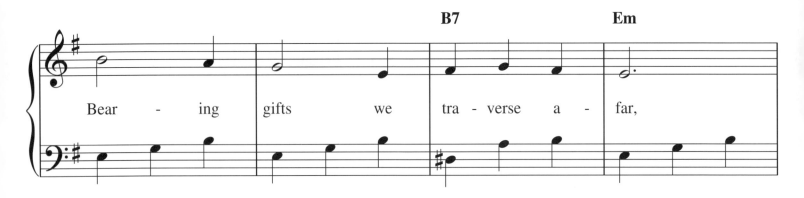

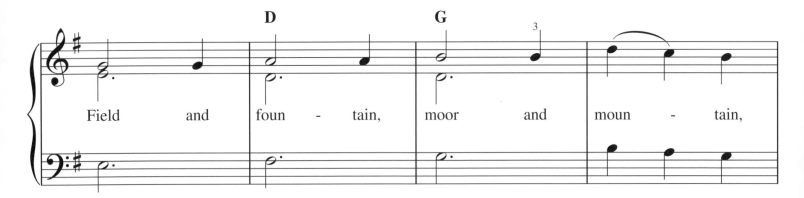

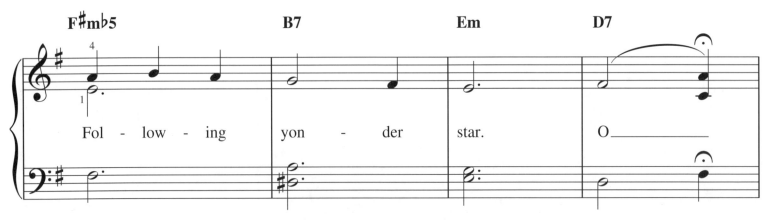

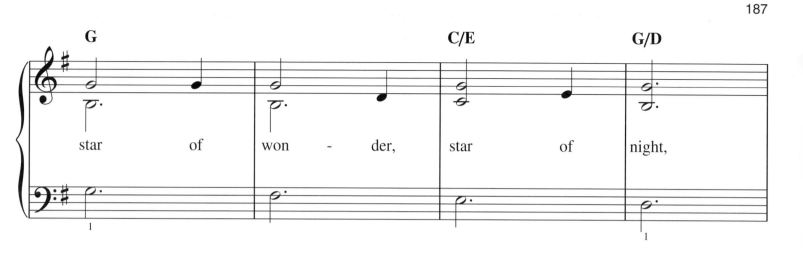

star of   won - der,   star   of   night,

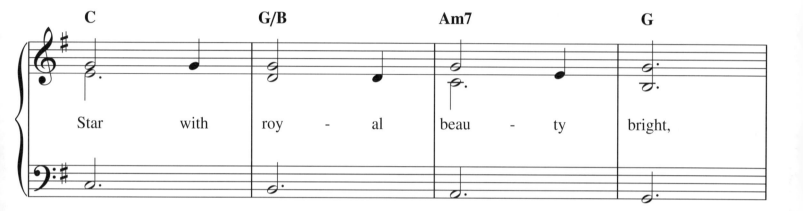

Star   with   roy - al   beau - ty   bright,

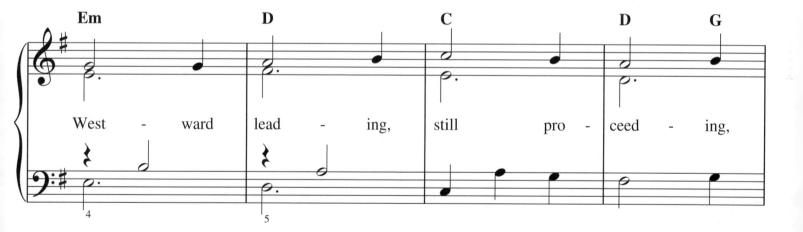

West - ward   lead - ing,   still   pro - ceed - ing,

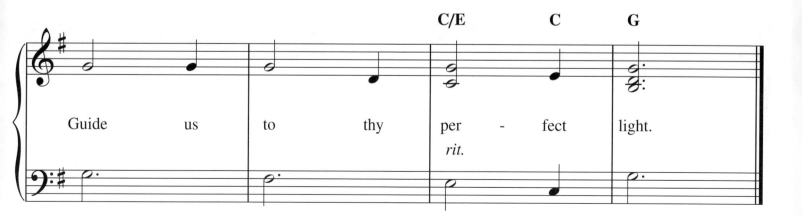

Guide   us   to   thy   per - fect   light.

rit.

WE WISH YOU A MERRY CHRISTMAS

Traditional English Folksong

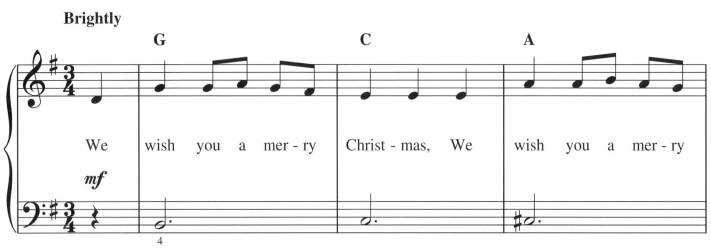

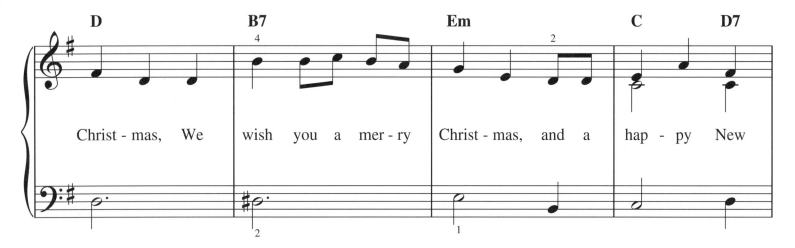

189

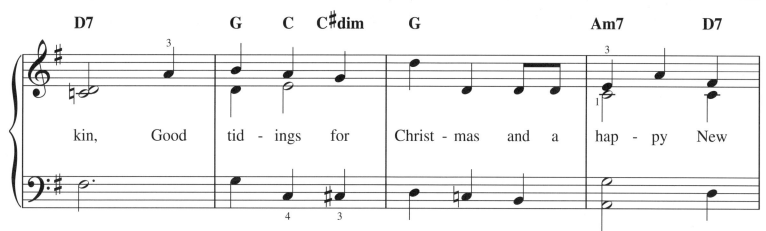

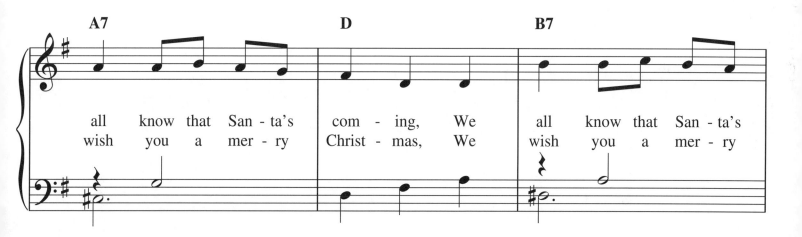

WEXFORD CAROL

Traditional Irish Carol

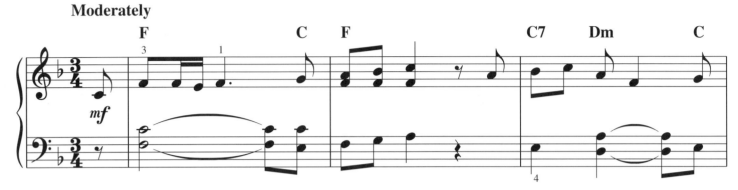

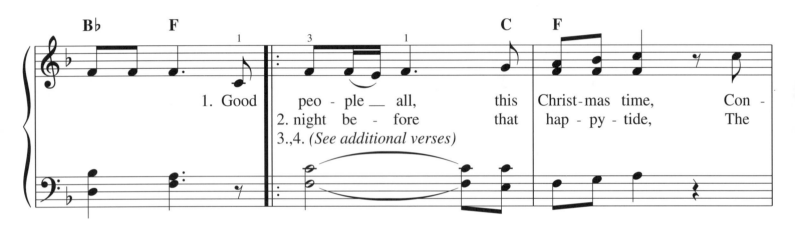

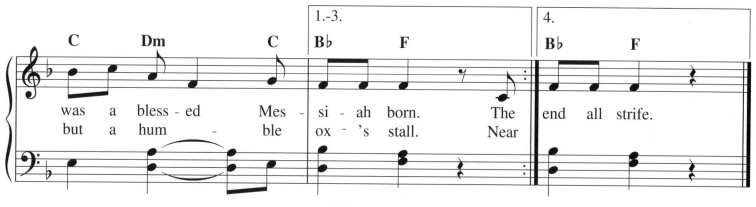

Additional Verses

3. Near Bethlehem did shepherds keep,
   Their flocks of lambs and feeding sheep;
   To whom God's angels did appear,
   Which put the shepherds in great fear.
   "Prepare and go," the angels said,
   "To Bethlehem, be not afraid;
   For there you'll find, this happy morn,
   A princely Babe, sweet Jesus born."

4. With thankful heart and joyful mind,
   The shepherds went the Babe to find,
   And as God's angel had foretold,
   They did our Saviour Christ behold.
   Within a manger He was laid,
   And by his side the Virgin maid,
   Attending on the Lord of life,
   Who came on earth to end all strife.

WHAT CHILD IS THIS?

Words by WILLIAM C. DIX
16th Century English Melody

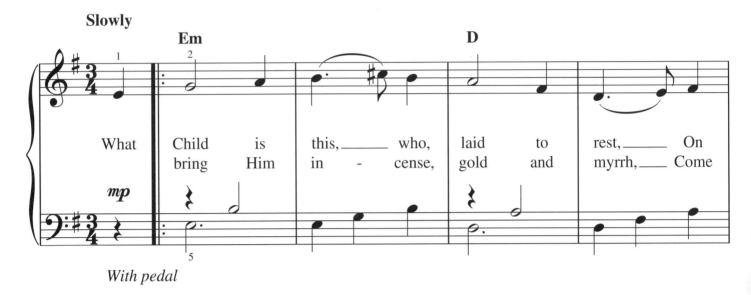

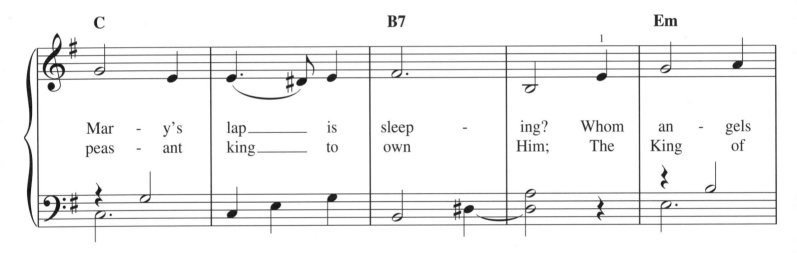

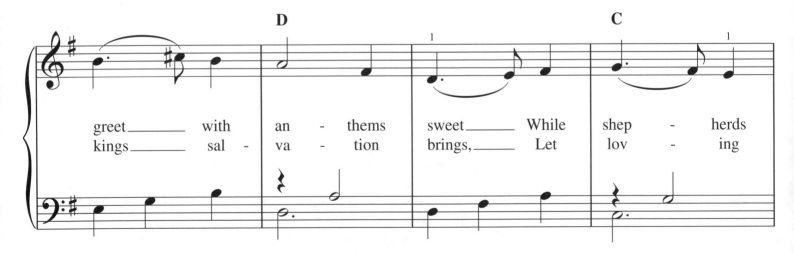

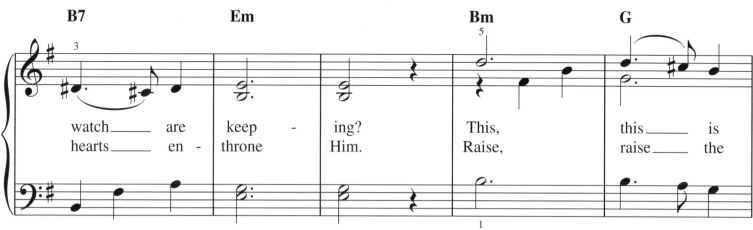

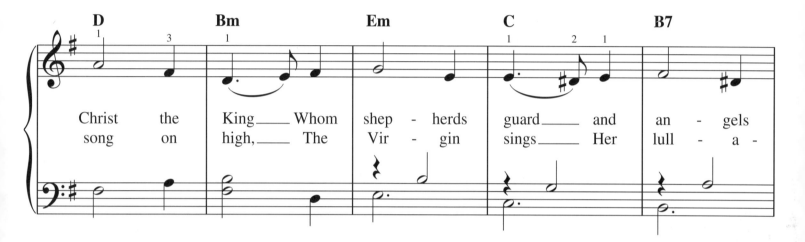

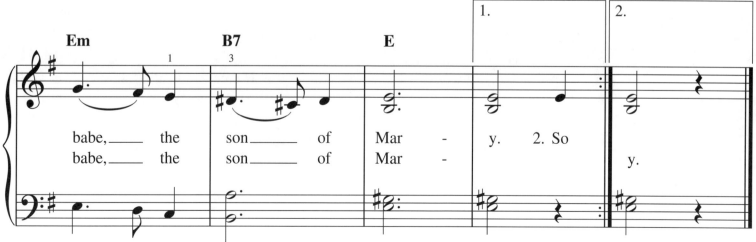

WHEN CHRIST WAS BORN
OF MARY FREE

Traditional English Carol

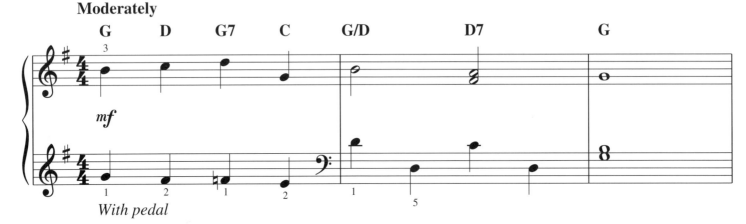

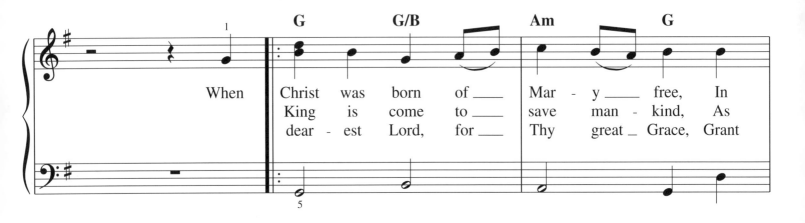

When
Christ was born of ___ Mar - y ___ free, In
King is come to ___ save man - kind, As
dear - est Lord, for ___ Thy great _ Grace, Grant

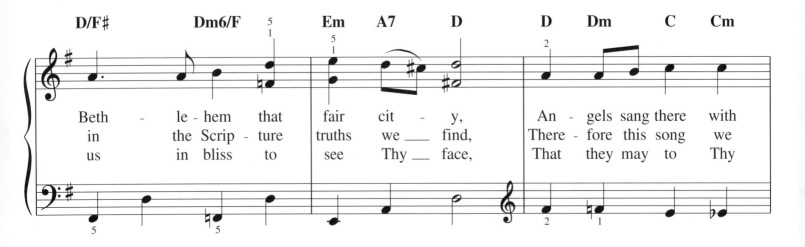

Beth - le - hem that fair cit - y, An - gels sang there with
in the Scrip - ture truths we ___ find, There - fore this song we
us in bliss to see Thy _ face, That they may to Thy

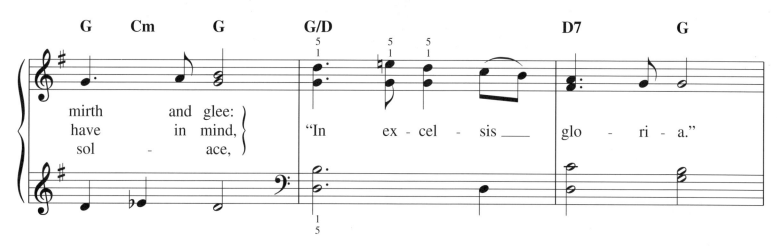

mirth and glee:
have in mind,
sol - ace,

"In ex - cel - sis ___ glo - ri - a."

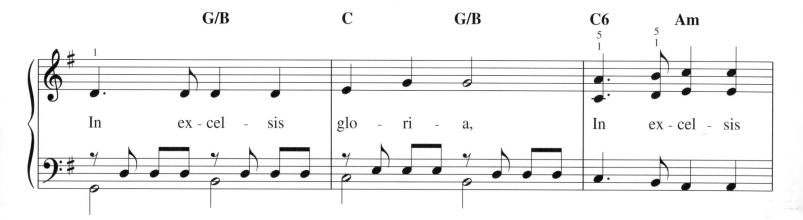

In ex - cel - sis glo - ri - a, In ex - cel - sis

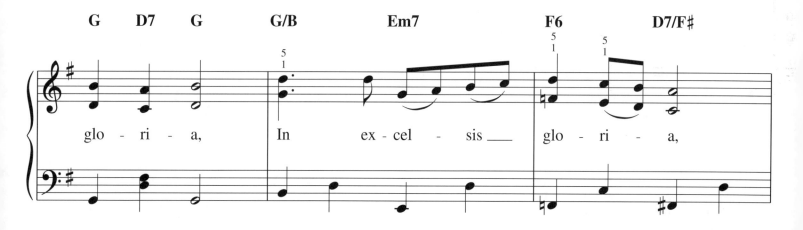

glo - ri - a, In ex - cel - sis ___ glo - ri - a,

In ex - cel - sis glo - ri - a. { The / Then, glo - ri - a.

WHEN CHRISTMAS MORN IS DAWNING

Traditional Swedish

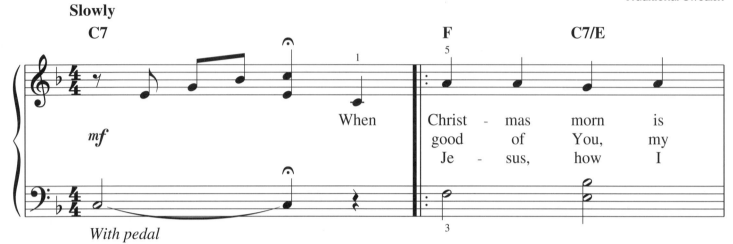

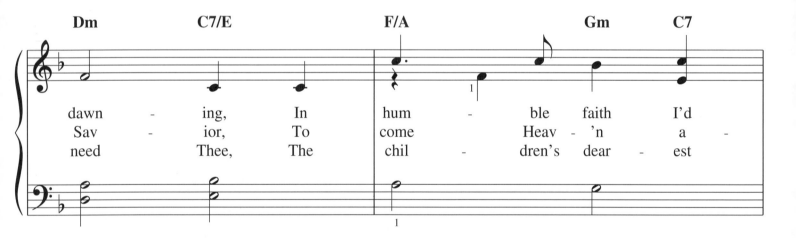

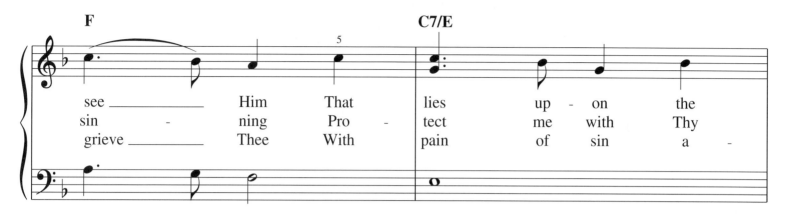

see _____ Him That lies up - on the
sin - ning That Pro - tect me with Thy
grieve _____ Thee With pain of sin a -

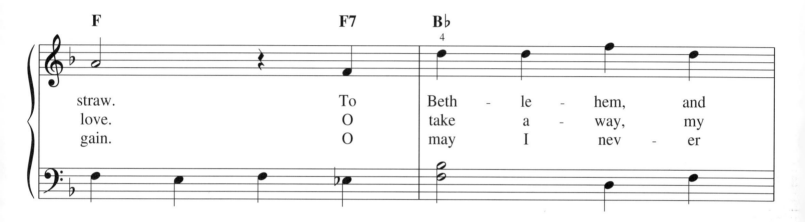

straw. To Beth - le - hem, and
love. O take a - way, my
gain. O may I nev - er

see _____ Him That lies up - on the
sin - ning That Pro - tect me with Thy
grieve _____ Thee With pain of sin a -

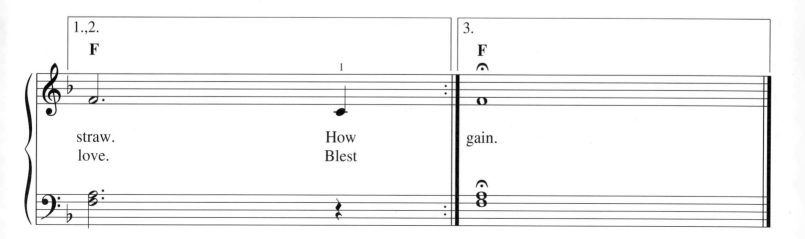

1.,2.

straw. How
love. Blest

3.

gain.

WHILE SHEPHERDS WATCHED THEIR FLOCKS

Words by NAHUM TATE
Music by GEORGE FRIDERIC HANDEL

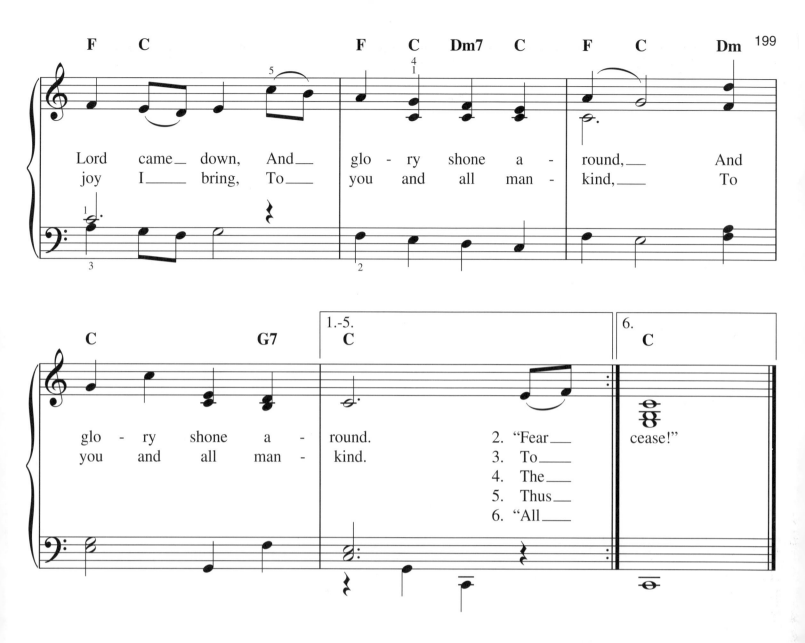

Additional Lyrics

3. To you, in David's town this day,
   Is born of David's line,
   The Savior, who is Christ the Lord;
   And this shall be the sign,
   And this shall be the sign:

4. The heavenly Babe you there shall find
   To human view displayed,
   All meanly wrapped in swathing bands,
   And in a manger laid,
   And in a manger laid."

5. Thus spake the seraph; and forthwith
   Appeared a shining throng
   Of angels praising God on high,
   Who thus addressed their song,
   Who thus addressed their song:

6. "All glory be to God on high,
   And to the earth be peace;
   Good will henceforth from heav'n to men,
   Begin and never cease,
   Begin and never cease!"

WINDS THROUGH THE OLIVE TREES

19th Century American Carol

Tender Waltz

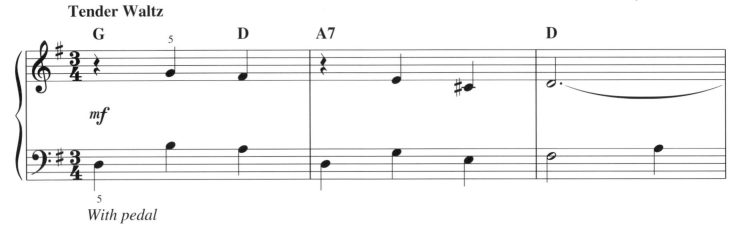

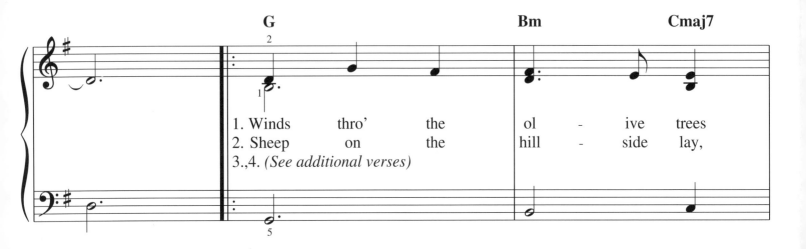

1. Winds thro' the ol - ive trees
2. Sheep on the hill - side lay,
3.,4. *(See additional verses)*

soft - ly did blow 'Round lit - tle
Whit - er than snow, Shep - herds were

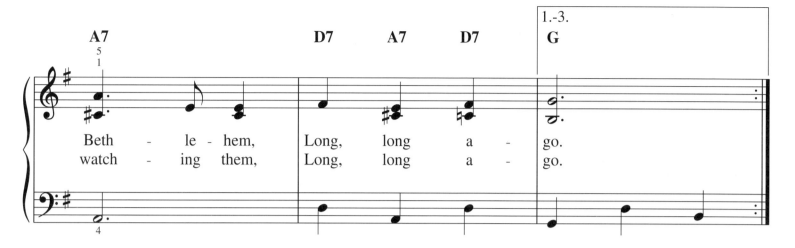

Beth - le - hem,
watch - ing them,
Long, long a - go.
Long, long a - go.

go,

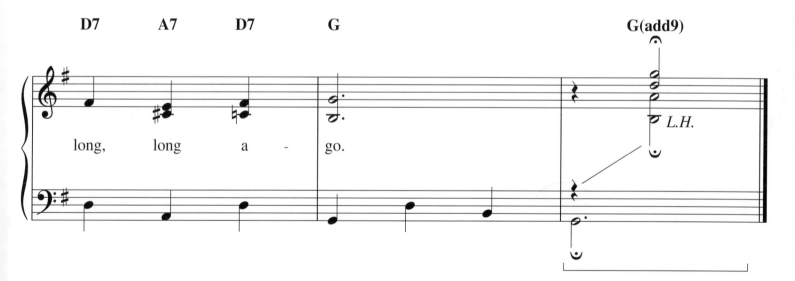

long, long a - go.

Additional Verses

3. Then from the happy skies,
   Angels bent low,
   Singing their songs of joy,
   Long, long ago.

4. For in a manger bed,
   Cradled we know.
   Christ came to Bethlehem;
   Long, long ago, long, long ago.

'TWAS THE NIGHT BEFORE CHRISTMAS

Words by CLEMENT CLARK MOORE
Music by F. HENRI KLICKMAN

Moderately

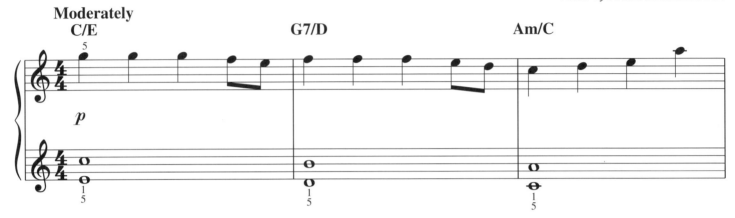

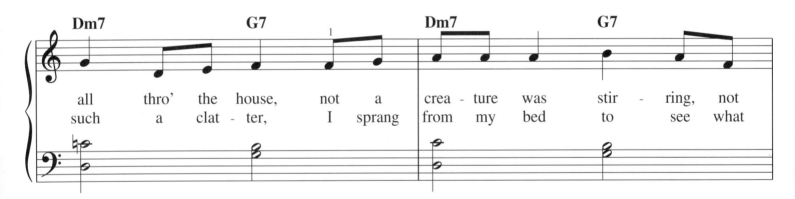

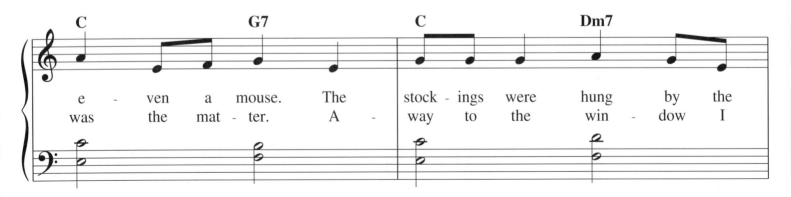

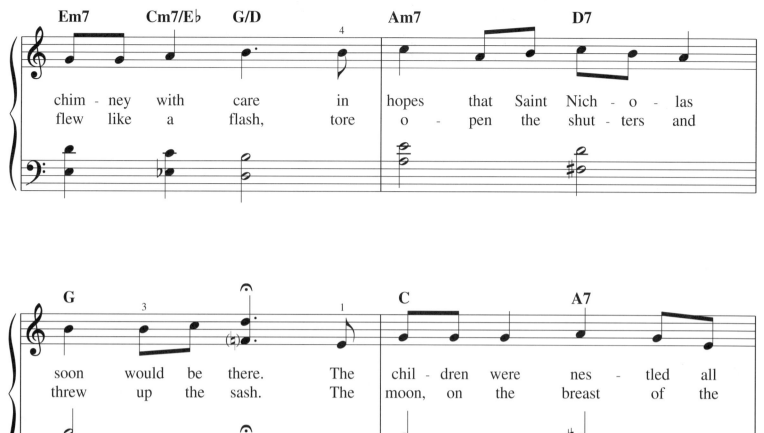

chim - ney with care in hopes that Saint Nich - o - las
flew like a flash, in tore o - pen the shut - ters and

soon would be there. The chil - dren were nes - tled all
threw up the sash. The moon, on the breast of all the

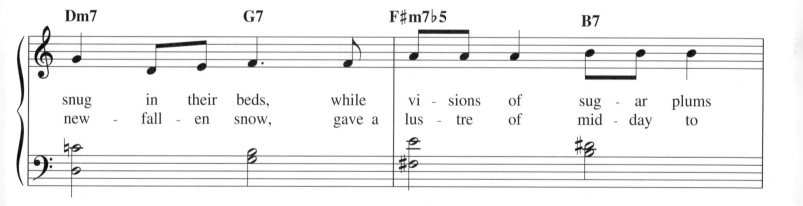

snug in their beds, while vi - sions of sug - ar plums
new - fall - en snow, gave a lus - tre of mid - day to

danced thro' their heads. And Ma - ma in her ker - chief and
ob - jects be - low. When what ___ to my won - der - ing

Additional Verses

3. With a little old driver, so lively and quick,
   I knew in a moment it must be St. Nick.
   More rapid than eagles his coursers they came,
   And he whistled, and shouted, and called them by name:
   "Now, Dasher! Now, Dancer! Now, Prancer! Now Vixen!
   On, Comet! On, Cupid! On Donner and Blitzen!
   To the top of the porch, to the top of the wall!
   Now dash away, dash away, dash away all!"

4. As dry leaves that before the wild hurricane fly,
   When they meet with an obstacle, mount to the sky,
   So up to the housetop the coursers they flew,
   With the sleigh full of toys, and St. Nicholas, too.
   And then in a twinkling I heard on the roof
   The prancing and pawing of each little hoof.
   As I drew in my head, and was turning around,
   Down the chimney St. Nicholas came with a bound.

5. He was dressed all in fur from head to his foot,
   And his clothes were all tarnished with ashes and soot;
   A bundle of toys he had flung on his back,
   And he looked like a peddler just opening his pack.
   His eyes, how they twinkled! His dimples, how merry!
   His cheeks were like roses, his nose like a cherry,
   His droll little mouth was drawn up like a bow,
   And the beard of his chin was as white as the snow.

6. The stump of a pipe he held tight in his teeth,
   And the smoke, it encircled his head like a wreath.
   He had a broad face, and a round little belly
   That shook, when he laughed, like a bowl full of jelly.
   He was chubby and plump–a right jolly old elf–
   And I laughed when I saw him, in spite of myself.
   A wink of his eye, and a twist of his head,
   Soon gave me to know I had nothing to dread.

7. He spoke not a word, but went straight to his work,
   And filled all the stockings; then turned with a jerk,
   And laying his finger aside of his nose,
   And giving a nod, up the chimney he rose.
   He sprang to his sleigh, to his team gave a whistle,
   And away they all flew like the down of a thistle;
   But I heard him exclaim, ere he drove out of sight–
   "Happy Christmas to all, and to all a Good-night!"

It's Easy to Play Your Favorite Songs with Hal Leonard Easy Piano Books

The Best Songs Ever
Over 70 all-time favorite songs, including: All I Ask of You • Body and Soul • Call Me Irresponsible • Crazy • Edelweiss • Fly Me to the Moon • The Girl from Ipanema • Here's That Rainy Day • Imagine • Let It Be • Longer • Moon River • Moonlight in Vermont • People • Satin Doll • Save the Best for Last • Somewhere Out There • Stormy Weather • Strangers in the Night • Tears in Heaven • Unchained Melody • Unforgettable • The Way We Were • What a Wonderful World • When I Fall in Love • and more
00359223 ....$19.95

Broadway Songs for Kids
19 songs, including: Be Kind to Your Parents • Beauty and the Beast • Castle on a Cloud • Gary, Indiana • I Won't Grow Up • It's the Hard-Knock Life • Little People • Tomorrow • and more.
00310354 ....$12.95

Contemporary Christian Songs
15 songs, including: Friends • Great Is the Lord • He Who Began a Good Work in You • Holy, Holy • Hosanna • How Majestic Is Your Name • I Will Be Here • In the Name of the Lord • Lamb of Glory • Lord of All • Love in Any Language • Love Will Be Our Home • O Magnify the Lord • Oh Lord, You're Beautiful • Thy Word.
00222501 ....$8.95

Contemporary Love Songs
27 heart-felt favorites: Breathe • Forever in Love • Here and Now • I Will Remember You • I'll Be • Just the Way You Are • My Heart Will Go On • Ribbon in the Sky • Tears in Heaven • Through the Years • Valentine • Vision of Love • When She Loved Me • You'll Be in My Heart • and more.
00310655 ....$12.95

Favorite Ballads of the '80s and '90s
25 contemporary ballads, including: Can You Feel the Love Tonight • Eternal Flame • From a Distance • Glory of Love • Hero • I Just Called to Say I Love You • I Swear • Just Once • Lady in Red • My Heart Will Go On • (I've Had) The Time of My Life • Up Where We Belong • The Way We Were • Wonderful Tonight • and more.
00310795 ....$10.95

God Bless America®
& Other American Inspirations
20 American classics: America, the Beautiful • Battle Hymn of the Republic • God Bless America • My Country, 'Tis of Thee • The Star Spangled Banner • Stars and Stripes Forever • This Is My Country • This Land Is Your Land • United We Stand • and more.
00310826..$10.95

Irish Favorites
From sentimental favorites to happy-go-lucky singalongs, this songbook celebrates the Irish cultural heritage of music. 30 songs: Danny Boy (Londonderry Air) • The Girl I Left Behind Me • It's a Long, Long Way to Tipperary • Killarney • My Wild Irish Rose • Too-ra-loo-ra-loo-ral, That's An Irish Lullabye • When Irish Eyes Are Smiling • and more!
00110011..$9.95

The Best of Andrew Lloyd Webber
11 of his best, arranged by Bill Boyd. Includes: All I Ask of You • Don't Cry for Me Argentina • I Don't Know How to Love Him • Memory • Mr. Mistoffelees • The Music of the Night • The Phantom of the Opera • Pie Jesu • Superstar • Take That Look off Your Face • Think of Me.
00290333..$12.95

Movie Favorites
20 songs, including: Beauty and the Beast • Endless Love • The Rainbow Connection • Somewhere Out There • Theme from "Ordinary People" • Unchained Melody • Under the Sea • What a Wonderful World • and more.
00222551..$9.95

The Really Big Book of Children's Songs
63 kids' hits: Alley Cat Song • Any Dream Will Do • Circle of Life • The Grouch Song • Hakuna Matata • I Won't Grow Up • Kum-Ba-Yah • Monster Mash • My Favorite Things • Sesame Street Theme • Winnie the Pooh • You've Got a Friend in Me • and more.
00310372..$15.95

FOR MORE INFORMATION, SEE YOUR LOCAL MUSIC DEALER,
OR WRITE TO:

HAL•LEONARD®
CORPORATION
7777 W. BLUEMOUND RD. P.O. BOX 13819 MILWAUKEE, WI 53213

Visit us online at **www.halleonard.com**
Prices, contents, and availability subject to change without notice

EASY PIANO CD PLAY-ALONGS
Orchestrated arrangements with you as the soloist!

This series lets you play along with great accompaniments to songs you know and love! Each book comes with a CD of complete professional performances and includes matching custom arrangements in Easy Piano format. With these books you can: Listen to complete professional performances of each of the songs; Play the Easy Piano arrangements along with the performances; Sing along with the recordings; Play the Easy Piano arrangements as solos, without the CD.

GREAT JAZZ STANDARDS – VOLUME 1

Bewitched • Do Nothin' Till You Hear from Me • Don't Get Around Much Anymore • How Deep Is the Ocean (How High Is the Sky) • I'm Beginning to See the Light • It Might As Well Be Spring • My Funny Valentine • Satin Doll • Stardust • That Old Black Magic.
00310916 Easy Piano $14.95

FAVORITE CLASSICAL THEMES – VOLUME 2

Bach: Air on the G String • Beethoven: Symphony No. 5, Excerpt • Bizet: Habanera • Franck: Panis Angelicus • Gounod: Ave Maria • Grieg: Morning • Handel: Hallelujah Chorus • Humperdinck: Evening Prayer • Mozart: Piano Concerto No. 21, Excerpt • Offenbach: Can Can • Pachelbel: Canon • Strauss: Emperor Waltz • Tchaikovsky: Waltz of the Flowers.
00310921 Easy Piano $14.95

BROADWAY FAVORITES – VOLUME 3

All I Ask of You • Beauty and the Beast • Bring Him Home • Cabaret • Close Every Door • I've Never Been in Love Before • If I Loved You • Memory • My Favorite Things • Some Enchanted Evening.
00310915 Easy Piano $14.95

ADULT CONTEMPORARY HITS – VOLUME 4

Amazed • Angel • Breathe • I Don't Want to Wait • I Hope You Dance • I Will Remember You • I'll Be • It's Your Love • The Power of Love • You'll Be in My Heart (Pop Version).
00310919 Easy Piano $14.95

HIT POP/ROCK BALLADS – VOLUME 5

Don't Let the Sun Go Down on Me • From a Distance • I Can't Make You Love Me • I'll Be There • Imagine • In My Room • My Heart Will Go On (Love Theme from 'Titanic') • Rainy Days and Mondays • Total Eclipse of the Heart • A Whiter Shade of Pale.
00310917 Easy Piano $14.95

LOVE SONG FAVORITES – VOLUME 6

Fields of Gold • I Honestly Love You • If • Lady in Red • More Than Words • Save the Best for Last • Three Times a Lady • Up Where We Belong • We've Only Just Begun • You Are So Beautiful.
00310918 Easy Piano $14.95

O HOLY NIGHT – VOLUME 7

Angels We Have Heard on High • Deck the Hall • Ding Dong! Merrily on High! • Go, Tell It on the Mountain • God Rest Ye Merry, Gentlemen • Good Christian Men, Rejjoice • It Came upon the Midnight Clear • Jingle Bells • Lo, How a Rose E'er Bloooming • O Come, All Ye Faithful (Adeste Fideles) • O Come, O Come Immanuel • O Hooly Night • Once in Royal David's City • Silent Night • What Child Is This?
00310920 Easy Piano $14.95

A CHRISTIAN WEDDING – VOLUME 8

Cherish the Treasure • Commitment Song • How Beautiful • I Will Be Here • In This Very Room • The Lord's Prayer • Love Will Be Our Home • Parent's Prayer (Let Go of Two) • This Is the Day (A Wedding Song) • The Wedding.
00311104 Easy Piano $14.95

COUNTRY BALLADS – VOLUME 9

Always on My Mind • Could I Have This Dance • Crazy • Crying • Forever and Ever, Amen • He Stopped Loving Her Today • I Can Love You Like That • The Keeper of the Stars • Release Me • When You Say Nothing at All.
00311105 Easy Piano $14.95

MOVIE GREATS – VOLUME 10

And All That Jazz • Chariots of Fire • Come What May • Forrest Gump – Main Title (Feather Theme) • I Finally Found Someone • Iris • Mission: Impossible Theme • Tears in Heaven • There You'll Be • A Wink and a Smile.
00311106 Easy Piano $14.95

DISNEY BLOCKBUSTERS – VOLUME 11

Be Our Guest • Can You Feel the Love Tonight • Go the Distance • Look Through My Eyes • Reflection • Two Worlds • Under the Sea • A Whole New World • Written in the Stars • You've Got a Friend in Me.
00311107 Easy Piano $14.95

FOR MORE INFORMATION, SEE YOUR LOCAL MUSIC DEALER,
OR WRITE TO:

HAL•LEONARD® CORPORATION
7777 W. BLUEMOUND RD. P.O. BOX 13819 MILWAUKEE, WI 53213

www.halleonard.com

Prices, contents, and availability subject to change without notice.

Christmas Collections
From Hal Leonard
All books arranged for piano, voice, & guitar.

Christmas Time Is Here
A 50-song Christmas collection! Includes: As Long as There's Christmas • Caroling, Caroling • The Christmas Song • Christmas Time Is Here • Do You Hear What I Hear • Emmanuel • Feliz Navidad • Let's Make It Christmas All Year 'Round • The Most Wonderful Time of the Year • Santa Baby • Silver Bells • and more!
00310761 ....$16.95

The Best Christmas Songs Ever - 3rd Edition
A collection of more than 70 of the best-loved songs of the season, including: Blue Christmas • Frosty the Snow Man • Grandma Got Run Over by a Reindeer • I'll Be Home for Christmas • Jingle-Bell Rock • Rudolph, The Red-Nosed Reindeer • Silver Bells • You're All I Want for Christmas • and many more.
00359130 ....$19.95

The Big Book Of Christmas Songs
An outstanding collection of over 120 all-time Christmas favorites and hard-to-find classics. Features: Angels We Have Heard on High • As Each Happy Christmas • Auld Lang Syne • The Boar's Head Carol • Christ Was Born on Christmas Day • Bring a Torch Jeannette, Isabella • Carol of the Bells • Coventry Carol • Deck the Halls • The First Noel • The Friendly Beasts • God Rest Ye Merry Gentlemen • I Heard the Bells on Christmas Day • It Came Upon a Midnight Clear • Jesu, Joy of Man's Desiring • Joy to the World • Masters in This Hall • O Holy Night • The Story of the Shepherd • 'Twas the Night Before Christmas • What Child Is This? • and many more. Includes guitar chord frames.
00311520 ....$19.95

Season's Greetings
A great big collection of 50 favorites, including: All I Want for Christmas Is You • Blue Christmas • The Christmas Song • Frosty the Snow Man • Grandma Got Run Over by a Reindeer • Happy Holiday • I'll Be Home for Christmas • Most of All I Wish You Were Here • Silver Bells • What Made the Baby Cry? • and more.
00310426 ....$16.95

Christmas Songs For Kids
27 songs kids love to play during the holidays, including: Away in a Manger • The Chipmunk Song • Deck the Hall • The First Noel • Jingle Bells • Joy to the World • O Christmas Tree • Silent Night • and more.
00311571 ....$7.95

Contemporary Christian Christmas
20 songs as recorded by today's top Christian artists, including: Michael W. Smith (All Is Well) • Sandi Patty (Bethlehem Morning) • Amy Grant (Breath of Heaven) • Michael Card (Celebrate the Child) • Steven Curtis Chapman (Going Home for Christmas) • Michael English (Mary Did You Know?) • Steve Green (Rose of Bethlehem) • 4Him (A Strange Way to Save the World) • Point of Grace (This Gift) • Scott Wesley Brown (This Little Child) • and more.
00310643 ....$12.95

The Definitive Christmas Collection – 2nd Edition
All the Christmas songs you need in one convenient collection! Over 120 classics in all! Songs include: An Old Fashioned Christmas • Away in a Manger • The Chipmunk Song • Christmas Time Is Here • The Christmas Waltz • Do They Know It's Christmas • Feliz Navidad • The First Noel • Frosty the Snow Man • The Greatest Gift of All • Happy Holiday • A Holly Jolly Christmas • I Saw Mommy Kissing Santa Claus • Jingle-Bell Rock • Mister Santa • My Favorite Things • O Holy Night • Rudolph, The Red-Nosed Reindeer • Santa, Bring My Baby Back (To Me) • Silent Night • Silver Bells • Suzy Snowflake • We Need a Little Christmas • and many more.
00311602 ....$29.95

The Lighter Side of Christmas
42 fun festive favorites, including: Grandma Got Run Over by a Reindeer • A Holly Jolly Christmas • I Guess There Ain't No Santa Claus • I Saw Mommy Kissing Santa Claus • Jingle-Bell Rock • The Merry Christmas Polka • Rockin' Around the Christmas Tree • Rudolph the Red-Nosed Reindeer • That's What I'd Like for Christmas • and more.
00310628 ....$14.95

Ultimate Christmas - 3rd Edition
100 seasonal favorites, including: Auld Lang Syne • Bring a Torch, Jeannette, Isabella • Carol of the Bells • The Chipmunk Song • Christmas Time Is Here • The First Noel • Frosty the Snow Man • Gesù Bambino • Happy Holiday • Happy Xmas (War Is Over) • Hymne • Jesu, Joy of Man's Desiring • Jingle-Bell Rock • March of the Toys • My Favorite Things • The Night Before Christmas Song • Pretty Paper • Silver and Gold • Silver Bells • Suzy Snowflake • What Child Is This • The Wonderful World of Christmas • and more.
00361399 ....$19.95